P9-CDI-454

"This book is a necessary read for any firm that is determined to implement customer-centricity, not just pay it lip service. It is not for the faint of heart – it pulls no punches in comprehensively laying out the effort needed to really effect customer-centric transformation."
Ian C. MacMillan – Professor of Innovation and Entrepreneurship at the Wharton School

"When you are ready to drive the change to become a truly customer-centric organization, look no further.
Let this book be your guide and your inspiration. It's terrific."
Larry Hochman – European Business Speaker of the Year and author of 'The Relationship Revolution' (2010)

"Doug's book should be part of your arsenal in determining and leading your crusade for customer-centricity!"
Jeanne Bliss – Author of 'Chief Customer Officer' (2006) and Co-founder of the Customer Experience Professionals' Association

"Like most of the English language just about everything has been turned into a bandwagon. 'Customer-centricity' is just such coinage but Doug has smartly sidestepped being just another book on the topic and created THE reference work – the guidebook for anyone wanting to understand, master and get after it. And it's a great read."
John Caswell, Founder and CEO of Group Partners

"In a business world filled with companies stumbling down the road towards customer-centricity, *The Customer-Centric Blueprint* provides both a GPS and a handrail. Doug Leather brings in a range of expert advice, but the best is his, based on many years of hands-on experience helping clients successfully reach customer-centric goals.
It is extremely well-written, no fluff and crystal clear."
Dick Lee – Founder of High-Yield Methods and author of 'The Customer Relationship Management Survival Guide' (2000)

"Customer-centricity can only be learned by practice and through example. Clear, well organized, simply put and straight talking – a solid way to deal with complex issues and to keep all organizations moving toward a common goal. An excellent piece of work – can be of great assistance to those willing to make the commitment.
If you can afford just one book on this subject, get this one."
Naveed Syed – Customer Strategist/Advocate

"The title is exactly what the book delivers – a thoughtful and thorough Customer-Centric Blueprint. Borne out of Leather's solid experience in the field and well supported with research and case stories, it is a handbook for any organization – large or small – to take a client-directed journey for success."
Cathy F Burrows – Director, Marketing Services at RBC Royal Bank

"Most business leaders say they want to be customer-centric. Yet if you ask 10 people to describe what that means, you'll get 15 different answers. In 'The Customer-Centric Blueprint,' Doug Leather gives sage advice regarding what business leaders must do to translate customer-centric rhetoric into business success. Two thumbs up!"
Bob Thompson, Founder and CEO of CustomerThink Corp

"Most companies try to deliver a differentiated customer experience – very few succeed. Doug offers a structured, systems-based approach to convert a strategic intent into reality – written in a very simple and accessible style."
Rob Shuter, CEO of Vodafone, Netherlands

"As more companies seek to become increasingly customer-centric and make customer management an integral part of "business as usual", they seek sources of insight, lessons from others, practical examples and applications of how leading organisations have overcome similar challenges. Mostly they seek guidance on how to approach this daunting task, what questions to ask and where to start. This book will supply such insights and guidance as they continue on their customer-centric journey."
Ica van Eeden – Chief Customer Officer, Sun International

"**This book is a manual**: By addressing the key questions of customer-centricity, Doug Leather provides tools and processes for successful implementation, honed by tough consultancy with the boards of some of the world's leading companies. Doug's manual stresses the elements that really matter in a holistic way – from leadership to culture, from planning to measurement, from brand and proposition to effective experience management execution. **But this manual is also a book**: It is crammed with distilled, inspiring, practical stories and wisdom for effective and profitable Customer Experience Officers and other C-Level executives. Organizations claiming to put customers at the heart of their businesses should equip everyone involved in this task with this blueprint, to be used as a real systems-thinking tool as well as a crash barrier when executing their programs. Doug Leather, as a constructive customer-centric activist, gives us vital reading for all those charged with customer-centricity, and for all managers wishing to make their companies really 'customer-oriented' ready."
Alan Price MBIDA, Chief Operating Officer, LAP GREENN Côte d'Ivoire and Non-Executive Partner at IMPACT & SOLUTIONS CONSULTING

"I have worked with Doug Leather over the last eight years, and one of the things I most respect about him is that he 'says it like it is'. I would highly recommend this book as it addresses head-on one of the biggest issues that businesses face today – paying lip service to customer-centricity! If you think you're customer-centric already, then you'll find out about the next level of building it into the DNA of the organisation; if you are passionate about it and work in a company that's on the journey towards customer-centricity, then you'll find a wealth of practical advice; if you think it's all about brand, product and quarterly sales numbers – and don't really care who buys them – then there are some inconvenient truths you really should consider. Above all, the book underlines that this isn't a fad or a quick fix – it's about a fundamentally better way of doing business."

Peter Lavers, MD of WCL Customer Management, REAP Consulting Associate and expert customer management capability assessor (completed over 100 assessments)

The
Customer-
Centric
Blueprint

Building and Leading the 21st Century Organisation

DOUG LEATHER

First Edition

REAP | publishing

Johannesburg, South Africa

The Customer-Centric Blueprint

Building and Leading the 21st Century Organisation

By Doug Leather

REAP | publishing

A Division of REAP Consulting (Pty) Ltd

P.O.Box 68520, Bryanston, Johannesburg, 2021, South Africa

reapconsulting.com

All rights reserved. No part of this publication may be reproduced or transmitted in any form or by any means, electronic or mechanical, including photocopying, recording or by any information storage or retrieval system, without written permission from the author, except for the inclusion of brief quotations in a review.

The moral rights of the author have been asserted.

Copyright © 2013 by Doug Leather

Managing Editor: Belinda Doveston
Copy Editor: Barbara Basel
Cover Design: Lauren Rycroft, Through the Looking Glass
Typesetting: Tracey Watson

ISBN: 978-0-620-55834-1

To Brigette, my gorgeous wife of 21 years,
and my two unbelievable kids, Brody and Christy, this is for you.
Without you I wouldn't have been able to do this.

TABLE OF CONTENTS

ABOUT AUTHOR

Doug Leather, CEO of REAP Consulting, is a leading international expert in customer-centricity, working globally to transform large blue-chip organisations into customer-centric leaders of the 21st century. He is known as a customer evangelist, activist and futurologist as a result of his intense passion for customer-centric transformation, and his broad multi-industry and multi-country insights. His primary focus is to help leaders and executives take the bold, transformative leaps required to build and lead a superior and sustainable 21st century organisation.

With a diverse engineering and commercial background, along with being an alumnus of the esteemed Wharton Business School at the University of Pennsylvania, Doug is relentless in his pursuit of knowledge and ground-breaking research. After many years employed at a range of corporates that include Barclays Industrial Bank, Hewlett Packard and the Primedia Group, Doug had the opportunity to work with Peppers & Rogers shortly after they were launched in South Africa in 2002. This experience inspired him to become truly focused on customer-centricity – a turning point he has never looked back on.

As a result, Doug then founded REAP Consulting so that he and his global network of associates could share their collective passion and wisdom with business leaders about just what it takes to become a truly customer-centric organisation and the practical considerations required to operationalize a customer-centric business model.

Doug believes that you should live life to the fullest. As an "adrenalin junkie", he is an active and passionate triathlete, whilst making time for spearfishing, water-skiing, golf and tennis. He is an avid reader with an insatiable appetite for good champagne and, hence, never has any. Doug is married with two children.

FOREWORD

Effective leadership, in any sphere of life, is about creating a vision that energises people and keeps them focused, despite all the challenges and difficulties they may face. This vision is critical in navigating your organisation through the unpredictable and ever shifting landscape of the global economy and the challenges brought about through increased competition, regulatory requirements, tough economic conditions and technological breakthroughs. It is my firm belief that the core success of any organisation and its vision rests with the customer.

Over many years, and after many meetings and discussions with Doug Leather, we have connected over a common understanding and belief that a customer-centric business model is a real driver for competitive advantage. In the 21st century, any business that cannot provide value to its customers that is superior to its competitors will not stay in business for very long. Advancements in technology have raised the stakes in the way business is done. Knowledge has become easily accessible. Customers have become more educated and aware, and as such, businesses are being held to higher standards and quality of service.

We live in a world of rapid change. For any organisation to survive in an environment of change it needs to adapt. As business leaders, the meltdown of the economy in the past few years has taught us that focussing on short-term profit at the expense of the customer can be disastrous with far reaching consequences. Bill George, writing for the Harvard Business Review, said: "Authentic leaders focused on customers are replacing hierarchical leaders that focus on serving short-term shareholders".

Transformation, specifically customer-centric transformation, is, therefore, key to building and leading a business in this time. Understanding transformation is one thing, but having the knowledge and tools to execute transformational change in an organisation, is quite another. In this book, Doug provides the blueprint as well as the business model necessary to operationalize customer-centric transformation. He answers all the "who, why, what, how and where to" questions. It is a guide on measuring the tangible, while reaping the benefits of the intangible.

One of the most simple, yet powerful, notions he puts forward in this book is that "to lead is to serve". In an "outside-in" organisation this appreciation of leading through service and customer experience is intrinsically connected. The organisation then exists to serve the customer and not the other way around.

Sustainability has become the buzz word of the 21st century. It's all about maintaining a sustainable social, economic, environmental and political system. As business leaders we are tasked with directly providing a sustainable business structure for our shareholders and customers alike, whilst also, indirectly, contributing in an ethical and sustainable way to the greater environments in which we operate.

Doug explores, through the REAP Customer-Centric Organisation Blueprint®, how to strategize, plan, and operationalize the future in a way that develops a sustainable competitive advantage for your business. It is everything you need to know to start on the path of extensive customer-centric transformation in your organisation.

Staying connected with customers means staying relevant. Staying relevant means providing greater value. Greater value means a satisfied customer. A satisfied customer will always come back and, more than likely, that satisfied customer will recommend your business. It is for these reasons that I believe in the customer-centric approach to doing business and why it is a driver for real competitive advantage.

Sifiso Dabengwa

Group President and Chief Executive Officer MTN

Johannesburg, 2013

PART ONE:
CONTEXT

CHAPTER 1:

CUSTOMER-CENTRIC TRANSFORMATION

Transformation Intent

Our world is undergoing rapid transformation, especially in the economic, political, social and technological arenas. In this tide of change and upheaval, your customers are also stepping into their power and making demands of business the likes of which have never been seen before. Building sustainable competitive advantage requires you to review your business models to ensure that the customer is central to its design.

I was running late, the traffic was heavy and I was double-parked outside the bank's head office. I ran into the main reception area to quickly drop off an envelope for the attention of a senior staff member. Looking fairly reputable in my suit, albeit somewhat harassed, I approached the counter and said: "Please, I'm in a rush and I'd like to leave this envelope here for collection." The woman to whom I'd addressed my request looked up at me and replied, "We're not allowed to accept that," and resumed tapping on her keyboard.

I was dumbfounded. This is a business overtly focused on customer experience yet here, when it really mattered, the person engaging with me, whether I'm a customer, supplier or potential customer, had absolutely no clue what customer engagement was about. She could have interacted with me in a multiple of different ways whilst still honouring "the rules". She could have said: "I'm very sorry, we are not allowed to accept 'drop offs' due to..." and then substantiated why. She could also have said: "Would you like me to call the individual and see if I can get her to come down to collect from you?" As I later learnt, she could have informed me about the drop off post box situated alongside the reception desk. Surely she knew I was frazzled and in a rush. I'd told her so! What she didn't know, and clearly didn't care about, was what I may have been worth to the bank.

This is a classic case that represents the antithesis of customer-centric thinking. Firstly, the woman was not a full-time employee of the bank. How can an organisation outsource frontline people, the first point of contact, without ensuring that those individuals behave according to the brand values and deliver the appropriate "defined" experience? Secondly, as a customer, I don't care about stupid internal rules, regulations or processes that make no sense to me. Why shouldn't I be able to drop off an envelope at the reception desk? Why would a business intentionally make it difficult for me to drop something off for collection by an employee? The mind boggles!

Sound familiar? Undoubtedly you've had similar experiences. Even in organisations outwardly committed to a customer-centric approach, there often remains a fundamental disconnection between the delivery of the intended customer experience and what is actually implemented and delivered at the coal-face. Transformation will only happen when ALL people are understanding of, and committed to, the hard work of change.

What about your customers? Do they experience this disconnection too? Do they have expectations that are not delivered against? Do they experience inconsistencies in your level of service? Are you even aware of their expectations and needs? Do you truly understand how you should be evolving in order to create a meaningful competitive advantage?

The world is changing

Disruptive technologies, social media, demanding customers and an interconnected global economy have altered the face of business forever. Since 2008 the global economic crisis has created widespread upheaval and change. In 2011 we witnessed the startling revolutions in North African and Middle Eastern Arab countries, and the social unrest and economic upheaval in unexpected places such as Greece and the United Kingdom. Even the "Occupy" movements indicated a revolutionary, grass roots social movement where power had started shifting from governments and large corporations to the individual.

While these revolutions have been spurred on by people's widespread frustration at how their governments and large corporates are getting richer while they get poorer, the rapid and drastic sweep of these revolutions could not have been possible without one key ingredient – technology. Internet-connected mobile phones and social media, through YouTube, Facebook, Twitter, Blackberry Messenger (BBM) and others, have been the primary reason that so many people have been able to mobilise as a unit with a common purpose so quickly. Gone are the days when the individual's voice did not count. Now, every person counts. This has created a massive challenge for governments, organisations and large corporates, many of whom still rely on the old order of the few controlling the masses. A new reality beckons where the masses control the few.

Tools of the Revolution: 800 million smart phones, 1.5 billion PCs, 2 billion people on the Internet, 3.5 billion mobile phones, 5 billion Internet-connected devices, 87 billion Google searches per month [1].

Your customer, as an individual, is also becoming more expectant of being listened to, responded to and being served according to their expectations. Individuals have their own specific needs and wants. Unfair or unacceptable treatment can result in instantaneous and broad-based communications via multiple online channels. This can sometimes be devastating for business.

A case in point is the well-known story of Dave Carrol, who in 2008 flew with his band on United Airlines from Nova Scotia to Nebraska. Upon arrival they discovered that Carrol's guitar had been destroyed at the hands of airline staff, with eye witnesses reporting purposeful malice. Upon being continuously refused compensation from United Airlines he turned to social media. Within three days of posting a song he wrote on YouTube entitled "United Breaks Guitars" he had received half a million hits.

Carrol relates: "There was a time in customer service where if you had a positive experience with customer service you would tell three friends. And if you had a negative one you would tell 14. Bad news always travelled faster than good news, but now things are off the rails and have gone exponential.

In my case, I basically told the story once with a video and over 100 million people around the world are now familiar with this song [2]".

Alongside this ability for customers to broadcast their customer experiences, is the fact that individuals are less trusting of government and corporate-generated communications and advertising and much more trusting of endorsements made by friends, friends of friends and colleagues. When looking to buy something, reviews through online and social media channels are treated with a much higher regard than any advertising statement or claim made by the supplier of the product or service. As United Airlines now knows, the cost of a guitar pales in comparison to the risk of a poor reputation.

Research provides further startling evidence that customers expect more from their experience than ever before [3,4]. The results reveal that:

Customers value a better customer experience	86% of customers would pay more for a better experience
A negative customer experience is much more likely to make a customer leave than it would have before	In 2006 the figure was at 68% and in 2011 it was 89%
Online complaints are not being resolved	79% of online complaints were ignored
A significant portion of customers would post a negative social media comment after a negative experience	26% would do so
Customers have a short time-tolerance for poor communication	50% of customers would cease business with the company if not responded to within one week
Customers will reward a superior experience by increasing their investment	73% would increase purchases by 10% or more in such a case
Customers who have a superior experience recommend the company to others	58% would refer to their friends and connections

Figure 1: Customer Experience Statistics [3,4]

These statistics clearly show that customers have become more discerning about the experience they expect. The impact of that experience is also much more significant than it has ever been, both positively and negatively. While customers will vote quickly with their feet in the case of a poor experience, they also indirectly create negative perceptions for potential customers. Get the customer experience right and the rewards are worth the effort – positive word of mouth, an ability to charge a premium, greater levels of customer retention and increasing customer spend.

Perhaps the scale of this shift in power from organisation to customer will be bigger than we can possibly imagine. Doc Searls, in his book *The Intention Economy* [5], posits that a revolution in personal empowerment is underway and buying will never be the same again. He makes reference to big business thinking that the best way "to get personal" with us as customers is with "big data", gathered by placing tracking files in our browsers and smartphone apps without our knowledge. We can be stalked wherever we go, with our so-called experiences on commercial websites being personalised for us. This approach does not recognise the massive changes taking place in the way that we expect to be engaged.

In the not too distant future we will, for example, be able to change our contact information with many vendors and suppliers at once, rather than many times over at different websites. We will declare our own policies, preferences and terms of engagement, and do it in ways that can be automated for us and for the companies with which we engage. We'll have software that can knit together apps with services offered by companies, saving work for us. We, as customers, will set the rules of engagement, delivery methods, pricing and terms of payment. The real question then becomes: is your organisation ready for this kind of customer?

"We believe it's because there are moments in time, stages of evolution and cycles of activity that throw up the need for radical thinking that we as a species just need. We know there are very scientific reasons, patterns and evolutionary forces at work, but on a very practical level we become aware that we just have to stop doing the same old things if we want to see different outcomes" [6].

Business is changing too

The world of business has been reshaped through the speed at which new technologies are created and copied, and through the loss of geographic advantage as a result of globalisation. The shake-up of traditionally stable industries, as a result of deregulation, creates additional pressure, and the rising power of the consumer and their ability to get what they want, whenever they want, from whomever they want, is changing the game.

One of the most important questions of our current time is: "How do we stay relevant in this uncertain and changing world?" The customer is central to this change. Standing in the way of the evolution towards a customer-centric approach, is the hallmark of competitive advantage of the past: product-centricity.

Peter Fader, in his book *Customer Centricity* [7], describes this product-centric view as one being followed by 99% of companies as they seek to maximise profit, market share and market capitalisation. It refers to organisations built entirely around competing in the market place through product innovation and branding. Profits are maximised through volume and market share. All strategic advantage is based upon product and the product expertise behind those products. The long-term focus is about strengthening the product portfolio and continually finding new ways to expand it. The brand is perceived to have greater value than the customer.

	Traditional Business	Twenty-first Century Business
Philosophy	Sell Products	Serve Customers
Orientation	Market Orientation	Interaction Orientation
Management Criteria	Portfolio of Products	Portfolio of Customers
Strategy Motivation	Increase Customer Satisfaction	Increase Customer Profitability
Selling Approach	How many customers can we sell this product to?	How many products can we sell to this customer?
Strategy Outcome	Sales Maximization	Customer Lifetime Value Maximization

Figure 2: Differences between Traditional and 21st Century Businesses [8]

What is absolutely clear is that goods and services are no longer enough. Our current world is saturated with product, largely undifferentiated. By 2020, less than 10% of brands will be able to provide meaningful differentiation through differences in their core products and services [1].

The world in which you and your company are doing business is, therefore, becoming increasingly demanding and competitive. New markets, new business models, extraordinary advances in communications and global sources of brainpower and skilled labour will herald an explosion in business opportunities. The majority of companies need to move beyond products and services to drive meaningful competitive advantage and sustainable profits. They need to find new ways to create and deliver value. They have to move beyond incremental changes towards real transformation. They need to view the world, and act accordingly, through the lens of the customer rather than through the way they "do" business.

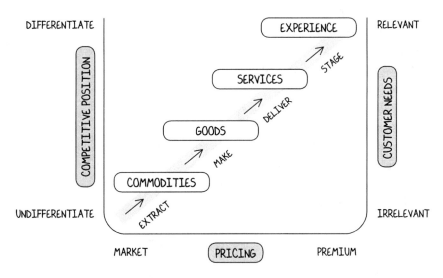

Figure 3: The Progression of Economic Value [9]

A customer-centric approach to business is rapidly addressing the multitude of issues that a product-centric approach is not able to solve. This approach, and the business model it requires, is based not on expertise in the realm of product development, yet rather on the deep understanding of what customers actually want, when and how they want it, and what they're willing to give you in exchange [7].

Sustainable business performance is the ultimate objective for any business, be it product-centric or customer-centric. There is, however, a greater opportunity to generate economic value and competitive advantage in a customer-centric business model, through designing and staging differentiated and relevant "experiences" at premium pricing.

An "inside-out" company is one that views its world from its own perspective and makes decisions that make sense to its own needs. An "outside-in" company is the opposite – it views its world through the lens of the customer and then engages with the customer community in a way that supports their needs. This "outside-in" perspective is the cornerstone of a customer-centric business.

Customer-centricity can, therefore, be defined as *the eco-system and operating model that enables an organisation to design and deliver a unique and distinctive customer experience.* This architecture enables the business to acquire, retain and develop targeted customers efficiently for the benefit of employees, customers and stakeholders.

The customer experience itself is a blend of the physical product and/or service and the emotions evoked before, during and after engaging with your organisation across any touch point. Decoupling the delivery of goods and services from the "staging" of experiences allows for tangible uniqueness and competitive differentiation.

"But in trying to escape the perils of commoditization, the company (GE) initially fell into a classic trap: It was seeking to solve customer problems but was viewing those problems through the lens of its own products, rather than from the customer's perspective" [10].

Amazon.com is a great example of a company differentiating itself through customer experience. Imagine for a moment that a competitor to Amazon.com launches tomorrow, providing almost exactly the same level of functionality through its web-site, offering a similar selection of books and pricing parity. What are the chances of you, as an Amazon.com customer, changing allegiance? In all likelihood, the chances are probably not that high.

So why is this the case? It's probably because Amazon.com has emotionally engaged with you. They remember things for and about you. They have a history of all your purchases and, in the event that you order a book that you've previously purchased, they'll advise you accordingly. There's a relationship, which speaks to the power of knowledge and the reward for the time you as a customer have made in providing that knowledge to Amazon.com. A new entrant cannot easily undermine the time invested in the relationship and the value of the relationship. And, don't forget about the trust created through that relationship too!

Jack Welch, the former CEO of General Electric, said that there are only two sources of competitive advantage – the first one being to learn more about your customers faster than the competition, and the second, to turn that learning into action faster than the competition [11].

Peppers and Rogers [11] refer to this as the learning relationship. It's a process during which you're talking with your customers and, based upon what you learn about your customers, you tailor your product, service or elements associated with it. Yet what you're really trying to do is give your customers a reason to invest time and effort in teaching you how to serve them better, and how to be more relevant to them. The more time your customers invest, the bigger the stake they have in making the relationship work. If they take the time to teach you how to serve them better, you can change the way you treat them.

Business transformation requires unique skills and resources working to implement strategies that competitors cannot implement as effectively. This will only be possible by adopting a new way of thinking and building capability to execute change across the business while implementing an alternative business model grounded in customer-centricity. Instead of trying to solve the problem with ad-hoc, customer-focused activities, we need to make an intentional and fundamental shift towards a holistic customer-centric business model. What is needed is a new blueprint that informs the company's DNA – a new genetic code that drives transformation in every area of our business. During the process we will reinvent how people and businesses work together and find new ways of solving problems.

> "What distinguishes customer-centric organizations from other companies that proclaim their customer focus? In short, they've moved beyond lip service and re-oriented their entire operating model around the customer, increasing customer satisfaction and their own profitability in the process" [12].

A model for transformation

Designing and executing a customer-centric business model requires end-to-end organisational alignment. This means building value by being innovative every day, focussing the whole organisation on a clear vision, developing a winning culture, being sustainable and encouraging efficiencies.

Being customer-centric is not simply a matter of appointing a customer executive, making bold statements about a differentiated customer experience, building a strong sales force or equipping your customer service representatives with new technology. Achieving customer-centricity means that you understand your most valuable customers intimately, you know their world and its challenges and you are able to speak their language. It means knowing when to be there for them and when to stay away. And when you are there for them, it means delivering on your promises.

Customer-centric capability development cannot happen in isolation to the rest of the business – it cannot be viewed as a project. For an organisation to become customer-centric, the principles of customer-centricity must become the essence of the ecosystem. In other words, the business model must be designed and executed with customer-centricity as the strategic outcome. This customer-centric outcome is then operationalized through organisational structures, processes, systems and measures. Building customer-centric capability requires an organisation to design "outside-in" thinking into every aspect of the business.

The REAP Customer-Centric Organisation Blueprint®, or REAP CCOB (see diagram below), is an approach that REAP Consulting has developed for strategizing, planning and operationalizing the future. As a business model it is the rationale of how an organisation creates, delivers and captures value. It's about thinking differently, challenging tradition, adopting a new approach, developing sustainable competitive advantage and embracing the transformative nature of the change required.

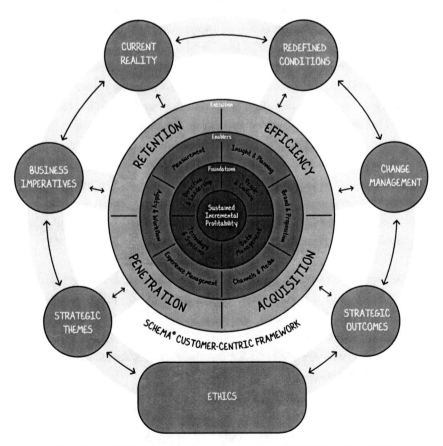

Figure 4: The REAP Customer-Centric Organisation Blueprint® (REAP Consulting, 2013)

The REAP CCOB consists of two parts. The overall system (outer circle) addresses strategic context – the reality of business of today versus business of tomorrow through effective leadership based on an ethical foundation. The second part (inner circle) is the SCHEMA® Customer-Centric Framework that describes the "business system" that underpins effective customer management. SCHEMA®, developed by The Customer Framework Limited, is by far the most sophisticated and integrated customer management model available, providing the framework that organisations need in order to build their capability and their performance.

There are three sub-systems within SCHEMA®. The *Foundations* layer includes the fundamental building blocks that support or limit your transformation. They require broad-based input and alignment, without which the operationalization of a customer-centric business model is almost impossible. They are components that can be difficult, slow and expensive to fix. Transformation of the *Foundations* elements may, therefore, be a long term undertaking. The *Enablers* layer explores the components needed to energise your transformation. They will invariably involve changes that can be planned for within the current business cycle, for implementation in the next budgetary or operating period. These components support your capability to implement your chosen customer strategies. The *Execution* layer relates to the capabilities and control levers needed to optimise customer value – Retention, Efficiency (understanding cost to serve), Acquisition and Penetration (customer development, cross-sell and upsell) – referred to collectively as REAP. These are capabilities and initiatives that can be optimised in the short term.

Whilst there is a vast amount of material available on customer-centricity, success lies less in the uniqueness of the strategy, and much more in the strength of execution. There is, therefore, a need for a clear, succinct and practical approach for business leaders. This book provides the blueprint to enable customer-centricity as a powerful business driver of sustainable competitive advantage.

Part One, *Context*, explores the overall system of the REAP CCOB by defining customer-centricity and its role in the new world order, providing context for how such a business model interconnects and integrates all the parts of your organisation, and demonstrating that it is a fundamental requirement for sustainable business performance in today's business world. In Parts Two to Four, *Foundations*, *Enablers* and *Execution*, each chapter systematically maps out the design and plan you need, based on SCHEMA®, for that aspect of your customer-centric blueprint.

Every chapter in this book provides a clear definition of the transformation requirements, or the transformation intent, that working with that aspect of the model brings your organisation. Examples, case studies and transformation reflection questions further guide your insights and the practical implementation of customer-centricity.

Transformation questions

- Why are you reading this book? What are you hoping it will help you achieve?
- For what reason would you drive customer-centric transformation within and across your business?
- If you asked 10 people in your company what the company purpose is, how many answers would you receive?
- Are you crystal clear as to how your business creates, delivers and captures value?
- Does your board really understand what customer-centricity is about, as well as the scale of change possibly required to operationalize a customer-centric business model?
- What is required to keep the principles of customer-centricity at the top of the executive agenda?
- Do you understand the problems your customers are trying to solve?
- Would most people say that the world is a better place because your company exists?
- Does your customer have a seat at the boardroom table?
- Are you prepared to learn how to "be" a customer rather than to "have" customers?
- Do you focus on executing tasks or delivering experiences that customers will want to repeat and tell others about?
- Do you have an unconditional respect for your customers?

Case study - Amazon.com obsesses over its customers

"Start with customers, and work backwards. Listen to customers, but don't just listen to customers – also invent on their behalf. We can't assure you that we'll meet all of this year's goals. We haven't in past years. However, we can assure you that we'll continue to obsess over customers. We have a strong conviction that that approach – in the long term – is every bit as good for owners as it is for customers."

These were the words of Jeff Bezos, Founder and Chief Executive Officer of Amazon.com, in his April 2009 letter to shareholders. Amazon.com is a company that obsesses over its customers. It aspires to be "Earth's most customer-centric company", yet what differentiates Amazon.com from all the other companies that aspire to a similar goal? They actually deliver on their promise.

Testimony to Amazon.com's obsession over their customers is how they measure the results they are getting. In the 2009 letter to shareholders, Bezos reported that 360 out of their 452 goals had a direct impact on the customer experience while the terms "net income, gross profit or margin, and operating profit" were not used once. While Amazon.com of course pay attention to what their competitors are doing, they do not let it detract from focusing on what their customer really needs. Their entire business is customer-centric. Bezos claims that putting the customer first is the biggest reason that Amazon.com is as successful as it is today.

Another winning strategy is Amazon.com's focus on invention as a means of solving any problem and accepting that it is not the customers' job to invent for themselves. Understand your customers' needs yet create the solution for their need before they know they need it.

Thinking long-term is the third aspect of its strategic success. It often takes Amazon.com's projects five to seven years before the return pays anything for the shareholders. Yet these projects create immediate value for the customer and the long-term perspective creates higher calibre thinking.

This shows us that the immense benefits of customer-centricity are won after a long-term, consistent, commitment to transformation across the organisation. The reality is that any success can be quickly and easily lost in the short-term panic for market share, cash flow, and not being left behind.

Not everyone agrees that Amazon.com is holding onto its customer-centric mission. Peter Fader, a leading customer-centricity specialist and a Professor of Marketing at the Wharton Business School, believes that Amazon.com's dabbling in the tablet market with the Kindle Fire may just indicate that they are stepping outside a customer-centric view [13]. He concludes: "Customer centricity is a winning strategy. Introducing a 'me too' product into an already crowded marketplace is not."

● CHAPTER 2:

● A SYSTEMS-THINKING APPROACH

Transformation Intent

When it comes to customer management, as with any system, the whole is greater than the sum of its parts. Treating a business as a holistic system is the only way to ensure end-to-end integration of a customer-centric approach. This requires that the right foundations are in place to deliver customer-centricity, and that your approach is driven by a comprehensive framework that practically connects your strategic objectives to the delivery of sustainable business performance.

The whole is greater than the sum of its parts

In 2009 I was privileged to meet Dr Russell Ackoff while studying at the Wharton Business School in Pennsylvania, USA. Although he sadly passed away not long thereafter, Dr Ackoff is still considered today to be a leading pioneer in systems-thinking and its application to management and organisational improvement. As a friend and contemporary of such business gurus as Peter Drucker, he produced extensive research, insights and knowledge into how systems-thinking is the only way to approach organisational development. Dr Ackoff reinforced my long-held view that the lack of systems-thinking is exactly the problem that organisations face when implementing improvements in customer management.

Systems-thinking is an approach that views an organisation or situation as a whole comprised of many parts, yet, at the same time, it is more than the sum of its individual parts. Dr Ackoff added that a system is also defined by the function it fulfils in the wider system. We can liken this idea to the system of the body, in which we are defined not by the functioning of our parts but on our function in the greater system, be that our family, community or life.

There are a number of principles that apply to this concept. The first is that each part affects the behaviour of the whole. If your heart or lungs are not functioning correctly then this will affect the wellbeing of your entire body. The second principle is that no part has an independent effect on the overall system. This means that the way your heart affects you depends upon how your lungs are functioning. The ability for your muscles to get you to walk in a straight line will depend on the balance maintained by your inner ear. Thus all parts are interconnected and interdependent. The third principle is that the system itself has properties which none of its parts have. Dr Ackoff uses the example that if you were to cut off your hand, your hand itself would not be able to write. You, as the whole system, are the one who writes. You, therefore, cannot take a system apart and understand correctly how it works. Understanding the whole requires you to understand the interaction of its parts and the resultant capabilities that the entire system has.

Taking the analogy further, Dr Ackoff explains that the challenges we face come from our approach in attempting to understand our organisations, using analytical thinking. This approach is akin to taking every type of motor car apart and analysing which one has the best engine, the best transmission and the best steering. If you took the best out of every car and put it together you wouldn't even have a car, as none of the parts would fit. If we scrutinise every part of the system and aggregate our understanding of the parts, we will never be able to understand the whole or make improvements to it. Instead, according to Dr Ackoff, we should use systems-thinking to truly understand how the pieces fit together.

"In our work we see organizations seemingly concretized, frozen in the headlights — built and organized for much more stable and predictable times. It seems too facile to repeat the mantra that the world in which we inhabit and need to evolve is increasingly dynamic and unstable because of the increasing interconnectedness and interdependence of individuals, groups, organizations, institutions, and societies. But we worry that too many organizations will wither and die because they lack the vision and foresight to do anything. And if you haven't guessed it yet these rapid changes in communication, technology and our environments have become larger, more complex, and less predictable — in short, more turbulent" [6].

We are so accustomed to thinking about our organisations as individual departments or silos, that, while systems-thinking may seem like a simple philosophy, in practice, we continue to struggle to grasp the basics. Business units are designed around an unnatural and piece-meal view of people, processes and technology, not fully considering the interconnectedness of a business unit with every other part of the business. In our organisations we have a marketing department, an operations department and a human resource department. Each department represents a point of view, yet not the whole picture.

Einstein said that "without changing our patterns of thought, we will not be able to solve the problems we created with our current patterns of thought". While we have an analytical and dissecting way of viewing our organisation, we will not come close to understanding the grander purpose that it is possible for the system as a whole to achieve. In order to solve the challenges we face within our organisations we have to move towards "synthetic thinking", which is an integrated approach that recognises the complexity of interconnectedness. This requires being able to grasp the nature of the whole system and its overall behaviour. From this holistic perspective we can identify the roles and components within the system, understand the interactions between the components and, lastly, understand how those interactions affect the whole. This will result in a far better understanding of what we should be doing to achieve an obvious outcome, namely superior business performance over the short term and long term.

A systems-thinking approach to customer management

Customer management is the business model that enables your organisation to design and deliver a unique and distinctive customer experience. In turn, this model or ecosystem allows you to acquire, retain and develop targeted customers efficiently for the benefit of all stakeholders. Saul Kaplan [14(xiv, xvii)] eloquently describes this need for a new business model: "The most exciting and best opportunities require entirely new business models or ways to create, deliver and capture value. New business model ideas come not by looking through the lens of the current business model, but by learning how to look through the lens of the customer."

In alignment with systems-thinking, customer management is systemic in nature — the whole being greater than the sum of its parts. Unlike a motor car, customer management is a living system built upon the complexity and interconnectedness of people, culture, attitudes and behaviours. An analytical and component view of customer management is a curse that prevents us from really understanding the dynamics of delivering superior and differentiated customer experiences.

There are some fundamental principles that are essential in our quest to understand customer management from a systems perspective. Firstly, customers are an economic asset that yields future cash flow. Secondly, any cost incurred within an organisation to build a customer asset base is an investment and not an expense. This comes from the fact that, in most cases, all of your existing revenue streams, today and tomorrow, are going to be realised through the customer. Thirdly, good management of your customer assets is critical for your long-term success and profitability. These principles are specifically addressed in the next chapter of this book as a critical focus area for the business case on customer-centricity.

In order to fulfil these customer-oriented principles, your organisation needs to develop interconnectivity across all the areas of the business that touch upon and affect the customer. This practice extends way beyond merely linking functional areas. It requires the deep integration of your customers' experience end-to-end across the entire customer life cycle, from before they first become customers, right through to until after they have left and you are trying to win them back. Across every channel that interfaces with the customer, such as a call centre, a retail outlet, an intermediary partner, or web site, there needs to be a consistent and differentiated customer experience.

"One way to forge those connections is to do away with traditional silos altogether and create new ones organized by customer segments or needs. Many companies, however, are understandably reluctant to let go of the economies of scale and depth of knowledge and expertise associated with non-customer-focused silos" [10].

If you are not adopting an end-to-end and integrated perspective of your customer you will never be able to deliver a consistent experience. At the same time, embracing a systems-thinking approach to customer management brings with it the acknowledgement that the very foundation of your organisation may need to change in order to sufficiently support the complexity and interconnectedness required by this approach. Gone are the days when a marketing department can reduce their budget or initiate a new campaign without due consideration of how such decisions will affect the entire customer management system. No part is independent or without impact on the whole.

The REAP Customer-Centric Organisational Blueprint® or REAP CCOB

In Chapter 1 the need for a customer-centric business model was established as a critical success factor for your business transformation. The REAP CCOB was suggested as an approach for strategizing, planning and operationalizing your organisation for a future customer-centric state in order that you find new, sustainable ways to create, deliver and capture value.

In this chapter we explore each area of the REAP CCOB in a little more depth, creating an integrated context of this organisational blueprint and highlighting the interdependence that supports customer-centric transformation. Group Partners' approach [6] supported the development of this greater level of insight.

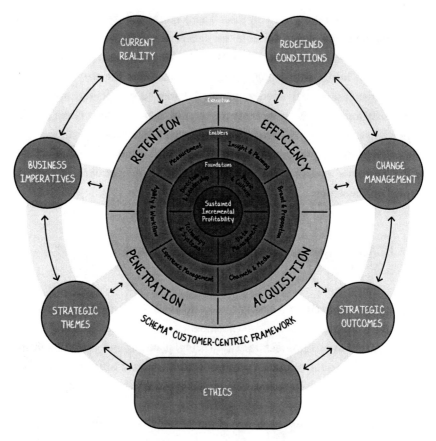

Figure 5: The REAP Customer-Centric Organisation Blueprint® (REAP Consulting, 2013)

Current Reality

Developing a deep understanding of your organisation's current reality uncovers important clues that will be fundamental to your transformation. This is about understanding your core assets and infrastructure and being able to define what assets the business has along with understanding its ambition to deliver and perform in its current state. Clear and consistent answers to the following questions are required:

- What do we do today?
- What assets do we have today?
- What are our core processes today?

- How do we operate today?
- What are our key systems and facilities, resources and unique competencies today?
- What are our key capabilities today?
- What or who are our priority stakeholders?
- Are there any trends that we should observe?
- Are there any key traits that exemplify the critical stakeholders that we specifically need to observe?
- What are the "points of pain" for the key stakeholders?
- What key issues do the key stakeholders have?
- What are the insights that will inform us of the key stakeholders' needs?
- What causes stakeholder satisfaction?
- What causes stakeholder dissatisfaction?
- What are the external drivers that influence our stakeholders?
- What are the definitions by which we should profile or segment our customers or citizens?
- What are the priority customer or citizen segments?
- Are there any key traits that distinguish the critical customer segments?
- What are the needs of our customers/clients/citizens/beneficiaries in their association with us and our offer?
- What are their hopes and ambitions in their dealings with us?
- What are their aspirations in their dealings with us?
- What are the drivers of customer satisfaction?
- What are the drivers of customer dissatisfaction?
- How well do we truly know and understand our customers?

You need to gather deep insights in order to evolve from your current situation. This requires recognising the burning issues and pressures that will be important to take account of as you consider the future. Business today consists of a tangle of issues and challenges as well as "oceans" of opportunity. It's important to understand the root cause of these issues. Political, economic, technological, environmental and social forces impact business, both positively and negatively. Organisational complexity, competition, "silo-based" thinking, lack of business alignment, standards, prioritisation, risk aversion, "short-termism" and measures that may drive inappropriate behaviours, all impact current performance and sustainability.

Business Imperatives

These are the themes and "must do's" that will focus and clarify the direction you must take to achieve your declared strategic outcome or future vision. You need to answer the question: what is absolutely critical if we want to achieve our vision or strategic outcome? These imperatives are the foundation for all planning, and the achievement of them will determine success. You need to properly define, understand and agree upon these imperatives in order to ensure you can create metrics and KPIs that contribute to the successful delivery of your strategy.

Strategic Themes

The strategic themes are those major themes of work underpinned by the projects and initiatives that you need to deliver in order to achieve your organisation's strategic outcome. Importantly, there must be a direct correlation between these themes, your strategic outcome and your redefined conditions. They are few in number and should be well balanced across those areas in which sustained competitive advantage can be developed.

Redefined Conditions

Redefined conditions are the resulting outcomes of your transformation, the beginning of the understanding of what it'll be like when you succeed as a team. They are the key metrics, measures or effects (KPIs) that you will be striving for across your organisation. There is a direct "line of sight" between the redefined conditions and the actions and initiatives that underpin the strategic themes. Through your redefined conditions, you decide what you believe to be your intended outcomes in the future. These conditions will be the new experiences that result directly from the effort and changes made over the given period. The redefined conditions result in measures and metrics that highlight the meaningful and measurable results that you demand. This provides confidence that you are developing a fully aligned and measurable solution and will enable you to know when your organisation's strategic outcome is in place.

Change Management

The failure rate of strategic transformation programmes is overwhelming. The implementation of a revised business model results in re-occurring waves of strategic transformation. The transformation management process involves the task of managing change, using an ethical and professional approach. Appropriate knowledge and common sense, a control mechanism and a layout of a well-planned organisational communication system are critical to its success. It is imperative to estimate what impact a change is likely to have on your employees' behaviour patterns, motivation, work processes, technological requirements and finances.

To operationalize the REAP CCOB, a number of imperatives need to be addressed in order to unify teams, inculcate the culture required and deliver the change that is needed for successful transformation:

- Clarity as to why you are engaging in change management – in other words, what is the logic behind the transformation?
- A clear definition of the end game and the vision everyone is working towards.
- High-level executive "buy-in" as their role is to convey the transformation business case and convince their teams to support it.
- Clarity and coaching regarding the behavioural change required by executive and functional leaders for the "new organisational way".
- A single view of what it will take to achieve this vision as a cohesive and effective team, while recognising the importance of diversity.
- Complete understanding of the implications of the transformation programme on the current "business-as-usual" policy.
- Moving in the right direction as one team aligned behind the same principles or guidance system.
- Transparency of the real issues and blocks that prevent or slow down the implementation of the business model across areas such as processes, responsibilities, measurement, reward and consequences.
- Focused commitment to make the changes necessary that will effectively implement the new business model.
- Clearly defined initiatives that will directly deliver on the change required for the new business model while ensuring the right level of empowerment

is in place.
- Transformation management components including governance, business alignment, programme planning and programme oversight.
- A mechanism to measure and report on progress to ensure that everyone stays focused on the vision and the agreed principles.

Strategic Outcomes

The strategic outcome is the overall ambition beyond your organisation's financial goals and often stated objectives. This is the highest order of "prize" – the supreme and primary reason for your existence. This is the "absolute clarity" of the end goal, sometimes voiced in your vision and mission statements. The strategic outcome evolves from having defined your challenges, problems and/ or opportunities and having a consistent interpretation of your ambitions and aspirations and what you're aiming for. This process involves the discovery of what you could do (as distinct and separate from what you are doing) and being united by a common purpose. It's about understanding what the business model or "way of working" will be in the future.

Ethics

Business ethics refers to the ethical values (responsibility, accountability, fairness and transparency) that determine the interaction between a company and its stakeholders. Responsible leaders build a sustainable business by having regard to the company's economic, social and environmental impact on the community in which it operates. They do this through effective strategy and operations, considering both the short-term and long-term impact of their personal and institutional decisions on the economy, society and environment. Responsible leaders do not compromise the natural environment and the livelihood of future generations. They embrace a shared value with all the company's stakeholders, both internal and external. They give direct rather than incidental consideration to the legitimate interests and expectations of their stakeholders [15].

SCHEMA® – the Customer-Centric Framework

Central to the REAP CCOB is SCHEMA®, the customer-centric framework upon which a large part of this book is based. SCHEMA® is a well-known model that provides a set of fundamental and critical building blocks that should be recognised as part of your overall customer-centric business model. These building blocks create a governing "architecture" for your transformation, ensuring that the initial intent is driven through to execution while staying true to the end goal. In totality this encourages you to think carefully about how you create value, and how you can improve and transform your organisation. It's about designing tomorrow's organisation, today.

The next chapter of this book, being the last chapter of *Part One*, explores an area critical to the effective implementation of customer-centricity – understanding the compelling business case for a customer-centric approach and the key considerations of sustainability and stakeholder engagement in the drive to develop superior business performance.

Transformation questions

- Can you articulate your business model? How do you create, capture and deliver value?
- How do you stay relevant in a changing and uncertain world?
- In what ways do you use systems-thinking to ensure your business delivers a relevant and consistent end-to-end customer experience?
- Are you capable of really transforming, or do you settle for incremental improvements?
- What are you doing now to build the capacity and capability you require to design and deliver a unique and distinctive customer experience?
- What framework are you using to ensure your approach to customer-centricity is holistic, integrated and consistent across the entire business?
- Is serving the interest of customers a priority in the way you run your business?

Case study – Johnson delivers an end-to-end customer management approach

Johnson is a Canadian insurance provider that is widely recognised as a world leader when it comes to the integrated and effective implementation of a customer-centric business model. Founded in 1880 and employing over 600 people across more than 30 locations in Canada and in more than 40 branches, Johnson has, since 2000, focused on a high growth strategy that puts the customer at the centre of the business and at the forefront of all decision-making. The company's consistent and continued double-digit annual growth has been attributed by leading customer management experts as being directly due to Johnson's commitment to customer-centricity in all areas of the organisation.

A fundamental principle of this company's success has been the organisational alignment and interconnection between its strategy, employees, customers and stakeholders, which has focused on a common set of goals with the customer at the centre of these goals. In so doing, each individual component of the organisation is part of a bigger customer-centric vision, or a system within a system.

A key support structure for the company's success to date has been Johnson's effective use of an integrated customer management framework that has helped to develop and implement the end-to-end foundational capability within the organisation. This integrated approach has included:

- Creating an ownership and entrepreneurial culture
- Hiring the right people
- Conducting effective training and development
- Using customer-specific goals and measuring the appropriate results to gauge success
- Conducting extensive research
- Deriving deep insights from customer data
- Integrating the consistent use of clear customer segments across the organisation
- Using organisational communication structures such as brainstorming

sessions and employee forums
- Listening intently to customer needs and complaints
- Optimising customer engagement through effective technology
- Connecting the company's overall strategy to the customer strategy
- Many other activities aimed at the long-term transformational journey that customer-centricity brings

The results of Johnson's customer-centric approach speak for themselves. Besides the direct financial returns, Johnson has developed an exceptionally focused and motivated team. In 2012 Johnson celebrated winning the prestigious award of "Canada's Top 100 Employers" for a fourth consecutive year. This success underpins probably this company's greatest achievement in customer-centricity – the development of a truly customer-centric culture and supporting their employees to deliver a superior customer experience.

● CHAPTER 3:

● THE BUSINESS CASE FOR CUSTOMER-CENTRICITY

Transformation Intent

The traditional financial-based forms of measurement on their own do not adequately address sustainable business performance. Transform instead how you view customer value – the customer as an asset requiring investment as well as a unique experience to deliver superior life time value. Through this approach you will realise the compelling benefit of a customer-centric business model.

A world in crisis

In 2008 the global economy went into shock at the news of the collapse of Lehman Brothers, the fourth largest investment bank in the United States at the time. Considered the greatest bankruptcy in the history of the United States, the ramifications of this incident spread far beyond the borders of North America.

The demise of Lehman Brothers took place in the context of the widespread systemic problem in the United States real estate market, a bubble that could no longer be contained. High risk and overvalued bonds structured into securities, and used as investment vehicles worldwide, started to crumble as housing prices continued to decline and high-risk mortgages could no longer be covered by the value of the real estate bonded to it.

Lehman Brothers started to illegally use a repurchase agreement to move debt off and back onto its balance sheet at the end of every quarter, aiming to cover up the immense losses being recorded from these bundled securities. Debt became temporarily classified as a sale until the repurchase agreement was concluded and the transaction was reversed. At a point when JP Morgan called in its transaction loan, Lehman Brothers could not pay. Its $639 billion of assets could not cover its $768 billion of debt.

Sudden uncertainty in the market arose from the question: if this could happen to a large investment bank that seemed to be doing well, how deep did this problem go within the entire economy? As a result, almost all lending froze, banks no longer had sufficient working capital as a result of all following the same high risk practices; and, before long, government had to intervene. The wave of panic spread worldwide because it became apparent just how extensive the use of these overvalued securities had become. It also became evident that the entire economic and monetary system was based on a short-term, quick-fix view with no thought to the long-term impact on the growth of the global economy. The foundation of the economic and monetary system was broken.

The scale of the worldwide impact from this series of events further highlighted this immense systemic problem in global financial markets. With these markets being so interconnected and interdependent, no collapse or speed bump in any economy would go without repercussions for the whole world.

"CEOs have commented to us often about the uncomfortable relationship between the need for short-term returns, to appease the demands of shareholders, and the requirement for long-term investment and sustainability. When we first wrote about this in 2002, we learned from the Enron, Worldcom and Equitable Life scandals that the short term balance sheet can look good, but can be misleading. Sadly, in 2008 we now have a host of examples of this. A company can make excellent profits this year and look good on the balance sheet even though it acquires high risk customers, acquires a competitor which de-stabilises its core business, cuts customer service standards to decrease costs, fires 30% of its staff, encourages a hard-sell policy to existing customers, reduces its marketing budget by half, fails to invest in product development and cuts all of its IT development budgets" [27].

Sustainable business performance

Since the collapse commencing 2008, governments and businesses have been focusing on understanding what it means to be sustainable and, through that sustainability, deliver superior business performance.

Gro Harlem Brundtland, who headed the United Nations' World Commission on Environment and Development, defined sustainability as "development that meets the needs of the present without compromising the ability of future generations to meet their own needs" [16].

From a business perspective, sustainability requires strategic development that plans for and delivers on a business' long-term goals for growth and development, coupled with the effective measurement thereof. Furthermore, this long-term strategy should consider a broad range of risks and likely impacts on the natural environment and society, while delivering efficient management of assets and resources. This is often referred to as the "triple bottom line", also known as people, planet and profit. Holistic and integrated reporting should demonstrate the extent to which the business is operating in a sustainable manner [17].

Sustainability is also showing that it can deliver results. A recent study has shown that companies delivering a high level of sustainability, when compared to their counterparts, delivered a significantly higher return over an 18-year period across criteria such as return on assets and return on equity [18]. Even stock market returns of these successful companies were 4.8% higher than those considered to be on a low level of sustainability.

> "What differentiates sustainable companies from traditional ones? Sustainable organizations are effective at engaging with external stakeholders and employees. They have cultures based on innovation and trust. They have a track record of implementing large-scale change" [18].

From a systems-thinking perspective, a sustainable approach to business recognises the interconnection between the business itself and the stakeholders and communities it engages with. There is a link between customer, strategy, risk, sustainability and performance.

The quest for profit at all cost is a disease suffered by many businesses resulting from their obsession with reflecting the value on paper that shareholders expect at the end of every financial quarter. Lehman Brothers certainly suffered from this obsession.

This often misdirected and singular focus on financial results, and the negative impact therefrom, is one of the reasons that *Ethics* has been included in the REAP CCOB. In so doing, the customer-centric business model encompasses a balanced approach to managing both the triple bottom line and stakeholder interests through the effective implementation of the ethical values of responsibility, accountability, fairness and transparency.

Sustainable business performance, therefore, demands ethical leadership. Richard Bellingham describes this powerfully in his book entitled *Ethical Leadership*:

> Ethical leadership has one outcome: sustainable development. We cannot sustain progress if our corporate culture does not support our policies. We cannot sustain growth if we do not invest in our people and treat them as whole persons with unique gifts. We cannot sustain profits if we fail to help our customers achieve their productivity and profitability goals. We cannot sustain development on a global basis if we do not treat the environment more respectfully and help transform developing countries into healthier, productive, and more prosperous communities, [19 (p93-94)].

Customers are an economic asset that yields future cash flow

Business performance means different things depending on which stakeholder perspective you have and this often results in conflict [20]. Shareholders may become excited to learn that your company has reduced its costs, yet for customers this may mean longer queues, reduced quality of merchandise or

– the classic irritation of customers – a cost-saving hidden in a non-obvious reduction in size, volume or feature of their purchase.

Shareholders may welcome increases in revenue and put pressure on your board and management to keep increasing revenue. Yet an excessive drive for revenue may tempt your organisation to take risks that it shouldn't in the Acquisition of new customers.

While a regulator may be satisfied that your company is complying strictly to regulations and legislation, adherence to those same regulations may mean customer inconvenience, which may have a negative effect on the overall customer experience.

While sustainability requires balancing the diverse range of stakeholder expectations, it also requires measures that reflect the delivery of the long-term strategy and the real driver of that growth – the customer. Measures of performance such as profit, return on investment, market capitalisation and net asset value are all valid yet do not represent the whole picture. While in most cases these factors are certainly easier to measure than intangible performance improvements, they focus merely on the outcome and not the means of generating sustainable and superior business performance.

"An analysis of US and UK consumers shows that customer experience is highly correlated to loyalty. Customer experience leaders have more than a 16 percentage point advantage over customer experience laggards in consumers' willingness to buy more, their reluctance to switch business away, and their likelihood to recommend. A modest increase in customer experience can result in a gain over three years of up to $382 million for US companies and up to £263 million for UK firms, depending on the industry" [26].

Dr Claes Fornell, an expert on customer satisfaction and asset measurement, founded the American Customer Satisfaction Index (ACSI) in 1994. The ACSI is a monthly measure of customer satisfaction across the United States economy. 17 years of ACSI data has led to startling insights that are steadily influencing the importance CEOs and shareholders are placing on the customer [21].

Fornell's research exposed a correlation between companies with high ACSI scores and the performance of said companies on the New York Stock Exchange (the Dow), the NASDAQ and the S&P500. Fornell found that selecting a sample portfolio of stocks chosen for the high ACSI results outperformed the market average results from these three stock exchanges. This finding provides further evidence that excellence in customer satisfaction is directly linked to the value of the business and its potential for sustainable business performance.

Fornell's work further revealed that the very structure of the balance sheet is changing. In 1930, 80% of the market value of companies (for Dow Jones industrials) was reflected as tangible assets on the balance sheet, the remaining 20% comprising intangible assets. In 1970, intangible assets had increased to 50% of the market value and by 1999 a staggering 80% of organisational value was reflected as intangibles [22]. Intangible assets are, therefore, a critical component in measuring market value and are an excellent indicator of future cash flow.

There are three types of intangible assets:

- Employee competence including values, knowledge and loyalty;
- Internal structures that include patents, management systems, models and culture; and
- External structures such as customer knowledge and relationships, and brand value.

Ranjay Gulati, Professor of Business Administration at Harvard Business School, conducted research into the correlation between companies focused on their customers and their business performance. He tracked companies between 2001 and 2007 as part of his research for his book *Reorganize for Resilience: Putting Customers at the Center of Your Business* [23]. When he compared the performance of "outside-in" companies, or those that viewed their organisation from a customer perspective, to the average performance of the S&P500, he discovered massive differences as illustrated in the table below.

	Shareholder Returns		Sales Growth	
	Outside-In Companies	S&P500 Performance	Outside-In Companies	S&P500 Performance
Study between 2001 and 2007	150%	14%	134%	53%
Extended time period study from 1999 to 2007	130%	0.6%	233%	10%

Figure 6: Differences between Outside-in Companies and S&P500 Performance [23]

With shareholder returns of over 10 times the industry performance standard and sales growth of 2.5 times that of the benchmark, the argument for the business case on customer-centricity is compelling. Gulati [23] then extended his research to take into account a wider time range, factoring in the longer term perspective. The gap between "outside-in" companies and the average increased even further. With a review period of just two years longer, shareholder returns of the "outside-in" organisations were over 200 times that of the standard and sales growth escalated to 23 times.

This research shows the value of the customer as an asset that, if managed correctly, can deliver superior business performance for an organisation's value and profitability. The question then becomes – what is the value of your customer equity and what investments are you making to develop it?

Costs incurred to build a customer asset base are investments

Customer equity lies at the very heart of customer-centricity. It is the sum of the customer lifetime values across a company's entire customer base. Developing customer equity requires a dynamic, integrative marketing system that uses financial valuation techniques and data about customers to optimise the Acquisition, Retention and selling of additional products to a firm's customers. This maximises the value to the company of the customer relationship throughout its life cycle.

One of the methodologies used very successfully over approximately the last 12 years to measure customer-centric capability globally was CMAT™ (Customer Management Assessment Tool). CMAT™ was an objective, quantitative and benchmarked assessment of the current customer management capability of an organisation.

In research commissioned by QCi, the developers of CMAT™, the correlation between how well a company managed its customers (CMAT™ scores) and overall business performance was examined. The results showed a strong correlation (0.8) between good customer management performance and business performance (Figure 7) [22].

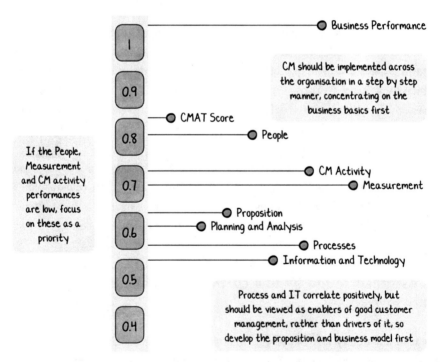

Figure 7: Correlation between CMAT™ Scores and Overall Business Performance

The highest correlation was with the overall CMAT™ score itself, implying that the greatest business performance was achieved by carrying out a number of priority business activities across the whole model, rather than focussing deeply on one specific area such as *Planning and Analysis*. Whilst correlation does not necessarily mean causation, all the combined evidence from the various performance studies suggests that striving for "best in class" across the "system" delivers a sound return on investment.

In a second analysis [24] of the CMAT™ results from a much larger sample, it was investigated to what extent customer management impacted on more tangible measures of profit, such as Return on Capital Employed (ROCE), Operating Profit, Returns on Assets (ROA) and the like. Figure 8 summarises these results.

Measure	Correlation	Confidence
Return on capital employed	.61	99%
Re-investment rate total	.53	99%
Operating profit margin	.46	99%
Return on assets	.39	99%
Re-investment rate per share	.31	95%
Return on equity per share	.30	99%
Net margin	.27	99%

Figure 8: Correlation between Overall CMAT™ Scores and Various Financial Indicators

As can be seen from the results, and using ROCE as an example, if a company's ROCE score increases or decreases by 1%, we can be 99% confident that 61% of this variation is due to changes in the CMAT™ scores.

Good management of your customer assets is critical for your long term sustainability

Managing your customers as valuable assets through an effective customer management strategy will, therefore, result in improvements in business performance where it counts most – bottom line profit. Yet customer management strategies can't remain purely theoretical and strategic – they need to be translated into tactical interventions which deliver real results.

There are four underlying principles or levers behind the delivery of these results – Retention, Efficiency, Acquisition and Penetration, or REAP. The application of these principles in terms of specific focus and measurement works to improve business performance through the translation of strategy into action. Each of these levers is examined in-depth in the last part of this book – Part Four, *Execution*.

"Firms with high CXi (Customer Experience Index) scores tend to have more customers who purchase again, who don t switch to competitors, and who recommend them. Our models show that the loyalty-based revenue benefits for a firm going from a below-industry average CXi score to an above-average score ranged from \$31 million for retailers to \$1.4 billion for hotels" [25].

Implementing a customer management strategy and utilising the REAP concept begins with extensive planning and developing a deep understanding of the nature and value (actual and potential) of existing customers and potential prospects. This is not a trivial or instant process. Before any company embarks on this approach, clear commitment from the senior management team is imperative. Since the tools necessary to implement customer management may need to be able to extend to millions of customers, full support is needed from the information technology (IT) and information management teams. This commitment must be matched to an activity plan, further supported by access to the necessary skills and competencies. The whole exercise will be wasted unless it results in potential changes to business development activities and will involve challenging some long-held practices and beliefs.

What is of critical importance for business value to be achieved is the realisation that change must occur within the organisation. The existing financial metrics by which most companies are managed are not easily adapted to account for the balance between short-term revenue and longer term value. Consequently, an understanding of where business actually comes from is needed to determine whether the primary focus should be on customer Acquisition, improved services, new product development, Retention activities or cost reductions.

Extracting value from this understanding depends upon the creation of a realistic, robust and validated strategy based on REAP planning.

The success of this strategy also depends on the establishment of specific tactics to address each of the REAP elements in such a way that different value groups can be treated differently. It is then necessary to create measurement systems to monitor the effects of the chosen tactics to ensure these are providing real business value. It is critical that all sections of the business can see that they have a contribution to make to business development. Involving each business function in customer management measures is a good way to achieve this.

One of the most cost efficient ways to drive operating profit in any organisation is to examine the means of retaining good customers. However, this activity can't be conducted in isolation, because simply retaining customers at any cost can represent reduced value to the company. Both extremes must be examined in order to see where the greatest value can be created.

Without the planning and management of Acquisition activity, "acquisition at any cost" may result. Attention must be paid to the targeting of good quality new or previous customers and the managing of the relationship with them from their first expression of interest right through to their conversion to a customer. Also valuable is the tracking of enquiries and sales leads as well as looking for measures to prevent low value or high-risk prospects being converted into customers.

Equally critical to an organisation's return on its customer investment is Penetration, or the ability to develop more value from existing customers through cross-sell and up-sell activities. An investment in extending the value of existing customers can deliver much more value than the same investment in winning new customers.

The Acquisition, Retention and value development of customers cannot be carried out at any price. If the cost of the activity exceeds the value delivered to the organisation, profitability will suffer, hence the required understanding of the cost-to-serve the respective customer or customer grouping. An Efficiency plan focuses on calculating, allocating and controlling costs in a manner that adequately supports the objectives of the other three customer management strategies.

Customer management is an extensive and even onerous undertaking for any business. However, an improved understanding of the customer, the creation of strategies and tactics that enable your organisation to generate value for the customer, carry with it the promise of great rewards, improved business performance and the creation of real value.

In the next part of this book we will focus on the four *Foundations* you require in order to build customer management capability that delivers sustainable business performance. These include:

- Chapter 4: Direction and Leadership
- Chapter 5: People and Culture
- Chapter 6: Data Management
- Chapter 7: Technology and Systems

Transformation questions

- Do you understand how customer-centric capability drives profit?
- Do you acknowledge that being customer-centric is not just about making customers happy, rather it's about motivating them to act in a way that is valuable to your business?
- Do you see the link between customer management capability and the ability to influence REAP (Retention, Efficiency (cost to serve), Acquisition and Penetration (cross-sell and upsell) levers and a mitigation of earnings risk?
- Do you understand the importance of "trust" in delivering sustained, superior business performance?
- Are you giving your customers a voice, and listening to it?
- How much of your profitability is coming through new clients? How much from existing clients?
- How much of your profitability is coming from new products sold to new clients versus new products sold to existing clients?
- Do you put profit before customers?

Case study – the SCHEMA Value Estimator™ defines the business case for customer-centricity

One of the tools we use to build the business case for customer centricity is the SCHEMA Value Estimator™. This is one of the modules of the SCHEMA® toolset developed by The Customer Framework Limited. This module takes current key customer-related value and behaviour metrics to produce a segmented view of where value currently comes from. It shows the value of customers acquired and those being lost, how customer value grows and how much is spent on customers of differing values. It is generated from information provided by the organisation about its current Retention, Efficiency, Acquisition and Penetration performance, with briefing and support being given to the organisation in the sourcing of this data.

The SCHEMA Value Estimator™ then drives the development of a realistic, precedent-based estimate of the potential value uplift from adopting various types of customer strategies. It enables the fast and robust testing of a wide range of "what-if" scenarios against a set of industry-specific value drivers under the "Retention, Efficiency, Acquisition and Penetration" dimensions upon which the module is based.

The testing is made even faster by the provision of a series of start-point strategies, based on approaches known to have worked in other organisations and supported by statistics and precedents from the SCHEMA Knowledge Base™. The results can be extended to cover periods of up to five years, taking into account the build-up and decay patterns of different type of benefits. Cost data can also be added if a full ROI view is required to support a business case.

While many executives may feel overwhelmed with the task of proving the business case for their customer strategies, as a methodology and tool, the SCHEMA Value Estimator™ brings the element of scientific planning back into customer value management. It creates a "line of sight" between your organisational strategy, your specific REAP strategies and the financial performance they will deliver to your organisation.

A business case approach to customer management and the optimisation of the customer as an asset is, therefore, more than a nice to have – it is a critical part of activating customer-centricity in your organisation and driving sustainable business performance.

SCHEMA VALUE ESTIMATOR

PERFORMANCE UPLIFT

Value Driver Strategies

2	Increased Market/Share
0	Better Acquisition Mix
0	Increased Activation
0	Higher Winback rate
2	Reduced Losses
0	Reduced Dormancy
1	Increased Cross-selling
0	Higher Purchase Value
0	Higher Purchase Frequency
2	Lower Cost-to-Acquire
2	Lower Cost-to-Serve
0	Lower Cost-of-Failure

Segment Strategies

0	HV Customer Focus
3	Marzipan Layer Focus
0	Mid-Ground Focus
0	Manage Up The Tail
0	Manage Out Loss-Makers

Reset STRATEGY Changes
Reset MANUAL Changes

Total Full Year Value 16,889,279

Value Segment		RETENTION		EFFICIENCY		ACQUISITION			PENETRATION	
		Lost Customers	Customers Going Dormant	Cost to Acquire	Cost to Serve	New Customers /Year	Activation Rate	Customers Won Back	Core Usage Revenue	Products/ Customer
Critical Few	Current Performance	50	38	135.00	255.00	55	97.30%	3	2,958.00	2.32
	Potential Performance	46	38	135.00	244.80	57	97.30%	3	2,975.75	2.33
Very High Value	Current Performance	2,181	1,588	135.00	125.00	2,345	96.40%	117	1,237.00	1.98
	Potential Performance	2,181	1,493	126.90	12.50	2,580	102.18%	138	1,266.69	2.03
High Value	Current Performance	10,343	7,833	97.00	125.00	11,238	93.80%	543	366.13	1.76
	Potential Performance	10,343	7,363	91.18	12.50	12,362	99.43%	641	374.92	1.80
Medium High Value	Current Performance	17,884	12,001	55.00	45.00	19,987	90.50%	999	316.18	1.43
	Potential Performance	16,453	12,001	55.00	45.00	20,786	90.50%	999	318.07	1.41
Medium Value	Current Performance	43,550	34,330	55.00	45.00	54,323	90.10%	2,544	153.36	1.29
	Potential Performance	40,066	34,330	55.00	43.20	56,196	90.10%	2,544	154.27	1.30
Medium Low Value	Current Performance	43,005	30,459	55.00	45.00	43,234	89.30%	1,987	94.80	1.22
	Potential Performance	39,565	30,459	55.00	43.20	44,963	89.30%	1,987	95.57	1.23
Low Value	Current Performance	33,202	27,998	15.00	45.00	35,432	81.50%	1,767	43.98	1.16
	Potential Performance	30,546	27,998	15.00	43.20	36,849	81.50%	1,767	44.25	1.17
Very Low Value	Current Performance	18,995	16,549	15.00	45.00	22,123	83.40%	1,111	6.76	1.09
	Potential Performance	17,475	16,549	15.00	43.20	23,008	83.40%	1,111	6.80	1.10
Marginals	Current Performance	13,440	11,454	8.00	45.00	15,432	89.60%	780	1.45	1.04
	Potential Performance	12,365	11,454	8.00	45.00	16,049	89.60%	780	1.46	1.05
Loss Makers	Current Performance	8,942	5,443	8.00	65.00	6,578	94.30%	313	3.55	1.05
	Potential Performance	8,208	5,443	8.00	65.00	6,841	94.30%	313	3.57	1.06
TOTAL/AVERAGE	Current Performance	191,572	147,693	57.80	84.00	210,747	90.92%	10,164	518.12	1.43
	Potential Performance	177,248	147,128	56.41	79.76	1,421,544	92.06%	10,283	524.11	1.43
Driver Value		1,266,804	987,262	97,687	4,558,033	1,421,544	1,910,283	60,288	2,048,867	3,429,361
Dimension Value		38%	42%	16%	37%	50%	34%		6,955,211	
Driver Value										
Dimension Value		38%		16%		50%			33%	
		42%		37%		34%			33%	

Figure 9: SCHEMA Value Estimator™

PART TWO:

FOUNDATIONS

CHAPTER 4:

DIRECTION AND LEADERSHIP

Transformation Intent

The keystone of an effective customer-centric foundation is an innovative, integrated, customer-centric strategy that is driven by leaders passionate about, and committed to, transforming the organisation, while delivering sustainable and superior business performance. This focused direction will enable you to demonstrate the compelling business case for customer-centricity through meaningful customer value metrics and realistic customer planning. Change management, in turn, supports you to develop an intrinsic customer-centric culture that activates the transformation required.

Leadership in the 21st century

Business leaders of the 21st century have a challenging job on their hands. We live in anxious times marked by uncertainty. How to stay relevant in this world is a big question. Leaders grapple with how their organisations will stay abreast of the tide of change, while continuing to deliver superior business performance and the expected results for their shareholders. At the forefront of this paradigm shift are the three main buzz words of the 21st century — innovation, sustainability and stakeholder engagement.

Innovation is no longer reserved for new start-ups and dynamic venture capital incubators. Every organisation has to be innovative in order to create and sustain competitive advantage in their market. Globalisation, consumer awareness and technological advancements are pushing the boundaries of those organisations not ready to innovate, internally and through their products and services. This drive for innovation means that you invent on behalf of the customer, while collaborating with customers in that process. Leaders have to be able to identify where future value will be created. It's a proactive journey, rather than a reactive one.

As was explored in Chapter 3, the need for companies to be sustainable is changing the criteria used to evaluate a company's success. The lessons of companies such as Enron, Worldcom, Lehman Brothers, Stanford, AIG and others, have shown just how unsustainable big player leadership has become in the drive for profit, market share and market capitalisation, while still avoiding accountability for business failures. Authentic leaders are now expected to demonstrate a commitment to long-term, sustainable development of their corporations. More importantly, leaders are expected to govern their organisations based on a moral compass that leaves the world a better place.

> "When leadership commitment drives the process, it usually comes from the personal resolution of a CEO to create a more sustainable company. In general, top executives have the ability to create an enterprise-wide vision and the clout to see that it is realized. Without this commitment, becoming a sustainable company is a 'nonstarter'" [18].

In the shareholder capitalism era, the drive for profit and delivering returns to shareholders was considered the reason business existed. Now, the broader view is that success only comes when you add value to all key stakeholder groups, including customers, employees, suppliers, communities and, of course, investors. Stakeholders do not exist in isolation and their needs have to be considered in light of their interconnected interests and how best to serve them across the board. The challenge is to find the pivot point that unites the core needs of all stakeholders.

In reflecting on Chapter 2, systems-thinking would illustrate that each stakeholder group is part of the whole, and when all parts are rallied together for a common purpose, the whole is worth more than the sum of its parts. A business focused only on one particular stakeholder view, as in the profit-or-die perspective of shareholders, cannot effectively deliver a result.

In the book entitled *Firms of Endearment* [25] the authors explore companies that are guided by stakeholder relationship management as their business model and posit that companies that focus on meeting the needs of all its stakeholders vastly outperform ones that do not. While a widespread holistic stakeholder perspective is still in its infancy, it is integrally linked to customer-centricity and will soon become a business model that followers in the market will attempt to play "catch up" on.

Those inspired leaders who appreciate the criticality of customer-centricity, sustainability and a broad stakeholder view will create a distinct competitive advantage in the market and an endearing position in the hearts and minds of customers. Enlightened leaders support this intent with a clear understanding of the purpose of their organisation that transcends profit and delivers on an innovative strategy that adheres to a set of underlying values. These values should fully link or create the "line of sight" between that purpose and authentic action.

While books on leadership are "a dime a dozen", leadership in customer-centric organisations must be understood from a new angle – that to lead is to serve. In an "inside-out" organisation the orientation of leaders is focused on how they can get something that they want from their customers. Their decisions drive the creation of hierarchical and silo-based structures that are not conducive to supporting customer-centricity or listening to the voices of those stakeholders directly influenced by or influencing the organisation. In an "outside-in" organisation this appreciation of leading through service and customer experience is intrinsically connected. The organisation then exists to serve the customer as a means of becoming truly sustainable and not the other way around.

The Chief Customer Officer

Demonstrating leadership and a commitment to the customer agenda requires the right calibre of individual who is positioned at an executive level and who has the total support of the CEO. This role, often referred to as the Chief Customer Officer (CCO), is rapidly becoming a key high-level position that addresses the customer as a critical asset that requires governance, focus and top-level commitment. According to an analysis from the Chief Customer Officer Council, the CCO position has enjoyed an overall average growth rate of 41% since 2000.

Jeanne Bliss, in her book *Chief Customer Officer*, states that the three goals of the CCO are to:

> Engage the organisation to purposefully manage customer relationships, revenue and profit; create a persistent focus on the customer in the actions the company takes; and drive the organisation to work together to create unified and optimum delivery to customers [26].

Having a CCO sit at the board room table will fundamentally change the calibre and focus of executive meetings. With someone specifically representing the customer at that level, leaders will view the organisation and the decisions they make from a different perspective. In his article, Don Peppers [7] shared a story from Siemens where a senior sales manager carried a folding chair into a meeting to represent the customer and to create awareness of how decisions made on behalf of customers impacted those customers. Attendees at the meeting very soon began to ask different types of questions than they normally would, such as "Would we say this in front of our customer?" and "What would a customer think of our plan in dealing with this issue?" Without customer visibility at an executive level, customer-centric thinking is not possible.

For organisations that do not appoint a CCO, the customer governance or customer experience role is oftentimes positioned as a direct report of the marketing or sales director. Customer management is far too important to be positioned anywhere other than at executive level. Delegation of this responsibility, within a single functional unit and below executive level, significantly increases the risk of failure to build the required cross-functional, customer-centric capabilities. Imagine a marketing director who is a passionate brand "brain-child", specialising in design and cutting-edge thinking in the area of brand and brand development. To him or her, the cross-functional requirements of customer management and the need to integrate sales, service and marketing may not be a top priority.

The CCO role is challenging in that it is multi-dimensional in the way it cuts across business silos, functional areas and organisational processes. This requires a unique approach to customer governance and building bridges with the customer in mind. The appropriate integration of marketing, sales, customer service and delivery ensures that all touch points across the life cycle of the customer, deliver a consistent experience in alignment with organisational intentions and the expectations created with and by the customer.

While the CCO role itself may not have its own bottom line responsibility, it is required to influence the perspectives and behaviours of every aspect of the business that touches the customer. This involves a constant process of creating customer awareness, while motivating and justifying a customer-centric approach to business. In turn, the CCO should drive changing behaviour in such a way that the organisation integrates its end-to-end structure and all functions that have an impact on how the customer is engaged with. This action will improve how the customer experiences the business, both physically and emotionally.

The CCO position is, first and foremost, about improving business performance through maintaining and enhancing the value of the customer base. This is best done through the operationalization of a customer-centric business model.

An effective customer management strategy

It goes without saying that if your organisation pledges to become more customer-centric, your business strategy will focus on how to deliver a customer-centric business model. The reality is that many businesses claim to put the customer first yet are still trapped in inside-out and product-centric thinking.

"How many times have we, in The Customer Framework, heard proclamations from Senior Management Teams that they are going to drive their organisation to be far more 'Customer-Centric'? And how many times have we seen a reference to Customer Focus as one of the three critical strategic areas for the year? Needless to say, we hear this in virtually all of the clients we work with and many of the other organisations with which we engage in research or benchmarking activity. But only when we dare to ask the simple question 'So, what exactly do you mean by that?' does it become clear that these bold statements are often meaningless at best and likely to drive severe value destruction at worst" [28].

A customer-centric organisation, therefore, has a very clear picture of the customer dimension of its strategy. When it comes to the customer, a business strategy should create absolute clarity on who the customer is and what they are worth to the organisation across all segments. This includes recognising a foundational principle of customer-centricity — not all customers are the same. An organisation that looks at their customer base as a "unit of one" is demonstrating their lack of awareness on just what customer-centricity means. As Peppers & Rogers [11] advocate, being customer-centric is about "treating different customers differently".

There is also often confusion for internal departments as to who the customer actually is. Time and time again I'm told by senior individuals within large organisations that they "don't deal" with the customer, instead their "customers" are internal departments or people. For example, the Human Resources department's customer is the employee. Let's be clear. The customer is the end user of the product or service being offered. Irrespective of how many channels, functions or layers you have to go through, there is only one definition of the customer – the ultimate end user of your product or service. Everything you do within your organisation needs to be in support of the experience provided to that end customer. So a mind-set shift is required – how are you supporting every level within your business to enable them to deliver the customer experience promise? A customer-focused business strategy should, therefore, create clarity across the entire organisation and unite everyone behind a common purpose.

You can also observe the level of customer thinking when you look at the customer metrics. Measures emphasising the quality of the customer base indicate customer-centric thinking, while those that only emphasise the size of the customer base do not. Another measure of a customer-centric strategy is how the different parts of the strategy and, therefore, the parts of the business, are referenced and interconnected through that strategy.

A customer management strategy must take into account the internal and external barriers as well as the opportunities that may be present. Clarity within management teams on just what this strategy means is essential so that everyone understands how customer-centricity will be delivered through the implementation of the strategy. Communication plays a critical role in ensuring there is widespread understanding and acceptance of the organisation's approach to the customer. It can be challenging to develop a customer management strategy, however, the real challenge is likely to be the execution thereof.

Every organisation's customer management strategy should be unique because they all are starting from differing positions of strength and weakness and all have, or should have, something unique in their vision or value proposition. However, there are some critical components that consistently appear in the best strategies, which, therefore, become a useful checklist to ensure that all the aspects are covered in your own strategy. I usually approach customer management strategy development in three distinct steps with 12 explicit components, as summarised in the diagram below.

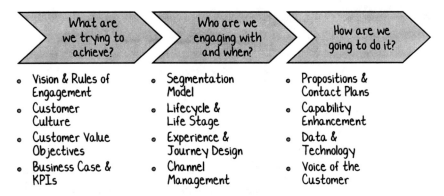

Figure 10: Components of Customer Management Strategy (WCL Customer Management)

Step 1: What are we trying to achieve?

Vision and Rules of Engagement
It is vital that leadership interprets the corporate vision for what this actually means for your customers and their experience. Too many businesses still don't mention the customer in their vision statements. Some don't even have common agreement on the definitions of key terms used, such as customer, partner, channel, proposition and value. In other words, there are no agreed "rules of engagement".

Customer Culture
Your organisation's culture can make or break your customer management strategy. The culture determines how customers are really esteemed in your business. It's not about grand statements and posturing. Your customer culture will show up not just in direct customer interactions, but also in the levels of priority and focus that customer-centred initiatives receive in terms of management time and effort. This culture also needs to evolve. In the last decade the customer experience landscape has been transformed. Cultures that haven't changed with it will appear stale or aloof.

Customer Value Objectives
It is vital that your customer management strategy has value objectives that are distinct from sales targets, phrased in ways that all stakeholders can immediately see the benefits of. Such objectives tend to fall into a few categories: *Acquisition* – more first-time buyers or improved conversion; *Loyalty* – more repeat purchasers and fewer lost or lapsed customers; *Cost-to-serve or acquire* – managing expenditure in proportion to value or potential; *Cross-sell or up-sell* – increasing share of wallet; *Winback* – drawing lost or lapsed customers back into active relationship; and *Advocacy* – positive word-of-mouth, including via social networks and the net promoter score.

Business Case and KPIs
New, customer-led initiatives often struggle to compete for budget with traditional marketing programmes because they often can't predict ROI as accurately. This should not be the case if customer value and benefit areas are well defined. Customer management teams should be challenged to build

a compelling business case and value tracking (KPI) model for the strategy, including "soft" benefits, yet not using them as an excuse for inadequate rigour or governance.

Step 2: Who are we engaging with and when?

Segmentation Model
Your organisation's segmentation should be 100% embedded in both strategy and execution. Best practice involves having one segmentation model even if it is supplemented by analytical or campaign groups. Segments should be clearly defined, described and understood by employees, with dimensions that go beyond transaction value, such as needs, attitudes, behaviours, profitability, share-of-wallet and lifetime value. A critical part of your strategy should be the management and tracking of migration across segments.

Life Cycle and Life Stage
Your models and approach to managing product life cycles and customer life stage must be explicit in your customer management strategy. Too many companies just offer the "same thing" because that's what the customer bought last time and this demonstrates not anticipating that their needs might have now changed.

Experience and Journey Design
Experience designers must understand how the customer felt about the experience and these feelings are very often more important than what was physically done. Many companies concentrate their journey mapping efforts on getting the processes right. They see quality and consistency improvements, but often at the cost of the customer feeling "processed". The other common mistake is to design the experience from the "inside-out", starting with corporate desired outcomes and internal processes. Customers, however, often view their journeys differently to the way organisations do and, therefore, experience design must be "outside-in". Sophisticated companies design blueprint experiences for key journeys and segments. These are based on customer needs and wants, and the journeys almost always extend beyond the internal processes of the company. Sometimes they cover important elements of the experience that are not within the company's control.

Channel Management

How well is your organisation adapting to the changing world of multiple communication and service delivery channels, and "real-time" connected customers? Commentators are already forecasting the demise of e-mail, saying that it will soon join the fax and telex in the history books. Your customer management strategy must prepare your business to deliver a consistent, high-quality customer experience across established and emerging media and channels. However, many organisations are still having internal battles about issues such as: "who owns the relationship?"; "how do we implement transfer pricing on our costs for communication-only channels?"; and "where do we credit the sale when the client has touched every channel in their purchase journey?"

Step 3: How are we going to do it?

Propositions and Contact Plans

There is often confusion within businesses about exactly what the proposition is. This is partly because a customer proposition has several objectives: attracting new clients, converting sales to new and existing clients, and making client experience and service promises regarding day-to-day interactions, transactions and complaints. Clarity and definition around these is vital to your customer management strategy, which must then direct how the propositions and offers are to be made to customers. These should be database-driven and triggered, based on segment, lifecycle and life stage management.

Capability Enhancement

Strategies, programmes and initiatives will only be successful if your organisation and people have the capabilities to enact them. To date, customer management or customer-centricity isn't a specialist academic subject. Perhaps it should be. These capabilities must, therefore, be raised systemically across the business system and trained vocationally. Your customer management strategy should contain a clearly agreed definition of the capabilities required to deliver its experience and value objectives, and to manage the quality of all the basics of service delivery – responsiveness, turn-around times, first-contact resolution and so forth.

Data and Technology
Effective management of customer information, and the systems that store and share it, is fundamental to excellence in customer management and the delivery of an appropriate, intelligent customer experience. People can cover up poor data and systems, yet systems can't cover up poorly managed and motivated people. It is vital that your organisation delivers appropriate data to the people and teams that need it to design and deliver the right customer experience and value-enhancing initiatives. Future information requirements (e.g. Skype, Twitter ID) should also be explicitly included, based on the channel management requirements.

Voice of the Customer
Customer satisfaction surveys have evolved in recent years from traditional questionnaires into multi-media, real-time, client-agenda driven feedback mechanisms that give real insight into both the physical and emotional aspects of product and service delivery. Traditional methods (surveys, mystery shopping and back-to-the-floor exercises) need to be supplemented and eventually replaced with newer and more insightful approaches, such as instant and continuous feedback, commitment measurement and effort scores. Your customer management strategy needs to set out how the organisation will clearly hear the customer's voice and track the elements of the experience that actually drive loyalty and value.

Once you have drafted your customer management strategy, the next stage involves stakeholder engagement where you present and confirm your draft customer management strategy with appropriate stakeholder groups throughout the organisation. Once you have stakeholder buy-in, the third and last phase is embedding that strategy. This ensures that the on-going socialisation and implementation of the customer management strategy, and the increasing influence of your customer management team in operational planning, become a crucial part of your organisation's overall management activities.

The transformational journey

Embracing and implementing customer-centricity requires a radical shift across your entire organisation to enable long-lasting, sustainable change. This transformational journey can be a daunting prospect as it requires you to bridge the sometimes massive gap between your current customer management capability and the future capability you require to deliver on your desired strategic outcome. This will call for the cessation of various activities, the continuance of others and the introduction of new initiatives and actions.

Your ability to drive this change is dependent on various factors. Is there increasing pressure for change? Where is it coming from? Is it externally driven, coming from the market due to declining competitiveness or a poor set of financial results? Or is it predominantly internal, coming from leadership itself? Or from an enlightened CEO who has recognised that the real source of sustainable business performance and competitive advantage is customer-centricity? These leaders recognise the importance of innovation and the need to change their business models to maintain excellence. In the event that business performance and/or competitive differentiation are mediocre, leaders should create "a burning platform" for continuous improvement.

A clear, shared customer vision is key to effective change management. This vision is created and maintained by leadership. Senior management ensures the vision is operationalized through empowered and focused teams. Without the capacity to change, your organisation's vision will not become a reality. This means that your organisational structure, culture, resources in people and capability and emotional readiness are essential supportive components. Knowledge already held, tacitly or explicitly, helps to identify the new approaches you require. The barriers to changing the customer relationship and the drivers that will overcome those barriers need to be identified and fully understood.

Taking those first steps on the customer-centric transformational journey can be the toughest. Planning is essential, and should take into account the likelihood of change occurring and the resultant costs required for the transformation.

This supports the development of a customer management business case that indicates the return on investment. Appropriate and realistic time horizons should be established in order to drive and implement change whilst business activity continues to ensure achievement of financial objectives. Effective decision making structures support the adjustments that need to occur as the organisation develops the level of its understanding of customer-centric principles. Furthermore, the customer-centric transformational journey calls for a formal approach, a structure and a framework, effective customer data translated into knowledge, and an in-depth understanding of customer needs, wants and unmet expectations.

Underpinning all these aspects of the transformation is the critical need to develop an understanding of the systemic nature of a customer-centric business model and the interconnection this creates between your customer, strategy, risk, financial performance and sustainability.

Small steps in the right direction are key. Clear symbols of success will support and motivate your organisation to build and sustain the momentum it requires to break old belief systems and "inside-out" customer practises that prevent change from occurring.

Proving your business case

Any business strategy requires both a clear direction and a sound business case that justifies the activity and investment required. This requirement is no different in customer-centricity. As explored in Chapter 3 there is compelling and growing evidence for the powerful business justification of a customer-centric business model. Your organisation has to prove what its own customer-centric strategy is worth and what the return on investment is likely to be.

Clearly identifying the gap between current customer management capability across your entire organisation and understanding the level of capability to which you aspire, is the basis for developing your business case. A tool, such as the SCHEMA Value Estimator™ as explored in the Chapter 3 case study, can provide powerful support in developing a business case driven from customer value analysis.

Once you're clear as to your current financial performance as measured against your customer value analysis dashboard, as shown in Chapter 3 (SCHEMA Value Estimator™), you're in a position to review the outcome and potential financial uplift resulting from various strategic choices. This requires working with a number of "what-if" scenarios that analyse and optimise your REAP mix. Reliable customer data is critical, as is your strategic team who have to be in touch with global, market, industry and company-specific trends.

A sound business case is critical to support leaders on a path to customer-centricity as it asks the tough questions that really scrutinise the detail of the customer-focused strategy and the commitment of leaders to the transformational journey. In order to support the organisation to deliver on its strategic intent, your organisation needs to have the right customer-focused measures in place that report to the business and the market on just how effective your organisation is in managing its most critical asset — the customer.

Transformation questions

- Is there documented alignment, at the senior management level, on the nature of customer-centricity for which the organisation is striving in the middle to longer term?
- Are financial analysts and other important stakeholders actively lobbied about the importance of customer-related measures (attrition, tenure, product holding, etc.) in assessing the organisation's performance?
- Do you have a clear strategy, which everyone understands, on why your brand can be differentiated in the marketplace?
- Does leadership have the courage and the authority to make the radical changes needed to embrace the new and different business model demanded by customer-centricity?
- Are you aware and fully understanding of what drives relevance and value to customers?
- How do you embed an idea or principle that changes the way people think

and work?

- Is your organisation ready to be a leader in your industry and to hold the responsibility that goes with it?
- Does your board appreciate that customer, strategy, risk, performance and sustainability are linked?
- Does the board talk about and provide direction on the moral obligation to serve the best interests of customers?

Case study - Patagonia encourages its customers to buy used

Patagonia is an outdoor apparel and equipment company founded in 1972 by Yvon Chouinard and based in California in the United States. Its mission is to "build the best product, cause no unnecessary harm, use business to inspire and implement solutions to the environmental crisis". Since its inception, Patagonia has delivered on this promise to its customers. It has established itself as a leading example of a company that has positioned its strategy both for profit and for social responsibility through its sustainability initiatives and social entrepreneurship. Patagonia is a clear leader in its field and connects powerfully with its target market's clear desire to experience the beauty of the outdoors while minimising the impact on its future. Patagonia's customers are as passionate about this vision as its team is.

In a recent move, Patagonia has taken this mission one step further. In 2011 Patagonia launched its Common Threads Initiative, which aims at helping its customer buy and sell used Patagonia gear using eBay as a sales platform. With no profit to Patagonia, this initiative is aimed at helping customers to re-use, rather than buy new, a key principle of sustainability. At first glance this seems to contradict what you think companies should be doing, yet is this really so?

Andy Hoffman, a professor at the University of Michigan's school of business, describes Patagonia's strategy as one that leads the pack when it comes to redefining capitalism through its sustainability initiatives. He emphasises that this move is consistent with Patagonia's vision and refers to it as an exciting and radical next step that flies in the face of conventional thinking about companies being solely profit-driven [29].

While strategic decisions are often driven by competitive forces, as in Porter's Five Forces Model, Patagonia is an example of a new, hybrid form of organisation that is driven by more than just profit. This deeper purpose engages long-term relationships with its customers, staff, channels and suppliers, who are all highly motivated by its cause and are passionate about making a difference. Hoffman adds: "What they're trying to think about is not doing this to the detriment of the bottom line, but recognizing fully that corporations have a more complex and nuanced purpose. To do everything solely by the profit motivation is not what they're talking about. They're trying to re-conceptualize what a company is. Money is a score at the end. How we get there is more important" [29].

In *Firms of Endearment* [25], Patagonia is referred to many times as a leading example of a firm of endearment through many aspects, such as their corporate social programmes, environmental impact programmes, unique employee scheduling needs, subsidized on-site child care, demands on suppliers to meet specified quality standards, moral construct and their criteria for selecting suppliers.

The Common Threads Initiative is the kind of move that loyal Patagonia customers expect and serves to deepen the commitment that existing customers feel for the company. It also attracts new customers who are drawn to a cause and not just a company trying to sell them more goods.
Although it is too soon to tell how this new approach will serve Patagonia and its shareholders, it certainly is an example of the bold moves that inspired leaders are willing to take to "walk their talk" — for customers, employees and the environment.

CHAPTER 5:

PEOPLE AND CULTURE

Transformation Intent

While conventional wisdom dictates that customer-centricity means customers should always be put first, in reality, it requires that employees are first and foremost given what they need so that they can deliver sustainable and superior customer experiences. To do that you need to transform your organisation's culture into one of customer-centricity, and then empower your team to deliver excellence in alignment with that culture. Customer-centricity also requires that you engage with your suppliers and channel partners as if they were part of your core team.

Employees first, customers second

Zappos.com is an online footwear and apparel store founded in the United States in 1999. The CEO of Zappos.com, Tony Hsieh (pronounced Shay), is a champion of customer service excellence delivered through highly engaged employees, the insights from which are encapsulated in his book *Delivering Happiness* [30]. Hsieh has managed to lead the meteoric growth of this business from its start-up phase in 1999 to where it is today — a two billion Dollar revenue company with the reputation for having extremely passionate employees who live the brand and deliver a superior customer experience.

In the 1990s, Hsieh co-founded LinkExchange and grew this company to 100 employees before selling it to Microsoft. Hsieh and his fellow co-founders' decision to sell this business was largely due to the realisation that they had not paid enough attention to the development of their organisational culture, instead hiring employees for their skill and experience. It became apparent that the downward slide in organisational culture could not be corrected. In his journey with Zappos.com, Hsieh pledged he would not make the same mistake twice.

Hsieh says that Zappos.com's business model is based on the philosophy that if you get the organisational culture right, most other aspects, including customer service, will fall into place. The company's investment into the development of the Zappos.com customer-centric culture and the engagement of employees is extensive. Every year they produce a printed Culture Book that encourages employees to contribute unedited opinions on what the Zappos.com culture means to them. This results in a company in which staff and their families work and play together, thus resulting in a strong sense of openness, family and unity. Even managers are required to spend 10-20% of their working hours relaxing with their employees outside the office.

A clear set of ten core values guides Zappos.com's business model, including the strategies, brand and, of course, customer-centric culture. These values are integrated into the recruitment process, where a "culture-fit" interview is given as much weighting as a "skill and experience" interview. Once a candidate has been successful and has completed training, he or she is offered $2,000 to resign. Zappos.com's confidence in the rigour of its company culture's clarity and fit assessment means that 97% of new employees turn down the cash offer. The company also offer a host of innovative employee benefits and the freedom to do what it takes to deliver excellent customer experiences. As an example, an employee was able to order flowers for a customer on the company's account, without prior approval, because the customer had returned her husband's shoes previously purchased at Zappos.com after his death in a car accident.

Employees are measured differently from what is considered typical. In a call centre environment, call wait times and call duration are frequently used as employee measures. Not so at Zappos.com, where call centre agents do not have scripts and no limits are put in place for call length. Zappos.com's consistent focus on providing the best customer experience possible is embedded in everything the company does. This is evidenced in its decision in 2003 to shut down 25% of the company's revenue that originated from warehouses not under its control. In *Delivering Happiness* [30] Hsieh says, "Outsourcing that [warehousing] to a third party and trusting that they would care about our customers as much as we would was one of our biggest mistakes. If we hadn't reacted quickly, it would have eventually destroyed Zappos".

In 2009 Zappos.com negotiated a $1 billion sale to Amazon.com and continues to maintain its focus on and culture of delivering superior customer experiences. Hsieh and his company are an excellent example of what is possible when a customer-centric culture is combined with highly engaged and motivated employees.

This principle of focusing first on the employee and the superior customer experience resulting from that, is one proposed by Vineet Nayar in his book *Employees First, Customers Second* [31]. In this book Nayar shares the journey of India's HCL Technologies, a global IT player, and how a change management programme, focused on making this shift, created dramatic results.

The customer-centric business model requires that you turn conventional thinking about employees upside down. If your organisation is committed to delivering superior and differentiated customer experiences, you need to first look at your organisational culture, the manner in which employees are engaged, how your teams are structured, the customer competencies you have, and whether your suppliers and partners are integrated into your customer-centric culture.

A customer-centric culture

Customer-centric thinking approaches the customer as a valuable asset that requires focus, investment and understanding — the same can be said for the culture of your organisation. Very few companies have a clearly defined set of values and a documented corporate culture that supports those values, and even fewer have a customer-centric culture embedded into everything that they do. Zappos.com is an example that it is possible to do this, yet the task of realigning an entire organisation to a new set of values and behaviours is very daunting.

In an article by Bruce Temkin, in which he explores culture as a corporate asset, Temkin [32] refers to a definition of organisational culture by Arthur F. Carmazzi: "The ability to do more than expected does not come from influencing others to do something they are not committed to, but rather to nurture a culture that motivates and even excites individuals to do what is required for the benefit of all".

While excellence in the engagement and development of employees is a keystone in the success of customer-centricity, the right customer culture is the game changer that makes the shift to customer-centricity much more dynamic and effective. Defining and implementing a customer-centric culture may not at the outset seem like a high value activity, yet the investment made into changes at this deep and foundational level create massive opportunities for customer-centricity across all parts of the organisation. When employees function instinctively with a customer-centric approach, the scope for change takes on new dimensions.

Temkin [33] further describes this customer-centric culture as the "the 6 C's of customer-centric DNA", namely: clear beliefs, constant communications, collective celebrations, compelling stories, commitment to employees and consistent trade-offs.

Clear beliefs

Any effective organisational culture is driven by the core organisational values that underlie that culture. While those values are unclear or undefined, the organisation becomes like a cart pulled by horses all going in different directions. When these values are hidden or assumed the direction being taken will only become apparent when it is too late. A customer-centric approach demands that values are explicitly agreed and communicated, and that these values speak directly to the needs of the customer. This requires that the values held are executed on a very deep level and not just in a list framed in the foyer. It is important to recognise that there will be those people within the organisation who do not and never will live the values the organisation desires or needs for customer-centricity. Once you have separated the wheat from the chaff, you can move forward with your organisation focused on deepening those values in every way. A recruitment process that specifically addresses and questions the right customer-centred values and culture will ensure that new employees are geared for customer-centricity.

Constant communications

While communications planning and training will develop skills and ability in communication, a customer-centric culture requires that constant and clear communication is the natural habit of the organisation. This includes the flow of accurate and timely information to employees, which is especially critical through the change brought about by a customer-centric approach, and the ability of employees to communicate their needs and the needs of the customer. Communication should also be used to deepen your employees' understanding of what customer-centricity means and what behaviours demonstrate its presence or absence. For example, you could provide your team with videoed customer interaction scenarios — those that demonstrate customer-centricity and those that represent the antithesis.

Collective celebrations

A customer-centric culture is one that seeks to recognise those individuals who deliver excellence for the customer and results in employees getting excited and inspired about these achievements. Very often an organisation's point of celebration is tied to the end of the year and the assessment of whether sales and other financial targets have been met. By focusing the company's corporate culture on celebrating financial success and not customer success, the opportunity to deepen a culture focused on the customer is lost. This aspect of corporate culture is closely linked to the way your organisation measures its success and effectiveness.

Compelling stories

Storytelling is rapidly becoming a business practice frequently used by organisations to engage their customers and employees. Facts and figures are not able to engage people's emotions in the way that stories can. Creating and sharing a powerful organisational story is a very effective way of creating the right customer-centric culture and sharing this culture on a regular basis. Stories may include how the company was founded, best practice examples of customer excellence, and values the organisation aspires to live by. When you are also able to engage your customer in the story you are then in a position to extend your culture of customer-centricity into the very experience they receive.

Commitment to employees

Creating a customer-centric culture requires a commitment to both rewarding the right cultural behaviours as well as removing the barriers that prevent that culture from developing effectively. Most often these barriers are unconscious and tacit. The development of a customer-centric culture, therefore, requires that these barriers are identified and overcome through the right support and positive reinforcement of culturally-aligned behaviours. As an example, I was part of a team that assessed the level of staff engagement with, and an understanding of, the principles of customer management for a large, blue-chip company. The objective was to compare the level of staff understanding of customer management as a principle with the degree to which they were enthusiastic about it. In one of the areas the results indicated that 79% of respondents thought that customers who spent more with their company expected to be treated better. Yet, 68% of respondents felt that all customers should be treated the same. These results indicate an alarming level of non-alignment! With a core principle of customer-centricity being to treat different customers differently, and the vast majority of respondents agreeing that customers expect that, the deeply-ingrained cultural belief that all customers should be treated equally was a barrier that needed to be overcome. Your organisation might also have these hidden cultural barriers that prevent you making the necessary changes.

Consistent trade-offs

A commitment to a customer-centric culture requires much more than a statement of intent. Employees observe the behaviour and decisions of the executive team and management, aligning their behaviour with what they see. If employees can see executives living this culture consistently, while making trade-offs when necessary to honour the organisation's values, employees will rise to the challenge and do the same. When the needs of the customer conflict with financial measures and promises made to shareholders, employees will look to the leaders to see if they are faking their commitment to the customer or if the customer-centred values are deeply held and demonstrated through their decisions.

It takes a long time to build the right culture for customer-centricity, yet along the way, specific actions focused on addressing cultural behaviours can create immediate and incremental improvements. Start by understanding your company's culture and where the unseen barriers might be. Focus on addressing specific cultural behaviours that do not resonate with your vision and work with reinforcing the right cultural behaviours that are already in place.

According to Jon Katzenbach, a senior partner of Booz & Company [34]: "Honour the strengths of your culture. I have never seen a culture in 50 years of working at them [cultures] that was all good or all bad. There is no such thing. So no matter how mad you get at your culture, it is not the villain. And if you do not honour the strengths of your culture, it's going to resist you time and again".

Engaging employees drives profit

Employee engagement is a principle that measures the extent to which your employees feel both an emotional and rational connection and commitment to your company's values and culture. This engagement is then demonstrated through their actual behaviour in delivering the strategic objectives of your organisation. Research indicates that there is a direct correlation between employee engagement and customer behaviour and, in one particular study with a retailer, it was shown that every 1% increase in employee commitment resulted in a 9% increase in the monthly sales [35].

The news though is not all good. Research conducted by Gallup [36], and corroborated by others, indicate that on average, for every one engaged employee there are two disengaged employees. For every person pushing for excellence, two are trying to actively undermine progress. In a world-class company this ratio is 9:1 – nine employees striving for growth while one puts on the brakes. Even though disengaged employees have a huge financial impact, the greater risk is their impact on the customer. Your customer-centric approach, therefore, needs to pay particular attention to the level of employee engagement and how your employees are demonstrating their commitment to the required values and culture.

The service-profit chain helps to illustrate just how interconnected employee engagement is with the delivery of superior and sustainable business performance. Each step or link in this chain serves to strengthen or weaken the links that follow. The diagram below is an extract of the Sears Employee-Customer-Profit Chain [37], which has been used to focus executives on the role of employee engagement in profit generation.

In using this approach, Sears discovered that a 4% increase in employee satisfaction over a 12 month period resulted in an increase in customer satisfaction by almost the same amount, translating into the staggering increase in revenue of $200 million over the same period and a resultant increase in market capitalisation of nearly $250 million.

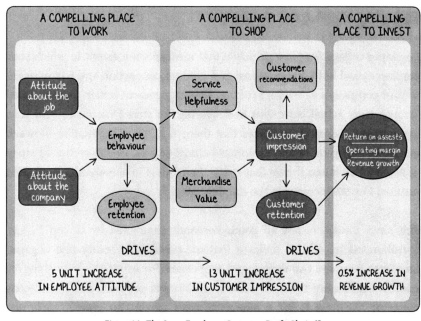

Figure 11: The Sears Employee-Customer-Profit Chain [37]

With employee engagement including considerations of satisfaction, loyalty and productivity, it is critical not to forget that employees do not become disengaged all on their own. Executives have the responsibility to ensure that the right climate and conditions are in place to support this chain of interconnected components in the delivery of customer value and, ultimately, superior business performance.

Changing employees' behaviour is best begun with a clear understanding of the perceptions, attitudes and beliefs they have about the customer. While we use the cliché that "the customer pays our salary" as a critical measure of customer-consciousness in employees, the reality is that the customer is often perceived as an annoyance to the employee. The language that employees use is telling. The verbal cues are easy to identify — "I hate that customer" or "I don't need to talk to another customer" — while the non-verbal cues, like rolling the eyes or sighing heavily when a customer has a certain issue, hint at a deeper disconnection between culture and behaviour.

The employee might also incorrectly view his or her customer as an internal department or business unit. Every single employee must have a crystal clear understanding that the customer is the end-user of the product or service, and must genuinely care about doing whatever is necessary to deliver a better experience. Simply knowing what you should do, without feeling strongly about it, does not suffice.

There are a variety of methods to support changes in behaviour and employee engagement in the implementation of a customer-centric business model. For starters, it is essential to create the habit of planning for employee engagement activities in any change that is implemented. This is especially the case when the activities demand a change in a fundamental or entrenched behaviour or mind-set. The more established the old habit is, the more extensive those engagement activities need to be.

The development of the right competencies for customer-centricity is an essential method to create powerful and sustainable change. You need to first investigate what customer management competencies you do have within your company so that you can plan to close the gap between what you have and what you want, and budget accordingly. Part of this process may include re-examining your existing training programmes to ascertain to what extent they really support the customer-centric strategy you are trying to implement. The advent of new markets and digital channels may also require employee training and development you have not done before. This is especially the case with social media platforms and the need to familiarise employees with the concepts around developing customer relationships through these online channels.

Communities of interest and internal advocates are two other opportunities that provide additional support to executives and management when seeking to engage employees on multiple levels.

A community of interest is a cross-functional group or community of people who share a common interest. These communities may be formal or informal, and based on personal or online interaction, depending on their purpose and function. Existing communities of interest should be assessed to evaluate their motivations and influence in the organisation so that they can support the effective transformation required. There is innumerable benefit in community leaders within the organisation (either formally appointed or influential in their own right) engaging with other stakeholders from across the business to focus on and develop customer-centric behaviour in all employees. If such a community does not yet exist within your company, you should create the opportunity for those passionate about the customer to demonstrate leadership through such a vehicle.

Internal advocates and opinion formers are powerful change-agents within teams, who through the respect they receive from their peers, are able to motivate their fellow colleagues to embrace the changes being required of them. Identifying these key people within the teams, acts as a catalyst to improve employee behaviour so that the end goal is always customer satisfaction.

Executives should also ensure that managers are provided with the right tools and authority to engage and motivate their employees. Besides what has already been suggested, this support should include the communication of strategic objectives and results, effective systems to support performing the job well and innovative reward structures. These create a level of internal service quality that, in turn, works to support employee satisfaction and hence a positive flow through the service-profit chain. Managers also need the authority to adjust the rewards structure and functions for customer-impacting employees to reflect changing priorities in the customer strategy. This includes ensuring across the board that employees are being measured for the right behaviour and results — rewards based on profit, sales and margin alone will not drive the customer-centric outcome you are striving for.

While the thought of actively engaging your employees in your quest for customer-centricity may seem daunting, in business the truism holds that small steps in the right direction are exponentially better than large leaps to nowhere. Start by knowing what level of engagement you have and where you need to be. Engage those who are motivated to deliver customer excellence to support your organisation to transform the relationship between employee and customer. And lastly, ensure the rewards you offer employees are directly linked to delivering an outstanding and consistent customer experience backed by the tools they need to deliver on this outcome.

Getting organised

Getting your team into gear for a customer-centric approach requires that you are ready as a team to deliver on the vision of customer-centricity. While your organisational culture and employee engagement is at the heart of what you need to get right, effective engagement requires the right working environment to make this change a reality. This transformative environment is made possible through structuring people and teams in the right way.

This restructuring means firstly ensuring there are no barriers in the delivery of customer-centricity in the functional and reporting structures currently in place. Part of this process, therefore, requires identifying what the barriers are, and where they are, so you can address them to release the obstruction. As an example, this could mean restructuring call centre agents' responsibilities so that they are empowered to service the customer to a specific level as opposed to handing over most calls to a separate service division, which delays the resolution for the customer. Long customer service processes spanning multiple departments can also lead to an impaired customer experience, especially when the customer has to deal with a multitude of people in order to have a question answered or to resolve a problem.

The weak point in any organisational design will almost always be in the way it manages hand-overs between people and across business units. Very often huge improvements can be delivered just through tightening up this aspect of the design so that customer issues do not fall through the cracks and service levels between units and functions are met. Any organisational changes should also be specifically assessed to determine their impact on the customer, with suitable plans put in place to manage such changes. A company that has an "inside-out" view of the world does not typically think through how its own internal changes may impact customers, suppliers and stakeholders.

The supplier universe

In the quest for customer-centricity and the engagement of your team it is all too easy to forget that your team also includes your suppliers and channel partners. The procurement and management of a supplier should, therefore, include the same level of attention to values, culture and behaviour as afforded to your own employees. This process is what I refer to as understanding your supplier universe.

Alignment in this area begins with having a clear understanding of which suppliers impact the customer experience and the service-profit chain, and defining a clear strategy for these customer-impacting suppliers. This approach permeates every aspect of this supplier relationship, including how you select your suppliers and channel partners, as well as how you engage with them — are they just there to provide a service or are they an integral part of your team. In addition, just as you ensure that your own internal measures are customer-focused, so too do you need to ensure that the terms of your service level agreements with suppliers are in alignment with the customer experience you have defined.

I have often noticed a disconnection between the organisation and its suppliers in outsourced call centres, especially where an outsourced call centre team handles a diversity of clients and products. In one case, the same team was managing service calls for both a fast food restaurant chain and an entertainment company (movie houses). The entertainment company moved its call centre back in-house and staffed it with movie-loving employees who were all given preferential screenings of latest releases. This created a massive improvement in the customer experience as customers could now have a real conversation with the call centre agent, who could share opinions and make recommendations on the latest movies.

In understanding the service-profit chain, including suppliers and channels, you are able to understand just how critical people and company culture are to the success of customer-centric behaviours and superior business performance. As Zappos.com did, if you focus on the people aspect of your organisation, you will most likely experience an immediate and rapid improvement in your bottom line results. However, developing the ultimate culture and engaging the right team does take time and continued effort.

Transformation questions

● Are real life examples of behaviours that have illustrated the desired customer culture regularly identified and widely communicated?
● Has a review of all training that could be customer-impacting been carried out to ensure consistency with the customer strategy and the training being provided in the customer management area?
● What are you doing to engage employees in delivering on the promise of your brand?
● Is your organisation one that is empowering and inclusive rather than one that manages according to a command and control approach?
● Does the corporate culture within your organisation recognise, where appropriate, the nature of the relationship with customers from a cultural perspective and what is the organisation doing to fix customer experience problems that result?
● Does your customer agenda appear on your board agenda and minutes?
● Is there a visibility of customer-related performance measures within your company? How do you measure people related to customer-centricity?
● What makes people heroes in your organisation?
● Are you really willing to reinvent how people work and think together?
● Has it become a way of life in your company to give priority to the interests and needs of customers?

Case study - Sun International thrills its employees

Sun International is a casino, resort and hotel group operating across over 27 properties and 8 countries. In 2006, the group realised how critical it was to sell experiences rather than just beautiful properties in order to compete effectively in the market and deliver superior business performance.

This strategic imperative resulted in a new brand promise for Sun International: "A Million Thrills. One Destination". Eight programmes were launched across the business to support this strategy and to implement it effectively. Sun International recognised that a critical success factor was the people aspect of their organisation. As a result, one of the eight projects launched was known as the One Sun Project that focused on bringing employee behaviour into alignment with the strong brand promise being made to customers.

Sun International's Chief Customer Officer, Ica van Heerden, led this project, which involved a multi-pronged approach across all properties and for all its 21,000 employees. This project needed to help employees understand the change in behaviour that was expected of them and why it was important, giving them a shared purpose. The organisation also needed to speak to their employees' hearts, creating a connection to the emotional component so critical if you want to change behaviour. Beyond getting the hearts and heads engaged, it was also necessary to create a new level of education and understanding that matched the "million thrills" experience that their brand ambassador, Charlize Theron, was able to convey through advertising. The right tools to deliver this expectation, and entrenching that behaviour so it became habit, were critical. Measurement and insight would then support Sun International's goal of being a learning organisation that is continuously improving and becoming more relevant to guests.

The answer lay in the innovative, practical and dynamic use of multimedia, training materials, on-the-job coaching and clear standard operating procedures. One of these innovative ways employed by the One Sun project, was the development of the acronym CLEAR (Connect with warmth, Listen with focus, Engage with intent, Act with ownership, Reconnect with sincerity) to create a language and interactive process that defined the expected behaviour. These criteria were identified as a result of asking guests what would delight them.

Other specific deliverables included video scenarios on what "good" looked like and what it did not look like, a talent competition, storytelling, the One Sun Magazine and a toolkit for trainers and managers to use in training.

While overall it has been an expensive exercise thus far, Sun International would not be able to deliver on its strategic intent and customer experience promise without the active engagement of their employees, unified through a customer-centric culture and equipped with the organisational structures and competencies to deliver.

CHAPTER 6:

DATA MANAGEMENT

Transformation Intent

Customer-centricity requires that you provide your customer with a consistent and integrated experience. Without the right, quality customer data that is consolidated across multiple sources into a single view, this is not possible. In order to transform your customer data management and deliver the business case for it, you need to measure, manage and report on your customer data as a vital and valuable organisational asset, while holding the protection of the trust placed in you as sacred.

Turning lead into gold

Every organisation today is swamped with data. Every engagement with every prospect and customer generates volumes of contact and transaction history and updates to core information. Technology fuels this avalanche through its ability to extensively gather, mine and generate new data sources. With the addition of social media and digital platforms, this flow of information has reached extreme levels. What organisations have not been able to do is to consistently integrate their sources of data into a consolidated view of their customer and, with a clear plan, transform their data into insight.

Using the analogy of transforming lead into gold, a customer-centric approach to data management requires that you inherently understand and recognise the value of data and then deliver on the compelling business case for the focused management of that data. This symbolic gold of financial value can only be achieved through meaningful data that has been consolidated across multiple sources and used to derive value for both the customer and the organisation.

There are many complexities and challenges in this quest for integrated and value-adding customer data. To begin with, companies may be under the illusion that data management is just about data source integration. They forget that it also requires good business processes to drive the collection and distribution of the right data to the right people. Diverse legacy systems, islands of information, poor data quality and increasing data privacy pressure all combine to make customer data management more complex. In addition, "the devil is in the detail" is a truism best applied to data management. Without a specific understanding and intention with every data element, and without a plan of how it will be used, the value potential of data is lost.

Critical to the success of a customer-centric business model is the ability to treat different customers differently. In order to do this you need to fully understand the segments and needs in your customer base and define the resultant change in behaviour required across customers or a segment of customers that will create the financial uplift to justify the investment. This financial uplift may necessitate retaining customers, acquiring new ones, getting existing customers to spend more, creating an easier channel for lower level customers to engage with you in a more cost-effective manner, or charging more for them to engage with you on a more expensive channel. Without the requisite data management to support these decisions, you simply cannot deliver insight or the results to warrant the investment.

Working effectively with a customer-centric approach to data management begins with the effective use of planning to define your data gathering priorities that are in alignment with your overall customer strategy. This is supported through the quality management of data captured at the source and the on-going delivery of reliable and cost-effective data. In addition, factors such as external data sources and the ever-present privacy question need to be addressed and managed. Through this specific and integrated approach to data it is possible to harness the real power of customer data rather than drowning in a sea of meaningless information.

"As of 2012, about 2.5 exabytes of data are created each day, and that number is doubling every 40 months or so. More data cross the internet every second than were stored in the entire internet just 20 years ago. This gives companies an opportunity to work with many petabyes of data in a single data set and not just from the internet. For instance, it is estimated that Walmart collects more than 2.5 petabytes of data every hour from its customer transactions. A petabyte is one quadrillion bytes, or the equivalent of about 20 million filing cabinets' worth of text. An exabyte is 1,000 times that amount, or one billion gigabytes" [23].

The customer information plan

The Customer Information Plan (CIP) is the foundation required to embark on the transformation of your data management capability. Clear data planning that links directly to your customer strategy enables you to build an effective framework against which you can assess and measure the performance of your data management practices and the value creation therefrom.

A CIP focuses your customer data management on core information and on specific strategic objectives, because the prospect of managing every field in every database is not only daunting, it is unrealistic. A thorough and detailed analysis of your data and its quality will reveal to you the level of information management actually taking place as opposed to a general sense from employees that data is inaccurate. Clear definitions of what is meant by "high quality" information will support this process by enabling a quality rating percentage to be allocated at field level and future improvements to be measured against this benchmark. The CIP will also work towards solving the problem of "information overload" by defining the priorities on the collection of new and enhanced information in the future. As with any plan, a CIP identifies and prioritises improvement areas in data management, sets targets for these and provides an action plan to achieve these targets.

The first step in developing your CIP is to fully understand the current reality in your data management capability. Core information across data sources is identified, and at a record and field level, data quality standards are defined and then assessed against those criteria. A clearer picture then emerges. Perhaps it reveals that a critical piece of information on your client record, such as an identity number, meets the quality standard only to 48%. What implications does that have on your statutory requirements? Or perhaps an address to be used to deliver your product or information to your client only has 23% accuracy. What happens if your revenue depends on the address being 100% accurate? Whatever your results, they will reveal a telling story of just where your data management efforts are needed.

The next step is to define what new customer data you need to collect across the customer life cycle in order to adequately support the needs of your customer strategy. A particular campaign or project may depend on a key set of data elements that can then be focused upon as part of that strategy. What is required will depend on the needs for each segment. An example may be specific online shopping preferences if you are planning to offer a digital channel to one or more customer segments and you need this data to plan adequately. This step also involves identifying the specific data elements that require on-going management so that sufficient processes and systems can be put in place to support this process.

Data collection and management is so often centred on statutory information, such as name, identity number, address and date of birth. It is seldom that you see an organisation that specifically has the capability and insight to recognise what they want to know so that they can use each appropriate customer touch point to gather that information, therefore being able to build a campaign to gather that piece of information.

Once you have defined and prioritised what data you need to collect and manage, you must identify the future capability you need in order to deliver on the defined customer data strategy and targets. This may include specific infrastructure, technologies and data warehousing tools, expertise and resources.

The last step is to bring all these elements together in a compelling business case that is specific about the value of data management and how the investment required in data management will deliver a financial return. Costs required may include staff, technologies, training, communication and external resources. Hard financial benefits are then derived in monetary terms based on reduced costs, such as savings on repeated communications and additional administration staff, and reduced risk from regulatory fines and statutory breaches.

Derived benefits in terms of increased revenue and opportunities, as well as the reduction of the perceived cost of poor data quality per customer segment, are also factored into this business case. The impact of a perceived error in customer data in a low value segment is very different to that in a high value segment, yet being specific can define the impact. Another aspect of this derived benefit lies in the value of being able to know and use specific information about a customer that enables a highly relevant campaign to take place that is almost certain to result in a positive outcome. It is possible to derive a relative value from inviting a high value customer to the kind of event they love attending, such as polo for those who love horses.

Building a reliable data asset

Most organisations will have multiple sources of data coming in from various points, including social, sales and contact centre channels. In order to build robust data repositories you have to understand exactly where the data is coming from and ascertain the accuracy of that data. This necessitates that the right systems are in place to support accurate data collection and that you are using various customer interfaces to support the collection of the highest priority data for those customers.

I cannot emphasise enough how often I have seen companies with customer data that is of such a poor quality that it really disables any opportunity for real customer-centricity. There is often no incentive or system support for those employees at customer-facing interfaces to capture the critical data that you would typically define in your customer information plan (CIP). The employees who capture the data are usually unaware that a crucial aspect of their role as data capturers is that of accuracy and thus they do not question data that is clearly of a poor quality. A case in point is an example I have seen first-hand — an insurance company that relies on accurate address details to deliver policy documents, thereby concluding the sale of the policy. When you see examples of the address being recorded as "next to the highway", you start to realise the dramatic, bottom line consequences of poor data quality collection and capture.

The system support in place for data management should enable automatic capture and field level validation that matches the quality criteria and data priorities defined in the CIP. In this way, you force quality and a focus on the right data at the point of entry into the system, thereby saving masses of work later to analyse and clean up the data. This is relatively straight forward for structured data, such as date of birth and contact numbers. What about unstructured data? Most systems provide text fields to capture notes about the customer or the contact made by the customer, yet what procedures and controls are in place to ensure that text and notes are captured at the required quality level? Your specific definitions and priorities for unstructured data should receive the necessary system support to drive the quality capture thereof.

With data capture channels extending into external sources, such as social media, you also have to be clear on how you capture specific customer information collected through external systems and how you use that data. For example, if someone signs up for your company app on your Facebook page, how will you use their registration information provided to Facebook? If they sign up for your newsletter on an external media site, how do you integrate that information with your overall customer repository?

If the extraction of data from external sources does not receive the attention, focus and system support it needs, this could result in poor data quality for your organisation. My experience has been that when a thorough and detailed analysis is undertaken of customer data sources and the quality of the data captured, the results are often quite shocking. As tough as it may be to face the reality of data sources and quality, the only way to start addressing the real issue is by "kick-starting" the actions required to turn raw data into a valuable, income generating asset.

"What do you need to fix this problem? IT organizations can't continue to drive technology investments with the ambiguous goal of 'cleaning dirty customer data' within CRM. Customer service and IT have to work together to change the conversation so that it focuses on articulating the benefits of sound data in business terms – like cost savings via agent productivity gains, reduced penalties for non-compliance and increased customer satisfaction scores using language that resonate with your executive management" [24].

Managing quality data

The on-going management of your customer data quality essentially revolves around the communication of quality levels expected and achieved, as well as the implementation of specific initiatives required to improve data quality. Your data dictionary guides this entire process, whether you have defined your definitions of quality in your CIP or you conduct a specific project to do so. From this benchmark, and with targets agreed in your CIP, you can begin to measure and report back on the actual results and improvements being seen.

Communication on the importance of information quality should include both employees and channel partners. It is not sufficient to focus only on your own team when external sources of data do not meet the standard. The key question to ask and answer is: what is the value of having accurate customer information at hand? If you can show the financial impact of having both the correct and incorrect information, you will create a very clear picture for those involved about what is at stake by not continuously focusing on meeting the defined levels of data quality. On the one hand, poor customer data will result in wasted paper, re-work, lost commissions, additional calls and lost time. The bigger impact, however, is on the customer, especially when it involves a high value customer segment that your business cannot afford to service poorly.

Your reporting systems should be able to provide feedback on your data quality, indicating the extent to which minimum levels of quality are being delivered. For example, if in your database you require at least 80% of a particular field to be populated, your system should report this to you when it drops below that minimum threshold. This may be required for a specific piece of information that you have identified as critical for a highly relevant campaign. Your customer management systems should also provide explicit support to update and validate information at the customer interface that may have become inaccurate over time. Data management therefore becomes a real time management process to continuously improve data quality and deliver on the defined targets.

The data management KPIs and the results achieved against your CIP initiatives and targets should be widely communicated to, as well as summarised for, executives. At an executive level, they should see a high-level reporting dashboard that also indicates the value that is potentially being missed as a result of poor quality data. By linking data quality to financial performance, it can receive the right focus and attention it needs. In some case, this may result in a prompt acceptance of your proposed budget for additional resources to improve the value of data and reduce the risk that poor data quality creates.

One of the key measures of your on-going improvement of data quality is the confidence of your employees in the quality thereof. On-going evaluation of this user perception compared to actual quality will reveal misconceptions that can then be managed and resolved. When users feel confident in system data, they are much less likely to create their own islands of data to manage data quality, which you often see as multitudes of individual spread sheets all storing the same information. When employees leave and their spread sheets leave with them, the value of that data asset literally walks out of the door.

Leveraging non-owned data

Non-owned customer data can be a very valuable source of insight to understand purchasing attitudes, behaviours and interests. This data might reside in other repositories, such as Facebook, Twitter, Foursquare and LinkedIn, or external sources and intermediary databases that you purchase or subscribe to. The question you have to ask yourself is: do you know about these non-owned data sources and how you can leverage them?

While non-owned sources may seem out of reach or too difficult to manage, they inherently hold considerable value both in terms of general buying behaviour and trends, as well as customer-specific data. For example, birth registries could be used to promote an education policy to new parents or a home purchase registered on deeds listings could prompt a relevant campaign. To make these non-owned sources deliver real value you need to find a way to merge their data with your own so that your data analysis is driven from a single, integrated customer perspective. You also have the inherent challenge of preventing duplication of data across multiple external sources once integrated.

Social media channels provide an interesting challenge in how you manage external data. While a person's profile may provide a wealth of information, it is only valuable if you can discover a way to duplicate that insight and data process for thousands and even millions of customers. However, a trend that will challenge this area of value further is the increasing use by customers of intermediaries and gatekeepers to manage their personal information, thereby taking control of how you engage with them. You need to take this trend into account in your customer information planning.

As in most things, there is a fine line that we walk in how we use non-owned data while honouring the laws of the land and the customers' right to privacy. There is immense value in these forms of customer data. As this sphere evolves so will your ability to derive value from it, yet at the same time, you must continue to deserve the trust placed in you by your customers.

Protection of the trust placed in you

Issues of data privacy extend far beyond ensuring there are no security breaches in your customer data. While a breach can be devastating to customer sentiment, as witnessed by some large online vendors, the greater risk is the on-going and inappropriate use and abuse of customer data.

Working with this aspect of data management requires a clear privacy and data usage policy that is widely available to everyone who has need of it, including the customer. This policy should be integrated into operational training and communication so that it does not become just a link on the web site that no-one really bothers to read, but a tool to build a balanced understanding of what they can and cannot do. This practice is as much about developing a culture and awareness of data respect as it is about just ensuring a policy is adhered to.

While to some extent your company cannot control a staff member with relevant access who downloads customer data and sells it, you can adhere to your privacy policy through your organisational decisions and processes that support them. This includes ensuring that your e-mail and mobile text listings only include those customers and prospects who have given you permission to contact them in that way. Customers are becoming more and more intolerant of communication without permission due to the onslaught of contact from every direction. This is especially the case in new and emerging channels, such a social media, where there are social norms and rules of behaviour that your organisation needs to honour.

In order to manage this aspect of data management effectively, you have to ensure that your communication permissions, and the management thereof, are up-to-date and integrated with your other systems so that you communicate with the customer in one voice and in the manner that your customer has agreed. It is not enough to just adhere to the law — you need to honour the trust placed in you by your greatest asset, your customer.

"Building trust with customers is a little like developing face-to-face relationships. In the beginning, we share a little. Then, once we show that we can be responsible with what the customer has shared, he or she will reveal a little more. And gradually the relationship deepens. This crawl-walk-run approach to sharing information is a sensible way for us to proceed in data collection and use. After all, as long as customer information is used to enhance the customer experience, taking small steps along the way can lead to big things. Gaining consumer trust requires shedding a lot of light--on your intentions, your practices, and your responsibilities. Do that and you can avoid the dark side of data" [25].

The scale and scope of this whole customer-centric journey can be overwhelming and this is especially the case in data management, where there is just so much of it to manage. If this is the case for your organisation, it might be worthwhile to step back, identify your highest value customers, and put those customers under management. Track their data manually and focus your efforts on where the highest rewards will be found. As you develop an awareness of how to do that effectively, you can look at expanding your customer information plan into other areas and segments for an organisational-wide approach.

Transformation questions

- Is there a documented strategy that recognises the financial, strategic and tactical value of customer information?
- Is there a senior level understanding of the issues surrounding customer information and the role that it plays within your organisation?
- Do you have a deep understanding of your data content, quality and usage as well as the customer information capabilities you have, as measured against best practice?
- How are you managing the increasing volume of data at your disposal?
- Have you recognised all of the stakeholders affected by customer data and are you gathering their input to inform your understanding of the challenges you face and the potential for creating value through data?
- Who is ultimately accountable for the customer information plan and do you understand the benefits of such a plan?
- Do you have a data management governance framework in place?
- Is there a common understanding of the value of customer information within the organisation and are you able to harness this effectively?
- Have you built a service-orientated architecture?
- Do you have the appropriate application services in place that can synchronise data across the different systems within your organisation?
- How can you unlock data, and gain access to it, so that you can use and store both structured and unstructured data?
- Do you have a plan that identifies the data that your organisation wishes to own versus that which it prefers to source from third parties?
- Does everyone within your organisation understand the criticality of data management, with the appropriate KPIs in place?

Case study – Target hits the bull's eye with their data analytics

Target is the second largest discount retail chain in the United States and is well-known for its focus on delivering an excellent customer experience, where each customer is treated as a special guest of the store. A recent initiative to push the boundaries of this customer relationship has created a great deal of media attention.

In compiling a research report for The New York Times, one of their writers, Charles Duhigg, had been interviewing one of Target's statisticians, Andrew Pole [38]. Hired in 2002 with the mandate to discover ways that Target's extensive repositories of customer data could be used to identify their habits and predict their behaviour, Pole was approached by the marketing team with an interesting question. They wanted to know if it was possible to predict whether a customer was pregnant. With birth records being publicly accessible, new parents are bombarded with promotions and coupons at the birth of their child by every retailer. However, the purchasing of pregnancy related products by pregnant women starts much earlier than that and thus promoting these types of products after birth is just too late.

Studies into the neuro-science of habit formation show that one of the opportunities to change a habit is when you go through a major life change. At this point, any change you make may very likely lead to a new habit that continues until another such change occurs. Being pregnant is one of the most significant of these big life changes. Target wanted to find a way to change the buying behaviour of a pregnant customer so that they would start buying more of their shopping requirements at Target, locking them into a new and extended buying habit.

Andrew Pole tapped into Target's vast stores of customer data that link extensive demographic data to a unique guest ID. He mapped the spending patterns of women who had used baby gift registries to ascertain whether there were certain triggers and products that indicated pregnancy. He started to notice a pattern. Increased purchases of unscented lotion and other items such as vitamin supplements added to a list of 25 products, which when analysed as a whole, allowed Pole to allocate a score indicating the likelihood of pregnancy. This data also allowed him to predict within a narrow margin what the due date would be.

The marketing team were ecstatic. They held in their hands retail gold — the ability to promote a targeted campaign to a pregnant customer months before other retailers would even know of it. They ran a test campaign on a targeted group that met the criteria. It was not long before they had a complaint — a father complaining that his teenage daughter was being sent copious promotions and coupons for pregnancy and baby products. What the father did not know was that his daughter was pregnant. The pregnancy model had worked.

Target suddenly realised the precarious position they were in and a prompt shut down of all communications on this project occurred. The journalist was refused access to Andrew Pole and Target staff, and they declined to comment and respond, other than to claim the report was inaccurate and misleading. They had understood the potentially damaging public relations that would ensue from pregnant customers feeling spied on and invaded. The promotions and coupons changed direction, with pregnancy promotions being mixed in with seemingly unrelated products such as wine glasses and lawn mowers. Target's management reasoned that if the customer could not detect the specific, targeted campaign there would not be a negative response, only a purchase.

It seems as if their plan worked. Although revenue from pregnancy and baby products is not specifically listed separately, Target managed to increase their revenues from $44 billion in 2002 to $67 billion in 2010. In 2005 Gregg Steinhafel, Target's president, boasted to investors about their ability to appeal specifically to the mom and baby market.

Target is an excellent example of the immensity of the potential to harness and use customer data in innovative ways that drives significant bottom line results. It also shows the treacherously fine line you walk in your ethical use of data and how your customers feel about their data being used in a particular way, even if you are just inside the laws of the land.

CHAPTER 7:

TECHNOLOGY AND SYSTEMS

Transformation Intent

While customer-impacting technology is a powerful tool to engage your customers in their experience and to efficiently manage their data, its role is to enable the activation and delivery of your customer strategy and not to drive the design and implementation of your business. Transform instead your use of technology and systems so that they support you to innovate the customer experience, take advantage of latest trends and develop both a single and an in-depth view of your customer.

Staying ahead of the curve

In the opening keynote address of the Gartner Customer 360 Conference [1], the speakers shared the top 10 trends that would affect businesses through to 2020: the economy, globalisation, the customer's desire for self-service (serving customers wherever they wish), the high expectations customers have of their experience, cloud computing, social interaction and software, mobile computing, predictive modelling, Internet-enabled and connected devices and privacy regulation. In this vein, a Gartner survey [1] of CIOs (Chief Information Officers) indicated that the top three technology priorities in 2012 were analytics and business intelligence, mobile technologies and cloud computing. Are these trends catered for on your strategic plan?

While the economy and globalisation may be out of your control, the other eight trends all directly impact the technology choices you make in the context of your relationship with your customers. The story that emerges from these trends points directly to the dramatic changes taking place in the way customers expect to engage with their world and, therefore, with your business. Without the innovation in customer experience that is increasingly being demanded across all aspects of the engagement process, you might just find that your organisation has fallen too far "behind the curve" and is playing catch-up with your competitors in the market.

A customer-centric approach to technology and systems is driven by a strategy and technology architecture that directly focuses on delivering the right customer experience while innovating that experience in alignment with the social, mobile and collaborative trends epitomised in Web 2.0. Innovation and strategy alignment alone are not enough. Your customer-facing systems must be monitored and managed on an on-going basis to ensure that a superior experience is being delivered and that a single view of the customer facilitates your active customer management capability. In alignment with one of the most critical trends for 2020 — data analytics and future forecasting — your systems must enable you to effectively analyse all customers from a variety of perspectives and across segments.

Customer technological implementations face the same challenges that all IT projects do. While IT projects still deliver a mediocre success rate at best, IT project methodologies and approaches have definitely matured and improved over the last 10 years. New business practises, such as IT governance, bring in a greater focus on improving IT decision-making and seeing projects through to their successful completion. Yet at the same time, the technologies themselves have become more complex and, with the rapid increase in data, the effective use of IT to deliver the required return has become a massive challenge. Added to this problem is the rapidly changing world that we live in and the demands that new trends place on IT teams to support customer-focused innovation.

Technology supports you to innovate and, at the same time, innovative leadership in customer-centricity allows you to choose the right technologies to deliver a superior customer experience and create a sustainable competitive advantage. Your technologies and systems are there to make your customer vision a reality and not to force your customer into doing business with you in an archaic manner, just because that is what your IT architecture dictates.

"However you decide to use technology, it changes fast. As many experts noted, the 'half-life' on digital innovations is short. Citibank was the first mover in mobile check deposits, but Wells Fargo just launched a similar service. Within the next year, all four of the largest US banks will enable customers to deposit checks by scanning with smartphones" [17].

Strategic customer technologies

Just as specific consideration of your customer in your strategy is a critical foundation for customer-centricity, so too is the customer-dimension vital in your technology strategy. Technology can play a variety of roles in fulfilling your customer strategy so it is important to be clear and specific on how you will make best use of both your current and new technologies to do so, while still delivering a return on investment.

According to Bob Thompson [39], 70% of "memorable" customer experiences are created by people and not technology, yet when technology does not work, the experience stays in the mind of the customer. He suggests that technology can play three roles — the star of the show, a supporting act or background support. Technology stars are those that "delight" the customer, such as Amazon.com's online store features or Apple's product-led innovation. Technology that plays a supporting role in superior customer experience includes examples such as Starbucks' planned use of Square for voice-recognition payment or Domino's Pizza's use of a mobile app for customers to track their pizza orders. In a background role, technology often goes unseen in its support of employees to deliver a superior customer experience, be that through an integrated customer view in the call centre or by seamlessly providing subtle personalisation of goods and services purchased. Whatever your use of technology may be, a specific strategy focused on the customer dimension of your technology architecture or road map is critical.

The end-to-end technology road map must be written in a way that it becomes a powerful communication tool across the organisation of how deep thinking and customer-led innovation will be implemented. This ensures that non-IT stakeholders within your organisation are able to understand the platform that is being built and implemented and how this will impact the customer experience. It also ensures that technology-focused teams always have customer-centricity as a focus area for their projects. In this way, the technology architecture seeks to bridge the gap between business and IT.

As highlighted by the Gartner survey [1], customer self-service is a top trend that will influence the way business works heading towards 2020. Self-service has typically been thought of as giving customers the ability to conduct transactions themselves, such as booking an airline ticket online. This does not take into account the other component of self-service — self-directed support through a variety of means and across channels. Customers now expect a consistent self-serve experience across channels. In the case of booking an airline ticket, this means customers expect to have the same functionality online as they would have speaking to an agent at a call centre or visiting a travel office. You, therefore, need to ensure that your current and future self-serve offerings have been built into your technology architecture and that your organisation can deliver on the performance expectations of your customers.

There is a clear trend that CIOs more frequently have customer experience solutions high on their priority list. The Gartner survey [1], confirms that this is the case. When you see customer-led technology planning in an organisation, you will also find leaders who are committed to a customer-centric business model and to creating competitive advantage through it. It can be said that CRM as a concept, to some extent considered a fad of the 2000s, has given way to customer experience-based solutions that seek to take advantage of the technological drivers of this decade — mobile and tablet app technology, cloud computing and social media platforms. While the big CRM and ERP players will still continue to dominate, visionary CIOs and their teams, through a clear and shared vision, will find ways to cost-effectively bolt together innovative applications that deliver differentiated and superior customer experiences across a diversity of channels and media.

"The consumerization of IT has now become social computing — and what does social computing mean — it means, "my world, my way." As Drucker points out, the big story here is about choices — people — everybody — now has choices, and they are taking advantage of their new ability to exercise those choices. They skip the advertisements on TV, they get their news from the Internet, they ask their friends what to do and share the dirt they discover. And there is plenty to discover" [16].

Managing your customer-facing systems

Besides the obvious role of IT in the innovation of your customer experience, IT plays a critical role in ensuring that your customers' on-going use of customer-facing systems is managed efficiently and still delivers on your promise. This requires building into your IT management approach the regular consideration and review of both the accessibility and usability of your systems, as well as giving customers the control they need over their systems' experience and ensuring that the experience aspect of any system failure has been considered.

The usability of your customer systems can be defined as: "… the extent to which a product can be used by specified users to achieve specified goals with effectiveness, efficiency and satisfaction in a specified context of use" [40]. In the context of customer-centricity, usability should also take into account the principles of user experience, which from an IT perspective include: "all the users' emotions, beliefs, preferences, perceptions, physical and psychological responses, behaviours and accomplishments that occur before, during and after use" [41].

Accessibility refers to the ability of your systems to allow your customers to have a consistent experience of these systems across your platforms. With mobile and tablet computing being a major trend, your IT department needs to ensure that your systems are ready for these platforms and have been optimised accordingly.

New technologies will continue to shift the "goal posts". As little as five years ago it was deemed unthinkable that mobile phones would be used to access your systems to the extent they are today. Now users expect that large organisations provide at least a mobile version of their web site to optimise accessing the information they need in a more convenient, immediate and effective way. In ten years' time who knows what new technologies your customers will expect. You, therefore, need to develop the capability to stay in touch with new technology trends and ensure your customer-facing systems support those trends.

Emirates Airline is a leading global brand and one of the fastest growing airlines, operating through their hub in Dubai. The usability and accessibility of their online booking web site was a critical concern in their strategy of continually growing their global market presence. They contracted a leading user-experience consultancy, User Vision, to evaluate the user-experience of their web site. A programme of usability testing with selected customers was conducted, where customers were observed in their use of the system to ascertain their responses and where they had challenges performing specific functions. The results of the exercise were outstanding. "Quick wins" for system improvements were identified and the long-term improvements planned for could be validated. The improvement in customer experience also created direct financial benefit, with visitors increasing by a staggering 70% year on year [42].

The management of your customer-facing systems, therefore, requires that you take a customer-experience view of your systems and that you embrace the principles of Web 2.0 in the design, development, implementation and management of your customer-facing systems. Web 2.0 was a phrase first coined in January 1999 by Darcy DiNucci [43] who wrote: "The Web we know now, which loads into a browser window in essentially static screenfuls, is only an embryo of the Web to come. The first glimmerings of Web 2.0 are beginning to appear, and we are just starting to see how that embryo might develop. The Web will be understood not as screenfuls of text and graphics but as a transport mechanism, the ether through which interactivity happens".

Since then, Web 2.0 has gained massive popularity as a term to describe the extensive, collaborative, decentralised and community-based network that the Internet has now become. In this light, customers expect that they can engage with your customer-facing systems in an interactive way that lets them control their experience. For example, customers may prefer to sign in to your customer-facing systems using their Facebook account so they do not have to share their e-mail address, or log in to your systems using an intermediary service so they can manage all their user accounts from one platform. If this kind of self-directed control is not yet possible in your organisation, then you need to ensure that you are planning to shift your customer-facing systems in this direction.

A customer-centric approach to your customer-facing systems also means that you consider the customer experience when your systems fail or do not work, planning for how such failures will be managed. This may mean building a proactive communication mechanism that lets customers know when there is a problem or providing them with the ability to find that information. Even the dreaded 404 error is getting a revamp. Some organisations are now using the 404 error, or "page not found", on a web site to continue the conversation with the customer and engage them with the brand even when a failure has occurred. This is the kind of innovative thinking that transforms a problem into an opportunity.

"Businesses tend to have a narrow view of customer needs or expectations. And, rather than design to evoke human emotion, journeys are designed with a 'mediumalistic' approach, where platforms and devices take precedence over the human connection or after effect. Products, pages, profiles, and entire click paths are narcissistic by design, taking into account the needs of decision makers and stakeholders over the customers they're designed to entice. The need to plug into trends trumps the opportunity to innovate and improve the customer journey" [26].

A single view of your customer

While systems play a crucial role in supporting your customer-facing employees to manage your customers effectively across a variety of interfaces, it is essential that they have a simple, single and efficient interface with which to do so. I am sure you have had the experience of phoning a call centre only to be told by the agent to please hold while they look up your details on multiple screens. As you wait endlessly for them to do so, you wonder why they have such a fragmented view of who you are. Do your customers also have that experience?

A single, integrated view of your customer and their information increases the capability to prompt your frontline employees for any customer management actions required alongside any transactions your customer may be performing. This allows you to naturally and seamlessly ask questions aimed at obtaining a specific piece of information that will drive further insights about that customer, also known as "golden questions". You could also use this capability to implement your customer information plan and improve the quality of your data through more regular updates of critical customer information, such as contact details.

The integration of customer data itself into a single view is quite complex. With there often being multiple sources of customer information, and updates thereto, across the organisation, business rules need to be in place to determine which version of data is the correct one and how to resolve conflicts between sources of data. Added to this scenario is the complexity of timing and the real-time, or close to real-time, updates and replication of customer data.

While the seamless integration of customer data offers many benefits, it is important not to forget the users of customer management systems — your employees. As users of your systems, your frontline employees should be engaged in determining whether your customer management systems are "fit-for-purpose" and do the job they were designed to do. This should be done through the user acceptance testing of a new system before you launch it, and on a regular basis with your existing systems. For long-term projects this practice is even more critical because business needs and even the customer strategy may have changed during the project.

As customer needs, trends and technologies evolve so quickly in this rapidly moving world, it is necessary for your systems development methodologies and platforms to be flexible and quick to respond. Long development lead times may result in a critical opportunity being lost or changing needs may render a system less effective. It is preferable that your development approach breaks larger projects down into smaller, ring-fenced units that can be rapidly developed and deployed. Very often this task requires the creation of highly-skilled, cross-functional teams with clear accountability to deliver their particular unit quickly and according to specification.

These development considerations will continue to challenge IT departments to find ways to implement the customer element of the technology strategy while ensuring the continued integrity of existing customer management systems. New platforms, such as those used for the development of apps for mobile devices and tablets, will also go through their own stages of evolution as they mature in use. There will always be something just around the corner. The customer is getting sharper at expecting you to be ahead of the curve.

Analytics of the future

As explored in the previous chapter, *Data Management*, organisations are flooded with customer data from a multitude of sources. Transforming your data into value is dependent on your ability to derive meaningful insight from that data so that you can deliver a superior customer experience. The Gartner survey [1] predicts that data analytics and future forecasting will be a major trend leading into 2020, yet organisations are not ready for what this means. A 2011 IBM survey of CMOs (Chief Marketing Officers) revealed that 71% of CMOs felt they were unprepared for the data explosion their organisations face — the highest category of unpreparedness in the survey [1].

IT has a major role to play in supporting this technological challenge, especially as the kinds of questions being asked are changing. In the past, data analytics was used to understand the past and what had already happened through data mining of transactional data and reporting dashboards. This process has now shifted towards seeing data in real-time so that you can understand what is happening right now and take immediate action. In the future, data will be used to predict what may happen and how your customers are likely to behave. Technologies are readily available to support this ability yet they are only as effective as the data you have and the team that drives your analytics.

In order to prepare your organisation for this future view of data you need to have a single analytics data warehouse that integrates all your essential customer data into one source. This includes transactional data as well as the behavioural, attitudinal and experiential dimensions of your customers. If you cannot do this you will not be able to see the bigger picture of your customers and their experiences across all segments and channels. This task becomes tricky when you consider that a large percentage of customer behavioural data is sitting in text note fields, customer surveys and focus group reports.

Whatever technology solution you choose it must support you to quickly access the right information you need and also have enough flexibility to meet your real needs for a customer-centric approach. There is no time in this fast-paced world to apply for a report and wait for weeks for it to return. By the time you are ready to act on that new insight, your competitors have already taken the gap and the opportunity is lost. Part of the IT team's job is to find ways of using technology to deliver analytics capability to those executives and decision makers that need it. The alternative is that the analytics function remains the sole responsibility of a few analysts, who may be brilliant statisticians, yet may also not fully grasp the relevance of the customer insights blinking at them on the screen.

In order for IT to deliver real value through its management of data you also need a connection and integration between your warehouse and your operational systems that employees use to engage with customers. This means that insights derived from data can be quickly deployed to the right people so that action can be taken and value can be delivered. If your analytics process identifies a customer as being at a high risk of loss, that insight should be delivered to the person who can do something about it. Without this level of interconnectivity, the insights derived give a "big picture" view yet cannot translate into meaningful action with the individual customer.

A customer-centric approach to IT, therefore, needs to deliver real value to the business in the areas deemed most critical for delivering a superior customer experience and creating competitive advantage. You can have the latest cutting-edge technology, yet without applying those tools for the direct benefit of the customer and their experience, the true value of technology and systems cannot become a reality for your organisation.

Transformation questions

- Is there a clear "customer strand" to your organisation's overall technology strategy?
- Are systems that are accessible to prospects or customers monitored and managed with a clear customer focus and are they evolving in a way that delivers according to the principles of Web 2.0?
- Are the systems used at all customer interfaces able to provide a common view of each customer in addition to performing their specialist role and can they be upgraded or changed rapidly enough to support the Customer Management Strategy?
- What mechanisms are you using to capture customer feedback across various channels and how are you utilising those insights for immediate action?
- Is your technology platform supporting the creation of an environment where customers can be successful in using and accessing the right product, information, help and channel?
- Does your IT strategy have a specific objective focused on improving customer experience and how is the organisational gap between IT and customer-facing units of the business being bridged?
- Does your technology enable you to understand what customers think, feel and experience when they engage with your organisation?
- In what way is your technology enabling a differentiated customer experience?
- Do you have technology capability to analyse text and translate it into

insights?

- Does your technology architecture support online communities and virtual worlds as a mechanism to prototype products and gather feedback through community participation and interactive design?
- Does your organisation make use of business process stimulation tools to optimise process design to positively affect customer experience?
- Can you use your customer database to customise offerings for your high value customers so that they can be segmented, based on both value and behaviour?
- Does your technology architecture enable delight by reminding your sales and frontline people about personal customer details and their priority?
- Do you provide ethics guidance to staff on appropriate use of technology and information?
- Would your customers be comfortable with the way you capture and manage information obtained from them?

Case study - Hilton Hotels uses CRM for customer leadership

Hilton Hotels is a huge global player in the hotel industry with a variety of hotel brands within its group, delivering distinct customer experiences for a diversity of segments [44]. As the expansion of a hotel group is very capital-intensive, Hilton embraced a franchise model as a way of leveraging other people's capital to expand the group. As such, while Hilton's real customers are the guests that stay in their hotels, Hilton also has a commitment to support its hotel owners and operators in providing excellent service.

Such an operational model brings with it many challenges, namely ensuring that guests do have the desired experience and that brand standards are met. Good relationships with operators and the monitoring and quality assurance of their activity are essential. Hilton developed its own technology infrastructure, OnQ, to provide an integrated and comprehensive solution for every hotel in its group, regardless of its size, location or customer segment. They decided to build this system in-house as there were no technology solutions available to the lodging industry that would suitably integrate all aspects of the customer experience.

Hilton invested approximately $195 million in this project while making a commitment to hotel owners that they would not pass that cost onto the hotels in the form of additional fees. This action demonstrated Hilton's commitment to support their owners and operators to deliver outstanding results and highlighted Hilton's understanding of the value that technology can create for their wider strategic goals. They could now open more hotels faster, while ensuring that customers were consistently getting the optimum Hilton experience.

OnQ CRM was an application built upon the overall OnQ infrastructure that directly supported Hilton's customer strategy and related initiatives and enabled them to use CRM as a tool to solidify their relationships with their best customers. One of the key benefits of OnQ CRM was its ability to integrate customer data so that timely reporting could improve the customer experience. For example, the hotel front desk would receive a report first thing in the morning that listed all guests arriving that day ranked by importance, with additional customer preference information that staff could use to personalise the lodging experience. Rooms and facilities could then be prepared accordingly. This might even include a report of service issues the customer had previously experienced at a Hilton hotel, such as a broken air conditioner, so that their allocated room could be specifically checked to ensure that all was in working order.

Measuring the actual customer experience was also an essential part of the role of OnQ CRM. Customer surveys allowed management to track customer satisfaction and loyalty and, hence, the likely impact on growth. This has been essential in ensuring that the right quality and brand experience occurs in every hotel.

Yet, as with any customer technology initiative, it is really challenging to measure the tangible benefits that CRM offers through a personalised customer experience. As Tom Keltner, then executive vice president of Hilton Hotels, explains: "Our success is going to come down to execution. That's the reality. We know what the opportunity is, we have the infrastructure and the data, what it comes down to is how effectively to harness the promise of CRM, the potential of OnQ, and execute it consistently and flawlessly across the network" [44].

PART THREE:

ENABLERS

● CHAPTER 8:

● INSIGHT AND PLANNING

Transformation Intent

Whereas data management ensures that the quality and priority of critical customer information enables a customer-centric approach, insight and planning translates that data into meaningful patterns of customer drivers and behaviour. With this understanding you can transform your approach to defining your customers' needs from an outside-in perspective, thereby segmenting them correctly and, thus becoming capable of delivering a relevant and superior customer experience, while being mindful of your competitors' manoeuvres.

From knowledge to wisdom

In Part Two, *Foundations*, the building blocks that drive your successful customer-centric transformation were explored. These foundations included: dynamic leadership driving the organisation towards a strategic vision, highly-motivated employees rallying together through a unified culture, integrated and high-quality customer data, and efficient and effective systems and technologies. In this section, Part Three, *Enablers*, those foundations are extended to include the next layer required for customer-centricity capability development — the enablers or components you need to manage in order to operationalize your transformation. These enablers usually require broad discussion across the organisation and may result in changes to be planned for in your current period so that these changes can be implemented in your next budgetary or operating period.

The first such enabler is *Insight and Planning*. In Chapter 6, *Data Management*, the measurement, management and reporting on customer data as a vital and valuable organisational asset was explored. As highlighted in the case study for that chapter, Target's story of its pregnancy analytics highlights how it is possible to derive highly valuable insights about your customers' behaviour and likely future drivers once you can rely on the integrated and high quality sources of your customer data.

The core principle of an "outside-in", customer-centric way of thinking is to treat different customers differently. The insights derived from understanding customer behaviour allow you to differentiate your customer segments effectively according to their current and likely future value and to clearly articulate the needs of each customer segment. If you are able to understand your customer segments and their needs at a level deep enough to predict their likely future behaviour, you have a massive opportunity to create specific, focused and relevant engagements with them. Using this awareness, you can then effectively plan for the revenue and margin improvements to be delivered for each segment and how you will achieve that result. This translates your knowledge into wisdom and, as a result, into superior and sustained business performance.

The ability to see new trends and patterns in current and future customer behaviour also allows you to understand the extent of the threat that direct and indirect competitors pose to your unique value proposition. As you act to enhance the quality and relevance of your customer experience, so will your competitors be watching your every move — either copying you and being left behind, or finding ways to outsmart you at every turn. Finding new and innovative ways to leverage your customer data with an "outside-in" perspective is one way to create a gap your competitors will struggle to breach.

Mining transactional data for insight

Any organisation that mines its data to glean insights about their customers is moving in the right direction towards a customer-centric approach. Where the organisation lies on that continuum depends on the level of detail and segment-based analysis that provides the greater depth of insight required.

In a customer-centric approach, you would most likely mine your transaction data according to your customer segments, whether those segments are based on value, needs, behaviours or a combination thereof, and then analyse the data that is most relevant and valuable for each segment. Your insight and level of understanding then becomes much more refined than it would by just analysing general trends across your entire customer portfolio. Those specific insights allow you to focus on the patterns and trends that will most likely lead to the development of your key segments using the approaches you have defined. This method is more focused, deliberate and directly linked to creating more relevant offerings for your customers.

Looking for patterns and trends is not just about the visible and easily discernible trends in purchase behaviour. Some of the greatest value lies in being able to identify hidden trends that your competitors may not be able to see because they do not have the same perspective as you do. In the example of Target's pregnancy model (see Chapter 6), their statistician was able to model a new pattern not known about from the very transaction data that every competitor had at its disposal. Being able to really use transaction data for insight requires that you can rely upon the data you have. Besides the quality and relevance issues, you also need enough data to be able to draw statistically relevant insights.

There is also an immense amount of information to be gleaned from how your customers are transacting with you. If you had to analyse the nature of the transactions across your channels, online and offline, you would start to understand how each segment prefers engaging with you. Perhaps your high value segment prefers your online channels to the physical store or branch alternative. This segment may welcome being able to interact more with you through online mechanisms, thereby reducing their need to engage through their less preferable channel. It would be a mistake to assume that your other segments have the same preferences. Knowing your segments and understanding their transaction preferences, therefore, supports the delivery of more relevant experiences.

Integrating non-transactional data

Customer-centricity requires much broader thinking when it comes to the way that you approach deriving insight from non-transactional data. This is largely due to the opportunities and challenges posed by new social and digital channels, and the changing behaviour of customers in the dynamic and rapidly changing world we live in.

An important source of information can be found in customer behaviour research. This includes having access to data on the behavioural trends in your own market, as well as being in touch with changing industry and global trends, customer buying patterns and buyer psychology. Traditional research, customer surveys and focus groups should be supported with academic partnerships that deliver rigorous research. Once again, Target's use of habit psychology as a way to change customer habits is an example of this (see Chapter 6).

For online and digital channels, you should be able to capture the way your customers engage with your online channels and map it to their overall customer profile so that you can build a complete understanding of your customer's behaviour in this way. What pages have they viewed? What product areas do they visit? How long do they spend in any particular place? Having the right analytics expertise will enable you to translate this data into patterns of customer channel behaviour that has intrinsic value. Intelligent agents and alerts, such as Google Alerts, can also deliver meaningful behavioural data and even industry and competitor information, yet can only do so to the extent that you have clearly defined the behaviour triggers you want to track.

While your own channels may be easier to track and control, how do you then manage socially-sourced data generated through social channels such as Facebook, Twitter, LinkedIn and Foursquare? With social media becoming an increasingly important player in the customer's experience, you need to find ways to derive insight from customer behaviour, even if you do not own that data. In the sea of endless online conversations and activity, you have to be able to selectively integrate social data related to an individual customer into your other, more structured customer data sources. This creates a deeper and more valuable profile than you could ever achieve through your owned channels alone.

The challenge of integrating data, of course, is that in this digital world, customers are becoming increasingly hounded by "bots", "cookies" and "trackers". If your customers think that you are stalking their every move, at worst, they may cut their ties with you permanently, and at best, they may become disgruntled and dissatisfied customers. Instead you have to find a way to derive meaningful insight while providing a positive experience for your customers that ensures they are willing to keep giving you information because they trust you with it.

Researching your market

From a customer-centric perspective, research into the needs of your customers and your market should extend far beyond your typical customer survey. Your qualitative customer research should be designed in such a way that it uncovers your customers' deep and real needs and wants. So often customer research takes the form of a tick-box "product or service features and benefits survey" or has been designed in such a way to drive a predetermined outcome or to put ideas in the mind of the customer. If so, a real opportunity to identify those key drivers is lost. It is also quite common that customers who leave a company are asked for their reason for leaving and this data is then used in research. Perhaps you should consider that a much better source of research data would come from asking your long-term, loyal customers: "Why do you stay?"

Remember to consider your customer segments in your quantitative research. I have often been presented with research results from clients, where an ad-hoc sampling of their customers across the entire database has been used for an interview-based survey process. Frequently, significant decisions with a long-term impact are made on the basis of those findings without due consideration of the different perspectives provided by different value segments across that base. A customer-centric approach would be to derive a sample from each value segment and then to scale the relative importance of the needs identified across those segments. In treating different customers differently, it is critical to recognise that the needs of a high value segment, at a particular moment in time, probably carries more weight than the needs of a low value segment.

Your needs analysis activities should include non-customers and, in particular, should focus on understanding the factors that influence their decision-making early in the process. This will help you to learn more about the criteria that potential customers may be using to make their decisions. Through understanding non-customers better, you can refine your value proposition and plan accordingly.

Customer research, both qualitative and quantitative, should also be designed to test the depth of feelings that respondents have for their wants and needs, relative to market factors that will either help or hinder them in making a decision to purchase. Your research should determine the factors that impact each particular need and to what extent they do so. An example might be the ability for a customer to easily do online price comparisons across all players in your market. The job of your research may be to determine to what extent the customers' ability to conduct a price comparison exercise influences their decision-making.

> "In an effort to be more customer-centric, companies today often jump to apply their "customer intelligence" to guide product and service innovation. Armed with data, companies feel they "know" their consumers. But knowing about someone is not the same as knowing them. Confusing the two is the difference between a transaction and relationship"[45].

Besides the identification of needs for both customers and non-customers, your research should try to identify the impact that each need area has on the depth of commitment that your customers have towards your organisation. For example, hygiene factors are those needs that a segment considers to be a minimum standard, and failure to deliver against this standard would dramatically reduce the customers' depth of commitment. Similarly, with other customer preferences you should determine from respondents the degree to which they would forgive failures against each of those needs areas and, possibly, the degree to which excellent delivery in those needs areas would guarantee future business.

While truly understanding the needs areas of your customers and your market is an essential part of a customer-centric approach to deriving customer insight, it is important not to forget the other side of the same coin — as Jeff Bezos of Amazon.com says: "invent of behalf of your customers". This is something that Apple has done consistently well: innovating the market and blazing a trail for others to follow. Therefore, have a clear understanding of what your customers need and, in addition, be brave and bold enough to provide them with something they need before they know they need it.

Operationalized customer segmentation

Effective segmentation of your customers begins with creating a segmentation framework that can be consistently used throughout your organisation by the people who need it. This supports you to derive insights about your customers and target the right value propositions to them at the right time. Your segmentation framework in many ways becomes your customer architecture and should create a reference point for any conversation about the customer and related planning activities.

A good, albeit dated, example of a segmentation framework that I still find useful is that of Rolls-Royce and Bentley Motor Cars [46]. Their four scale SLVP Segmentation Framework was based on: Current Satisfaction (S), Repurchase Loyalty (L), Current Value (V) and Future Potential (P). The data used to calculate the scores was initially quite simple and, over time, the sophistication of the SLVP calculations improved. Customers were then placed into meaningful segments with clear descriptors, such as "Maintain Excellence" and "Nothing's Too Much". These descriptors then determined the level of management activity directed at different customers. So often I see organisations having a comprehensive theoretical segmentation framework that just cannot be operationalized. You need to have the ability to map customers to meaningful segments and to be able to recognise them when they make contact with you, so that you can deliver an experience on the frontline that is relevant to, and matches the needs of, that segment. This allows you to capitalise on that moment of truth.

Let's reflect on what this may mean from a practical perspective. Imagine for a moment that one of your high value customers contacts your call centre to complain about having been billed a fee that they do not understand. If your call centre agent understands their value in that moment and is equipped with the right decision-making tools, they could offer to reverse that fee without question. In the event that a lower value customer called in with the same query, the agent may reply that nothing can be done due to the fee being part of the standard terms and conditions. If you equip your frontline people with the knowledge and tools they need, they can support the effective implementation of your segmentation framework, inculcate consistency and optimise profitability because they possess the ability to treat different customers differently.

> "A customer-centric segmentation is just a nice idea unless you create a customer-centric IT operation capable of delivering. Rethinking and restructuring IT infrastructure and the development process now becomes critical" [47].

Customer value is not the only way to segment your customers. An effective segmentation framework should include attributes such as behaviours, life stage, needs and demographics. Your ability to do this effectively is dependent on the availability and quality of your customer data. You would be well advised to conduct research into robust segmentation methodologies that take these factors into account.

With the explosion of online platforms and social media, there is a new trend in segmentation – self-segmentation. The customer is likely to be able to segment themselves more accurately than you can with the definitions and categories you have defined for their value, behaviours and needs. Customers would, therefore, select their most relevant communities of interest, referred to as "tribes" by Seth Godin [48]. The opportunities that flow from this activity are immense – clearly and accurately defined groupings of passionate customers rallying together. The challenge is, of course, whether your organisation is ready to handle this new kind of approach with consistency and relevance.

While it might seem obvious that customers will move between segments over time, I do not often see organisations that track and analyse the segmentation history of its customers and the reasons for the movement. There may be great insight to be derived in understanding why and how customers move across segments. These insights may assist you to implement campaigns that result in customers moving into higher value segments if appropriate.

Customer-based planning

One of the key outcomes of your entire insight and analytics drive should be to enable you to approach business planning with a customer-centric mind-set. If you are clear as to the primary customer value management objectives of each segment, be that retention, efficiency (optimising cost to serve), acquisition or penetration (cross-sell and up-sell), you can develop specific plans that will deliver the intended results according to the business case defined.

With your outcome clearly defined, you can focus on the key value drivers or measures that are critical, such as win rates for Acquisition, attrition or churn rates for Retention, cross-sell ratios for Penetration and many more. For each driver you would then define the intended improvement target for that driver which would enable you to calculate the resultant business benefit in monetary terms. For example, if you could reduce your customer attrition rate from a hypothetical level of 2.4% per month to 1.8% per month, the derived business benefit may be worth $XX million. You could then, with very effective cost control, design specific initiatives and campaigns to facilitate the achievement of the target because you understand the financial benefit that will likely occur and can, therefore, plan for the costs to be incurred to achieve it.

Staying one step ahead of the rest

As you act on the insights and customer knowledge you have developed, you can be sure that your competitors are watching your every move. Your customer planning process needs to take this into account by predicting how quickly your competitors can react to your plan and to what extent you can create a time and value lag that they will struggle to catch up with. A massive investment in a project, where value created can be quickly duplicated by a competitor, will not be as cost effective as smaller investments that create distinct and compelling competitive advantage that is not easily replicated. It is well known that both Amazon.com and Starbucks have led in this area, focusing persistently in a niche market and creating such a wide gap before competitors woke up to the opportunity.

With a product-centric approach, it will become ever increasingly difficult to create and sustain competitive advantage through product. While Apple is an example of leading edge product innovation, it would only take a few releases of unexciting iPhones or lacklustre iPad upgrades to give competitors the opportunity to differentiate through a customer-centric approach or even compete directly through innovation.

It may also be necessary to widen your view of who your competitors are. Who would have thought ten years ago that the mobile banking platform would become such a threat to the traditional "bricks and mortar" banking practises? Could banks have foreseen that Facebook might one day become your bank?

"This will create a greater need to consider the user experience — not just in terms of current offerings or other close competitors — but also in terms of more aggressive competitors from outside your conventional competitive set and even from other consumer facing providers in other industries. It s not just about how your client-facing technology stacks up against your closest competitor, but how it compares to Amazon, Google and Wikipedia" [47].

Developing expertise in customer insight and planning allows you to approach your customer from a strategic perspective and with a mind-set focused on creating sustainable competitive advantage. Instead of making "knee-jerk" reactions to your customers, market and competitors, you can rather approach your customer from an experiential and scientific approach that seeks to quantify the value your customers add across segments, and how you can best work with your customer to leverage that value.

Transformation questions

- Do you fully understand the nature of customer transactional behaviour both on-line and off-line?
- Is there a clear customer dimension to your planning activity and a deep understanding of the value drivers that should be taken into account in this activity?
- What are the clues in your world today that you need to understand and that will need to be removed as barriers, or used as leverage, in achieving your strategic outcome?
- What criteria would you use in order to select from a set of alternative choices?
- What are the key time horizons and events that are driving your thinking?
- How will you know when your "strategic outcome" is in place?
- Are you clear as to what capabilities and culture you will need as an organisation if you are to meet your objectives through the delivery of differentiated products and services?
- What political, economic, social and technological pressures lead to insights which will help you think through what you need to know in order to change and transform your chances of success?
- How do you take your intended outcome back to the organisation and make it real?
- What is the highest order of "prize" – the supreme and primary reason for your existence? How good could it be?
- What role do the interests and needs of customers play in the way you do your planning?

Case study - Harrah's hedges their bets with analytics

Harrah's Entertainment, Inc., a United States gaming company, is a leading example of what it means to derive deep insight about the customer through integrating both transactional and non-transactional data [49]. Harrah's developed its WINet platform in their casinos to create a single customer view that integrated customer data from multiple sources, segmented that data and, then, linked targeted offers to customers directly from the insights derived.

A customer loyalty programme was central to this initiative because it supported Harrah's need to understand the buying behaviour and preferences of their customers. Customers earn points for their gaming activities and then redeem vouchers for a variety of products and services, such as cash, hotel accommodation, shows and meals. The higher the level achieved in the programme (Gold/Platinum/Diamond), the greater the rewards.

A variety of source data is integrated to create a single view of the customer. Hotel records document a history of customer stays, including their reservation details, room preferences and demographic data, such as address. Special events, like golf days, provide additional information linked to a unique customer ID. Customers also use their loyalty programme card to access all of Harrah's facilities, including slot machines, card tables, eateries and other services. Every bet made is recorded and tracked, and even the pace at which gamers bet on slot machines is recorded. Rapid fire betting tells a different story to the more slow and methodical approach. Vouchers that are redeemed also provide a wealth of customer preference information. All this data creates a comprehensive customer profile that defines the value of every customer and determines the experience preferences that would most likely positively influence their buying behaviour.

This customer profile allows Harrah's to tailor-make specific campaigns directed to suit a particular customer and the value segment they form part of. A low value customer might be offered food and beverage vouchers relative to their preferences or a voucher for free gaming chips linked to their gaming profile and preferred game of play. An out-of-state high value customer could be offered overnight accommodation, whereas the same value customer who is a local resident may be offered tickets to a show.

As every bet, purchase and voucher redeemed is recorded and tracked, Harrah's can experiment with "closed-loop marketing" where different marketing campaigns are tested and evaluated. The feedback loop, gleaned from the vouchers redeemed, provides useful insight into what is really required to influence customer behaviour and which incentives are successful. This creates a learning cycle that drives high profitability campaigns and a more relevant customer experience.

In one example Harrah's experimented with two groups at the same casino. The first group was offered a marketing package of a free room, two meals and $30 in free gaming chips for the casino. The second group was offered $60 in gaming chips and no other extras. The second group's offer resulted in much more gaming than that of the first group and, therefore, more revenue and profit, indicating that all the extras were in fact unnecessary and not relevant to that target segment.

Harrah's results speak for themselves, including market share, profitability, market capitalisation and customer loyalty. In one study by Nuclear Research, it was gleaned that, in only one part of Harrah's programme, a $22 million investment made over three years resulted in a direct return of $208 million for the same time period [50]. This further supports the direct and tangible benefits of a customer-centric approach to deriving insight from an integrated and consolidated customer data source.

CHAPTER 9:

BRAND AND PROPOSITION

Transformation Intent

Customer-centricity recognises and encourages the value of brand equity as an intangible asset, which is not created through gimmicks, but through an emotional connection with customers that communicates a clear value proposition and engages their participation in the creation of that proposition. Transform your approach to the design and development of your products and services by embracing customer-focused change and innovating on behalf of your customers, while keeping your eye on the competition.

To infinity and beyond

On 14 October 2012, the base-jumping dare devil, Felix Baumgartner, jumped from his Red Bull Stratos balloon capsule at 128,000 feet above the earth. Luckily for Red Bull, their gamble paid off. With bated breath and a relieved sigh, over 8 million people watched the live event, streamed on YouTube and on other traditional broadcasters, as Baumgartner dramatically, yet safely, descended to the ground. While Baumgartner celebrated still being alive, Red Bull celebrated the win for their brand because this was the largest streamed live audience in history, even beating President Obama's inauguration [51].

The significance of Red Bull's campaign lies in the changing landscapes of brand development that it heralds. In this case, Red Bull's brand is no longer about selling energy drinks. It is now also a media company, creating content and experiences for its target market that produces deep and enduring emotional connections. No matter if you never buy a Red Bull drink in your life, you will remember the tension and nervousness you felt when Baumgartner jumped and the relief when he effortlessly touched down on terra firma. That, in itself, was brand equity creation at its best.

Brand equity can be defined as "the brand assets (or liabilities) linked to a brand's name and symbol that add to (or subtract from) a product or service" [52]. It is an intangible asset and, as explored earlier in Chapter 3, it is estimated that intangible assets comprise over 80% of the market value of companies. Iconic brands such as Coca Cola and Apple know all too well the immense value of their brands. According to Aaker and Joachimsthaler [52], there are four dimensions that contribute to brand equity and the asset development thereof: brand awareness, perceived quality, brand associations and brand loyalty. With the effective management of these four aspects, future cash flow can be assured.

When it comes to brand and customer proposition development, customer-centricity requires a shift from an "inside-out" to an "outside-in" approach. In traditional branding and marketing, development of the proposition is approached from an "inside-out" perspective, as seen in the "4P" model, which defines the products and services for your target market according to their product features, price, promotion and placement. An "outside-in" approach places the customer at the centre of a clearly-defined proposition. At times, and when appropriate, customer participation in the creation of that proposition may occur. With this perspective in mind, the development of propositions takes into account the additional customer perspective of the "4Rs" — relevance of communication, receptivity or right timing, responsiveness to trends and customer needs, and relationships created with engaged customers [53]. When following this approach, customer propositions, in comparison to product propositions, consider the customer experience as well as the features and benefits.

This idea of the "4Rs" also embraces the idea promulgated by Amazon.com's Jeff Bezos to invent on behalf of the customer. This requires a culture of innovation that embraces change, disruptive thinking and co-creative development, as well as providing customers with opportunities to tailor their proposition. This method also acknowledges that to truly understand your competitors' propositions you need to understand what customer experience they are offering and whether it is being delivered upon.

Just as Baumgartner and Red Bull planned for and reached the "near-edge" of space, so do you need to transform the focus of your brand and proposition development so that you too can take your organisation to "new heights", and becoming extremely relevant and competitive as a result.

The brand experience

A brand is a "set of physical attributes of a product and service, including name, design and features, together with the surrounding beliefs, perceptions and expectations that distinguish one product or company from another in the minds of the audiences" [53]. A customer proposition is a statement that clearly articulates both the functional and experiential promises of value, made to the customer about that product and/or service, which, in essence, defines the benefits and the emotions the customer should experience.

For a brand and proposition to work well they must speak the same language. Very often there is a disconnection between the customer proposition and the organisation's documented brand values or personality attributes, with the brand over-promising and the proposition under-delivering or vice versa. For example, if an organisation offers a low cost and limited support product or service yet the brand is all about exclusivity and personal attention, then there is an inherent conflict that will impair the customer experience. You should, therefore, ensure that your organisation's brand values have been correctly translated and articulated into what those values mean for the customer and, in turn, the proposition must ensure that brand values and personality are correctly represented.

Customer-centricity also requires that there is integrity between your brand promise and the actual experience your customers have of that promise. As an example, it is well known that the Volvo brand is associated with safety. Volvo says that every car it builds is the sum total of more than 70 years of a concerted safety focus, which means that "you are not just driving a car, you are driving a promise" [54]. Volvo was at the forefront of safety engineering before government safety regulations arose. While the specifications of all Volvo cars deliver on this safety dimension of its promise, one has to consider the "feeling" one actually experiences when driving a Volvo. Does the actual experience match the brand promise? In Volvo's case it does, because the cars are relatively heavy and solid, which creates the feeling of safety. The customer experience should, therefore, be a key consideration in developing your brand equity. The situation becomes more complicated when your business comprises multiple brands or sub-brands. Your brand architecture, or the structure that defines your brand portfolio, creates a map that clearly defines the attributes and the personalities of each brand and who your customers are for each brand. Using the Virgin brand as an example, each sub-brand, such as Virgin Atlantic, Virgin Mobile and Virgin Active, explicitly defines its target audience so that clear differentiation is defined for each brand within the architecture.

Visionary leaders appreciate that there is a direct and powerful relationship between customer experience, product offering and brand equity. In turn, such leaders understand that customer equity, or the total sum of the discounted lifetime value of all your customers, is directly influenced by brand equity, and vice versa. In a customer-centric organisation, brand teams will demonstrate their understanding of the crucial nature of the customer experience in building brands and the value thereof.

> "Many brands get into trouble by failing to notice the warning signs before it's too late. The military realized that intelligence, not firepower, was the central ingredient to counter-insurgency. Sophisticated software looked for exceptions, patterns and relationships that might reveal terrorist activity. Fortunately for brands, terrorists try to hide their tracks, but customers usually try to get your attention. All you need are some good tools for monitoring social media, a crack team of social analysts and customer advocates, and a genuine commitment to act on what they see and hear" [20].

Setting the bar

In bridging the gap between your brand and your detailed customer propositions, it is necessary to clearly articulate your overarching customer proposition in a way that is aspirational and simple to communicate. Some visionary organisations build this overarching proposition into their vision statements. The Royal Bank of Canada is one such company, whose vision statement is "always earning the right to be our clients' first choice".

A customer charter is a tool used by some companies to define this overall proposition to the customer. Companies such as NatWest, Royal Bank of Scotland and AAMI (an Australian Insurer) are using customer charters to define the standards of service that customers can expect. In AAMI's case, their customer charter is externally audited, annually reviewed and the results are publicly reported [55]. There are 8 promises made in the revised 2013 version of this charter and AAMI incur a penalty if the terms of the charter have been breached. This demonstrates true leadership and commitment to their overarching proposition "to always provide its customers with the highest standards of customer service". Does your organisation have a customer charter and can it be easily and effectively communicated with your customers?

In the interests of clarity and consistency, your purpose and core offering must be understood by all your employees. A great litmus test for every employee would be to be able to consistently communicate your core offering and how it creates competitive advantage. There is a well-known story that the then American President, John F. Kennedy, visited the NASA space centre in 1962 and came across a janitor with a broom. Upon being asked by Kennedy what he did, the man replied that he was helping to put a man on the moon. Imagine what this kind of clarity of promise would create for your customers.

Merely having a clear proposition is not enough. You need to regularly assess whether your employees have a thorough understanding of the proposition. It is also good practice to assess whether customers are able to understand your proposition. This enables customer understanding of the quality they should expect and employee understanding of the quality they should deliver. Remember – brand equity is not only about the functional components of your proposition, it's also about the experiential components of the proposition.

If mismatches between your brand and your detailed customer propositions are identified, these need to be addressed with urgency. This action will enable you to manage your customers' expectations, because you know when you are creating an expectation that does not match the reality of the proposition.

Invent on behalf of your customers

While the clarity of the proposition, both for customers and employees, is critical, its success is dependent on whether your proposition is really offering the market something unique. Do you have a distinctive customer experience or is your proposition merely "me too"?

So often companies think they are "leading edge" yet all they offer their customers is more of the same mediocrity offered by other competitors. I have too often seen companies invest heavily in projects that deliver nothing more than "better sameness" – a small incremental difference that in most cases is insignificant in the eyes of the customer. In order to deliver superior customer experiences and, consequently, sustainable business performance, you need to innovate and lead the pack. There is, therefore, a huge opportunity to leapfrog your competition through innovation, especially as most markets and industries are characterised by "better sameness". However, it also requires that the way you do business supports innovation leadership.

A culture of innovation and the existence of leadership that is willing to embrace "disruptive thinking" sits at the heart of innovative leadership. It is not enough to say that you are innovative or that you have an innovative product or service. What is more important is that innovation sits at the centre of everything that your company does and is integrated into your business model. This includes innovating the experience that your customers have with you, engaging their emotions and creating differentiated value through the experiences you stage, in addition to the physical product. To do this you need processes across your entire organisation that are designed to identify innovative ideas for service improvement and then move these ideas through a structured process during which they can be assessed, valued, prioritised and implemented. So many organisations claim to be "leading edge", "bleeding edge", brave and creative. Yet when you look under the surface you find a culture of mediocrity — a satisfaction with "the status quo", an avoidance of the conflict and discomfort that change brings — which does not embrace change and maintains a culture of "if it isn't broken don't fix it".

Your formalised business model of innovation should also extend into your supply chain and channel partners, who are as critical to customer innovation as your own team is. Very often innovative ideas are created by these partners, yet without the processes in place to capture and act on these, you'll be unable to leverage your stakeholders effectively. The more broad-based and inclusive your process is, the better the quality of innovation you can deliver to your customers.

Collaborative co-creation

Co-creation is an approach that enables and encourages customers to actively participate and collaborate in the creation of the products and services they choose to purchase. Customers are no longer satisfied with simply accepting the choices that you decide they need. It is a mistake to think that personalisation and customisation are examples of co-creation — they only allow the customer to adjust the offering you have already decided they should have. Instead, co-creation acknowledges that the customer is an expert in his/her own right and it seeks to implement a multi-staged approach to idea generation and problem solving across a broad range of stakeholders.

This multi-staged approach [56] begins with the exploration of trends and conversations on the web, leading to insights that initiate the co-creation project and set its direction. Crowd-sourcing and the engagement of online consumer communities are then used to collaboratively explore ideas and develop some clear opportunities that require further investigation. A target group of both customers and experts evaluate those ideas in greater detail through face-to-face workshops so that possible solutions are investigated, refined and concluded. The last step is to take the idea back into the consumer communities for validation.

Co-creation also requires the active involvement of your employees and partners. It always amazes me when an organisation embarks on an expensive, outsourced research project without bothering to gather input from customer-facing employees. Your own employees are very often in a far better position to provide insight into the experiential dimension of what customers actually need and want than consultants.

If you are embracing co-creation with your customers, the type of multi-staged approach referred to above could ensure that your processes, product features, promotions and pricing are all integrated into a cohesive and customer-centric development model. Co-creation projects such as Unilever's Axe "FRESH" [57], First Direct's debit card design [58], General Mills' collaboration portal [59] and Dell's IdeaStorm [60] are just a few examples of the outstanding results you can achieve for your customers and organisation through co-creation. Is your organisation equipped to truly co-create with your customers and employees?

> "For decades, consumers have been saving up their insights and rants about the stuff they consume, simply because they didn't have adequate means to interact with companies, or with other consumers for that matter. No longer. These fickle, wired, empowered, infolusty, opinionated and experienced holders of a MC (Master of Consumerism) are getting used to 'having it their way', in ANY way imaginable, which includes wanting to have direct influence on what companies develop and produce for them" [19].

Knowing your competition

Developing your customer propositions should not occur without regard to what is on offer in the market. Your customer proposition process must enable an understanding of what propositions your competitors offer and how these create or negate a position of competitive advantage when compared to your own proposition. Make sure you have researched what is being offered in the market. What you take to the market depends on what does or does not already exist.

In rising above "better sameness" you have to be equipped with knowledge of your competitors. In a customer-centric business model, this requires that the customer experience dimension of competitor propositions is fully understood. Very often I see propositions differentiated purely on price. Very seldom do I see deep investigation into the experience being offered by competitors, with a concomitant focus on delivering a unique experience and developing the customer proposition around this goal. For most businesses, a price war will only lead to winning the race to the bottom. Having the cheapest price is not a guarantee of success, especially if you are unable to deliver a differentiated experience while your competitors can, and that experience is highly valued by customers.

Vodafone UK is a great example of how you can gather the right insights about competitors' propositions to enable you to compare them against your own. In 2006, Vodafone implemented a competitor intelligence tool to reduce customer churn and increase sales [61]. While largely based on product features, their technology allowed them to dynamically integrate insights from over a dozen competitors on tariffs, handsets and deals. Frontline staff were equipped with comparisons and deal analysis that allowed them to explain to the customer "why we're better". This resulted in a staggering 18.6% reduction in customer churn in one year. The ability to counter competitive offers also enabled an improvement in the closing of deals, ensuring that Vodafone remained extremely competitive in a tough market.

Understanding your competitors' propositions, therefore, requires that you actively gather the right information about their offerings to enable you to assess all aspects of their propositions — features and experience included. This will help you to equip your customer-facing employees, in both sales and service channels, to act on that information and to engage with your customer in a knowledgeable way.

Tailoring the proposition

The hallmark of customer-centricity is to treat different customers differently. While your product development process may factor in co-creation and competitor intelligence, you still need to provide different customer segments with the opportunities to customise or personalise their purchase and experience, when appropriate. In some cases, you may even be able to identify special needs for a segment so that you can devise tailored versions of your propositions that specifically meet the unique needs of that segment.

Cunard Line, operator of the ships Queen Mary 2, Queen Elizabeth and Queen Victoria, launched a specific, tailored proposition in 2012 for a very unique need – wedding ceremonies at sea [62]. A basic wedding package was made available, including the wedding ceremony conducted by the Captain, and only a limited number of ceremonies are available per voyage. A host of additional extras allows you to further tailor this special package, taking into account the vast array of special needs that wedding couples may have. The luxury and style of this differentiated and tailored experience is a great example of the value of tailoring your customer propositions to meet their specific needs.

If you choose to provide specific tailored options that are available only to your high value customers, you have to guard against those options becoming too readily available to other segments. While your employees may feel that they are delivering a great service to those segments by doing so, it erodes your ability to deliver something extra special for those high value segments that the additional feature was planned for.

The choices you make on your propositions should be driven by an intimate understanding of your customers and the needs of each segment. Specific and targeted propositions that deliver your brand promise and develop endearing customer experiences will dramatically clarify your unique offering in the minds of customers.

Transformation questions

- Have your organisation's brand values been examined for what they could, should and must mean in terms of the customer proposition(s) and have the proposition(s) been checked against these values and personality?
- Are mechanisms in place to enable some customers (usually high value customers) to design their own proposition based on the elements that are important to them, such as faster delivery in return for lower level support?
- What does your organisation stand for in the public's mind and what is "your promise"?
- Have you initiated radical innovations that challenge your conventional business?
- What makes your organisation, or could make it, unique?
- In order to sustain innovation success do you have an R&D budget? What percentage of revenue is allocated to it?
- What statement best sums up the exceptional outcomes your organisation expects?
- Is there recognition that brand and reputation can be enhancers, differentiators and accelerators of organisational results?
- Is caring for customers and being ethical part of your brand and does this cascade through to the way your organisation is viewed in the market?

Case study - Godiva sweetens the deal

Godiva Chocolatier, founded in Belgium in 1926, is a leading, global brand of premium, high-quality chocolate. Godiva established a limited-access, online community called Chocolate Talk that provides it with a customer listening channel for feedback and ideas that in turns helps the company to develop the right products for its customers [63]. Members of the community can also interact with each other, giving Godiva insights into customer behaviour and the experience dimension.

In 2009, Godiva was concerned that as a luxury brand its customers would continue to turn away from its products in the wake of the global recession as this impact was already showing in sales. In analysing the lifestyle and shopping habits of its online community, Godiva was able to identify important factors that were influencing customer behaviour. For example, Godiva sold largely through shops in malls. With the economic downturn, less people were visiting malls and, therefore, less people were buying Godiva chocolates. It also became apparent that there was an increasing trend of buying chocolate for "casual gifting". Godiva's expensive range was well loved as gifts for close family and friends, yet was too expensive for more casual acquaintances, where the need was for affordable chocolate that still appeared to be very special. The biggest insight came when Godiva realised that one of the main reasons for their competitors' success, being Lindt and Ghiradelli, was their individually wrapped chocolates that they could share with anyone. It was revealed that people did not like sharing open chocolate with people they did not know.

With "sharing" and "casual gifting" now being known as dominant needs for their market, Godiva was able to act on that knowledge by launching individually wrapped chocolates, or "Godiva Gems", while increasing access to their purchase in more convenient locations, such as grocery stores. Godiva could maintain its brand as a luxury, high quality chocolate, while offering their customers an affordable option.

The improved affordability resulted in customers purchasing self-treating and gifting chocolates more often. This would not have been possible if Godiva had not created a platform for customers to share their insights and if they had not been willing to try something different, while still honouring the values of their brand. The new product range and distribution networks have dramatically improved Godiva's revenue as well as helping this company to surpass Lindt's share of the market in 2010.

Rich Keller, a Godiva global business director, believes that the community members' input was critical in the success of this initiative: "The community provides us with the ability to continuously tap into our members' minds to be sure we are meeting their desire for Godiva chocolate. In addition, it was instrumental in getting Gems to market fast so we can stay competitive in the Premium Chocolate category" [63].

⊙ CHAPTER 10:

⊙ CHANNELS AND MEDIA

Transformation Intent

Channels are critical vehicles through which you deliver a superior, consistent and relevant customer experience. In order to do so effectively, your channels and the media you use to transmit your message both need to be integrated and individually optimised to manage this consistency and deliver an appropriate return on investment from a customer value perspective. Your organisation also needs to be dynamic and strategic in how you leverage the new forms of media and digital channels.

New channels, same principles

Channels are methods or vehicles through which you get your products and services into your customer's hands. In a business-to-business organisation, channels are largely comprised of distribution channels, such as dealers, brokers and account managers. In business-to-consumer environments, channels include retail outlets, branches, contact centres and online facilities. A direct channel is one where there is face-to-face engagement as in the case of account management, a retail store or a branch. A call centre is often used as both a service and sales channel, while a web store would be an example of an online channel. Media are the mechanisms through which your information is transmitted, such as television, radio, web sites, blogs and podcasts.

While it is often said that the new and evolving channels, such as mobile and social media, are changing the way customers interact with businesses and vice versa, these new channels reflect changing customer needs. Customers are also using existing channels and their touch points in a different way. If you are buying a motor car, it is unlikely that you will visit the dealership – a touch point for a direct channel – to understand the specifications of the models. You, in all likelihood, would have already undertaken that research through an online channel, with the purpose of the visit being to get a "sensory" experience to finalise or substantiate your decision.

Customer-centricity requires that your organisation focuses on providing a consistent, relevant and superior customer experience, no matter what new technologies become available or which channels you have or media you use. At the same time, your customers' need to socially engage, share, collaborate and advocate, fundamentally changes the way you operationalize your channels and media.

Effective channel and media management, therefore, requires a strategic and integrated approach that seeks to optimise each channel individually, based on knowledge of your customers and informed by quality research. This method results in a consistency of message and experience for your customers across all channels and media, while utilising customer relevant measures to evaluate channel and media success. As the utilisation of social media is now such a major trend, you need to find a way to manage your social engagement with customers effectively while ensuring your organisation delivers the relevant and content-rich media that customers expect.

> "Many marketers believe that social media and building a 'fan-base' (or, worse, 'earned database') replace conventional CRM and building a database of high value and/or influential customers. Some see Social and CRM as separate, with different teams driving two separate strategies. Despite all the talk about Social Marketing, Social CRM and the focus on 'engagement programs' and 'participation platforms', many businesses still fail to integrate their social and CRM efforts into one customer management strategy" [17].

Bridging channel silos

Developing a customer-centric approach to your channel development and media selection is only possible if your organisation is structured appropriately. Organisations are most often functionally or departmentally structured which, in turn, can create silos of business activity through their channels. For example, if your direct sales channel operates within the sales division, yet your online sales channel resides within the marketing division, and the organisation isn't operationalized with an "outside-in" perspective, it is a challenge to ensure that there is a consistency of experience across these particular channels unless a mechanism exists that bridges the two.

One solution may be a formal channel management function with the requisite power and authority to integrate the experience across channels and to manage any conflicts that arise. Without a cohesive, strategic approach across channels it becomes impossible to assess the real effectiveness of your channels in delivering on your company's goals for each customer. A silo-based approach very often encourages conflict and competitive behaviour between channels that may impact negatively on the relationship that your organisation, as a whole, has with your customers.

In order to create clarity you need a clear and focused channel strategy that is agreed on by all stakeholders. This strategy helps you overcome the inherent potential for conflict between channels by balancing the needs of each channel and clarifying the role each of them should fulfil in creating the desired customer experience for each customer.

This need for a strategic, customer-centric approach to the management of your channels extends into your strategy for the most appropriate media for your customer segments, be that owned, paid or earned media. Owned media is a media channel you control, such as your website, blog or Twitter account. The primary role of owned media is to build longer term relationships with existing or potential customers. The brand has complete control over what is posted. Paid media includes the traditional forms of above-the-line media such as advertising, both online and offline. Earned media relates to word-of-mouth created through social media channels such as Twitter, Facebook, Foursquare, Pinterest and others, both good and bad.

In days gone by, the term "earned media" referred to brand exposure through free media as opposed to paying for it through advertising. Sean Corcoran, an analyst at Forrester Research, says earned media can be most easily described as the result of paid and owned media – more of an effect than a cause [64]. This means that you could pay for an advertisement or you could run a campaign on your owned media, such as your Facebook page, and when people talk about it and share it, paid and owned media converge into earned media. The challenge is that no amount of advertising can force a customer to buy, share or promote your products or services. You have to earn their engagement and advocacy.

A strategic approach to your media, therefore, requires that you think less about your spend across an individual media channel and focus more on integrated media planning that can ensure optimal customer connections across the most relevant channels and touch points, at the most appropriate time. Relevance of both your channels and media in light of your customer strategy is, therefore, fundamental.

Research, relevance, results

The integrated and strategic approach to the management of your company's channels should also change the way you measure channel performance. A simplistic approach of viewing a channel from a profitability perspective only will not help you achieve this. Instead you have to understand the cost-to-serve in each channel in relation to your customer strategies and value levers — Retention, Efficiency, Acquisition and Penetration. If you consider a more costly direct channel — a face-to-face relationship manager for example — and you assess the channel purely from a profitability perspective, the profitability may not be optimum. However, when looking at the channel performance holistically and systemically through a customer lens, you may find that the value derived from immediate access to the relationship manager has made a significantly positive contribution in terms of customer satisfaction and, therefore, customer retention.

In using this integrated approach you can evaluate the extent to which an individual channel is supporting overall business performance. You can then optimise the channel by ensuring that the right processes are in place to keep it working efficiently and delivering the value required. A major challenge that you face is the fact that you cannot control the channel through which a customer may choose to engage with your company. To meet this challenge you need to optimise each channel and its costs, in light of understanding the customers who choose to use that channel and the overall profitability of those customers, rather than focussing exclusively on channel profitability in isolation of overall business performance.

As the saying goes, "you get what you measure". In one case I have seen an organisation use a call centre as the contact and sales channel for a direct sales campaign, involving expensive television advertising. A primary success measure of the campaign focussed on the number of leads the campaign generated. The number of leads was calculated according to the number of people who contacted the call centre in connection with the product being advertised, during the period the advertisements were flighted. From these results, the "cost per lead" was calculated and tracked. Yet, the capacity of the target market (very low income individuals) to commit to on-going monthly payments, the accuracy and clarity of explanation of the product proposition by the sales agents, the data capture quality and the back-end fulfilment processes, were all poor. A significant number of the recorded leads, therefore, failed to convert into monthly revenue over a sustained period. Whilst "cost per lead" in isolation may have been acceptable, the take-up rate was poor and many callers who did take up the offer failed to make payments beyond the first couple of months.

Your customers' attitudes towards your different channels and types of media will influence their experience of using those channels. Research in this regard will support you to determine which channels are most appropriate for your focused messages per customer segment. Your customers also increasingly expect that you record and remember what their channel preferences are. Perhaps they prefer text messages to e-mails, or online statements to printed ones. Should you offer the option, their chosen channel preferences should then be consistently applied. If you can't do this, it will only frustrate them. This need for consistency also applies to the experience you provide across channels.

If you use one or more channels and a variety of media for marketing campaigns, there needs to be an alignment of people, process and technology so that campaigns can deliver effectively across all your channels using relevant and optimised media. Your ability to do this is dependent upon the technology infrastructure that supports the operationalization of your marketing campaigns, known as marketing resource management (MRM). MRM refers to software that supports planning, design and production within your marketing function and it is necessary to ascertain your effectiveness in these areas by asking critical questions of your campaign results. In your cross-channel campaigns, how are you making sure that you've deployed the right blend of media and channel? Do your campaigns deliver useful insights that allow you to improve how your channels and media are used to engage your customers? The need for integration across channels and media, supported by technology, is the key to ensuring the right return on your investment and a consistent and superior experience for the customer.

Integrating channels and media

There is a direct relationship between your channels and your brand strategy. Across every channel, your brand values, attributes and materials need to communicate the same message. This does not imply that pricing should be the same across channels, rather that it is important that pricing is consistent. For example, it is acceptable that a purchase through an online sales channel is priced lower than the direct sales channel because, in all likelihood, it has a lower cost.

The task of delivering brand consistency across channels becomes more challenging when you consider that your channels may include suppliers and partners who might adjust the customer experience according to their own standard or design, or in alignment with their own brand promise. In reflecting on your non-owned distribution channels, do you have a clear agreement with your suppliers and partners regarding how much they can influence and adjust the message, the pricing and the customer experience? What aspects of pricing are out of your control and how do you manage these factors to ensure consistency? Even in your own channels, you might find that some channel managers, directly or indirectly, compete too aggressively with each other for the customers' attention, to the detriment of your overall business.

Integration then is the key to effective channel management, and this applies too in the movement of customers between channels. You should allow customers to initiate a transaction on one channel and move that conversation across to another channel should they wish to. This requires effective collaboration between business processes and technology, supported by an organisation that welcomes customers switching channels. Does your platform allow your customers to contact you through the web site and respond to an e-mail by calling the call centre, with a consolidated history of that communication thread easily available for the call centre agent? Can your customers order online yet collect from a branch or retail outlet if they so wish?

> "A recent study by Pew Research Centre showed that 22% of US adults use their Smart Phones to look-up prices on-line for a product they've found in store before deciding to buy or not. The same proportion seeks product reviews on-line while in-store. Over a third call friends on their mobile for advice on buying a product while in the store" [16].

Another area that may require integration is your social media channel and your owned channels so you can activate a lead generated on social media as a prospect in your own systems. This capability allows you to create a direct relationship with the prospect and brings the prospect into one of your owned channels. You may need to implement specific processes that allow you to identify these prospects and manage their transition.

It is also important that you recognise the disruptive nature of the new social and digital channels. Do you have an intricate understanding of the impact of these new channels in terms of driving brand awareness, purchase preference, loyalty and advocacy? Within your organisation, are guidelines widely communicated and appropriate training provided to the marketing and sales teams to leverage this awareness?

Riding the social media wave

Social media is a grey area for many organisations. Perhaps your organisation is the same — not quite sure what to do with it yet not wanting to be left behind. Big budgets are being thrown at social media and digital consultancies are clinching lucrative deals as organisations' scurry to effectively implement social media strategies. As with any channel it has its own considerations that make the difference between success and a "#fail".

While trendy, your social media can only add value to your organisation if you understand the paradigm shift that it demands and you take cognisance of the latest trends, independent research, academic papers and published best practises. This knowledge, combined with an awareness of how your own prospects and customers use social media, will create the clarity you need to inform your social media strategy. For example, a "Generation-Y" segment will use social media in a dramatically different way to a "65 and over" segment. A continuous review of social media usage by an appropriate team will enable your organisation to trigger changes in how you adopt and leverage social media to your advantage.

It is also really important that your employees are clear as to how they should engage through social media as a representative of your organisation. Some organisations ban employees from using social media as part of their role. While reputational risk requires consideration, clear guidelines and good training on how best to make use of social media for maximum impact can facilitate employees positively contributing to the success of your digital strategies.

Another critical component of your approach to social media is how you reward your "fans" and "followers". Many companies focus so obsessively on growing their fan base that they forget to look after the fans they already have, whether through recognition, special promotions or value-adding content. You should, therefore, allocate the responsibility for "fan management" to a specific, competent team while allocating them a budget to maintain and deepen the engagement with, and the enthusiasm of, your fans. Part of this role is to consider what the value of the fan-base is and perhaps how high-value fans can be segmented and treated differently through rewards and special privileges, drawing them into your organisation through an owned channel. Maintaining and growing your high-value fans is not just about a like or a follow button, it's about how you manage and leverage that relationship after the click.

Such leverage goes hand in hand with making web sites "social" and integrating them with social media platforms. Your web site must be interactive and engaging, providing sharable content. Do you allow your prospects and customers to choose a diversity of social media platforms through which to share your content? Have you explored connecting the login to your web site to other platforms that make it easier for fans to engage with you? As we continue to evolve our understanding of social media and its implications, these questions will be answered while many more will arise.

"A study by Bain & Co. found that customers who engage with companies over social media spend 20% to 40% more money with those companies than other customers. However, there s more to social than just gathering likes and follows. As the interactions between organizations and their customers become more fragmented and dynamic, Social and Collaborative technologies can play a key role in helping organizations differentiate" [15].

Content is king

One of the biggest questions raised by digital and social channels is whether you are ready for the content-thirsty audience that is becoming ever more discerning of what they read, view and share. Great content is the keystone of digital success, yet sustainable content generation is often not given the prioritisation it needs. Initial enthusiasm to tap into this new world quickly fades when it becomes evident how resource hungry and complex content management can be.

A critical success factor is, therefore, the consistency that your organisation demonstrates in updating relevant content on a regular basis. This may require schedules driven by explicit content strategies where valuable and relevant content is drawn in from varying parts of the organisation, including channels, touch points and brand teams. Most organisations have a wealth of information to share, and so the issue is not about the availability of information but more about the mechanisms that drive, review and approve organisational content in alignment with organisational goals and the objectives of customer-facing programmes.

The integrated approach to your content, both internally generated and externally sourced, is significantly enhanced with an enterprise content management system that enables you to manage your content effectively across all channels. A customer-centric approach considers not just management efficiency, but also the ways you categorise, index and tag your content in a manner that supports your prospects and customers in finding that content efficiently.

As content, and the generation thereof, is such a dynamic process you also have to consider how you update your content, based upon user feedback and requests received. If your audience can tell that you engage with them, and not just broadcast to them, you can derive much greater value from your content. Another aspect of this dynamic approach to content is the "liquidity" of your content, which refers to the ease with which your content can be shared, edited, reused and re-published. The more "liquid" your content, the more value it has to others, and the easier it is for your content to be distributed widely on your behalf. Great, sharable content that is linked to your organisation really leverages the potential and power of content in this digital age. This approach requires that your content strategy is one that ensures that content is flexible, portable and easily shared. Do your social channels, web sites and e-mail marketing campaigns encourage and, in some cases, incentivise the sharing of content?

Customer-centricity, therefore, requires you to think carefully and differently about your channels and media. While you can take advantage of the new opportunities available, you still need to honour the key principles of strategic linkage, relevance, consistency, integration and return-on-investment. It is only through this approach that you can use your channels and media to deliver superior, consistent and relevant customer experiences.

Transformation questions

- Does your organisation manage its channel/media mix against a clear strategy that encompasses owned, earned and paid media/channels?
- Are your channels and media integrated so that they deliver consistent messages and feel, as well as allowing customers to be moved easily between them?
- Do you have a balance between evaluating both online coverage as well as analysing print and traditional media?
- Do you have predictable and reliable data that enables you to create channel and media KPIs that measure the overall health of the organisation and engagement with your customers?
- Do you have a defined channel management strategy for each segment, including the specific goals you have for each channel (Acquisition and/or Retention), policies for the administration of accounts or individuals within each channel, and products within your offering most suited for each segment?
- Are you clear as to what metrics are important to your team in order to make the decisions that drive improvements in your channel programmes?
- Are you aware of what channel and media measures actually matter to the bottom line as opposed to vanity metrics, such as friends, fans, followers and number of visitors, which explain little about the actionable effect?
- Do your channel and media KPIs define and measure progress toward organisational goals?
- Is your approach to channel and media driven from the customers' perspective, rather than your organisations' perspective?

Case study - KLM flies to new heights with social media

KLM Royal Dutch Airlines dipped their toe into the powerful potential of social media in a campaign called "KLM Surprise" in November 2010. Over a period of two weeks, they tracked approximately 40 customers who had checked in for a KLM flight and had mentioned KLM in a tweet or had checked in at the airport via Foursquare before going through security or boarding.

Flight attendants and team members allocated to the project searched social media platforms using a social media toolkit to find more information on their "target travellers" so that they could ascertain where they were travelling to and why. Customised gifts were then prepared for each traveller, who was then tracked down as they arrived at security gates or to board their flight. Some of the examples included a pack of energy bars and treats for a traveller going to Mexico to build homes, a fitness monitor for someone travelling to Rome on an adventure holiday, and even an elderly lady who was upgraded to an extra leg room seat as her neighbour tweeted about the travelling difficulties for the elderly. Every gift was unique and specific to something they had tweeted about or had broadcast on social media platforms.

KLM's experiment in social sharing paid off. Besides the obvious pleasure that 40 KLM customers received from their unexpected surprises in an industry where much is being cut back, the real win for KLM was that they received over one million impressions from this campaign in November on Twitter alone. That is a staggering result — their Twitter "feed" was, therefore, viewed more than one million times for the price of a creative approach and 40 gifts.

Not everyone, however, agrees that this campaign was a success [65]. While the experiment itself was successful, unless it moves from an experiment to an organisational practice, the true value to KLM's social community cannot be realised. For KLM's approach to their social and digital channels to really make a difference, these channels need to be integrated into the organisation across the board. This means that complaints and customer feedback through Twitter and other platforms become as critical to the customer conversation as the call centre is. If you activate these types of channels for your customers, and then do not deliver on the practical implications those channels bring, you might create more negative experiences than positive ones. For example, does KLM address complaints that arise from comments on their YouTube channel? Do they have an integrated and on-going monitoring and follow-up process in place for KLM mentions and hash tags? And not to be forgotten, can KLM measure the return on investment that their social campaigns and channels deliver?

Martijn van der Zee, the Vice President of E-Commerce for KLM, shared his insights from the campaign [66]: "When you engage in a real, authentic way, it takes more effort from the company, but the viral effect is so much bigger than anything we've done in a higher-volume or more organized way". His words ring true, yet the next level of insight for KLM would be to learn how to capitalise on this potential so that they can deliver a consistent and superior experience for the customer through these new digital and social channels.

● CHAPTER 11:

● EXPERIENCE MANAGEMENT

Transformation Intent

Achieving excellence in customer experience is about finding ways to create products, services and experiences that positively and profitably influence what people think, feel and do. This calls for the ability to design and deliver innovative, differentiated, economic and relevant customer experiences across every channel and touch point ensuring that both physical and emotional elements are addressed.

Relevant and consistent experience trumps a "wow"

Customer experience can be defined as a blend of the physical product, service or communication and the emotions invoked before, during and after engaging with the organisation across any selected touch point. A touch point is a physical or non-physical point of engagement with the customer. Examples include contacting your organisation through your web site, phoning your call centre, speaking to a staff member in a branch or retail outlet or reading your e-mail newsletter. It is very important that these touch points, or moments of truth as they are sometimes called, are positive.

In order to be cognisant of your customer's experience before, during and after connecting with your organisation across any touch point, you also have to consider the non-touch points. These are the moments of truth, including your customers' thoughts, feelings, expectations and assumptions, which occur outside of, or before and after, physically engaging with you at a touch point. For example, customers might feel trepidation in anticipation of incompetence and an inability to have their problem solved when having to call a contact centre. Alternatively, while a jewellery store owner can deliver an exceptional experience to the customer who walks into the store – welcome, advice, selection and wrapping – there is a limited ability to "romanticise the giving of a gift" after purchase, unless of course advice or a service in this regard is provided.

It is extraordinarily difficult for organisations to adapt their customer experience because, over time, an organisation adopts a way of dealing with itself and its customers and these behaviours become firmly entrenched in their "business-as-usual" practices. Furthermore, the majority of organisations approach the challenge of customer experience by mapping out and focussing on the experience they deliver at each of the touch points. In reality, it's not about the experience you deliver, it's about the experience the customers actually have that influences the choices they make in the pursuit of what they want.

An emotional connection is created with your customer through relevance, respect, consistency and a high-contrast signature experience, all of which serve to create uniqueness and differentiation. Without a strategy to develop these high-contrast signature experiences the outcome will very often be one of perpetuated mediocrity or "better sameness". Incremental improvements in customer experience tend to go largely unnoticed and in most cases are unable to transcend the dominant mediocrity. At the same time, for a strategy to deliver high-contrast signature experiences it, ironically, requires you to recognise that you should be deliberately mediocre at some things. After all, it's unrealistic to believe that you can be the best at everything you do.

Emotionally-engaging, relevant and consistent customer experiences create positive memories of your organisation. It is these collected memories that ultimately linger in the customer's mind. While you might obsess over designing and implementing the intricate details of every single component or element of the experience in the background, the reality is that your customer does not remember all the details for long. Instead, they walk away with a high-level feeling or sense of what the experience meant to them.

This behaviour is attributed to what is known as "gist processing" – a subconscious, pattern-mapping process that determines how the overall gist of an experience is recorded as a memory [67]. This helps us to perform tasks without having to think about them. In our daily onslaught of rich, complex and multi-dimensional information, this fuzzy processing preference focuses our attention on a few items only – usually those experiences that are important, high-contrast or surprising enough to attract attention. For your customers, this will result in them adjusting their memories or perception of their experiences by reconstructing their story from the high-contrast features of the original experience, together with a sense of how they felt. Once a perception has been created, it is very hard to change it.

Creating high-contrast signature experiences does not mean that touch points have to be "wow" moments, which in my opinion is not sustainable. A customer experience strategy built on "wows" creates expectations in the mind of the customer that get harder and harder to improve upon. One "wow" experience may reside in the customer's mind, yet it is often solitary and random. Consistency of experience can embed a wealth of positive memories for your customers and position your brand at the centre of those positive feelings. These kinds of emotions are the ones that drive long-term, sustainable, superior business performance and not the short-term, once-off "wows".

What makes experience management really challenging is that your customers are often pre-conditioned with negative emotions before they even connect with you. Customers bring into the engagement past experiences with certain types of touch points, such as frustrating call centres, and the expected experiences of the industry and society you are part of. Experience management requires that you understand the impact of those past experiences and pre-conditioned emotions and design your experience to influence a positive change in customer behaviour.

The key factor to bear in mind is consistency. Deliver a positive and relevant experience every time your customer connects with you across any touch point and this will deliver to your organisation customer loyalty, increased spend and new customers through referrals. Being able to deliver this desirable outcome requires absolute clarity of purpose and an in-depth understanding of what the customer experience should deliver at every touch point and non-touch point. Fundamental to this is a systems-thinking approach, an organisation that is connected and integrated, and a willingness to proactively design the desired customer experience, taking into account all its inherent complexity.

> "Consumers notice and financially reward companies that deliver superior customer experiences... 73% of consumers stated that they would expand their purchases with a vendor by 10% or more if the customer experience was superior. 55% of consumers agreed that they would stay with a company for 10 years or more if the customer experience was superior and 58% said they would recommend the company to others"[18].

Understanding experience excellence

Experience excellence requires having an awareness of what "best-in-class" in the world is and how you measure up against that benchmark. It's insufficient to only consider your industry and to attempt to draw industry comparisons alone. Every experience a customer has adjusts and informs what kind of experience she expects. For example, customers may enjoy a consistent experience flying Upper Class on Virgin Atlantic and may, subconsciously or consciously, identify this experience as their individual benchmark. The mere fact that Virgin Atlantic provides a service experience that is unique, differentiated and consistent is proof enough that other organisations should have similar capabilities. The end result is that it is likely that the customer expectation of your service offering is influenced in some way by their Virgin Atlantic experience. You, therefore, have to look beyond industry norms and adopt a more holistic view on what experience excellence really means.

While research can be an expensive exercise fraught with complexity and timing issues, it is also a critical part of understanding the customer experience you offer and in what ways there is a gap to fill. Voice of the Customer (VoC) is a well-known research approach that uses tools and techniques to understand customers' needs, wants, preferences, expectations and aversions. The outcomes are largely statements that express key customer needs and should be prioritised in terms of their relative importance and satisfaction with current alternatives.

Event-based research is an effective way to identify and interview people with a high involvement in your product or service category because it gathers data directly after an event so that immediate satisfaction feedback is obtained for a specific intervention. If you have just completed a transaction on a call centre, event-based research would obtain an understanding of your feelings there and then. As soon as time passes the relevance of this data diminishes and, therefore, gathering it "in the moment" is essential. Sample-based research involves collecting data from a sample or subset of individuals and using researchers' observations to make inferences about the entire population – a satisfaction "litmus test" at a given point in time. Both these types of satisfaction research should be conducted regularly enough to detect changes in the quality of experience being delivered, while not so often that it negatively impacts your customers. A consistent set of questions will enable you to compare the results across different types of customers and time periods. It is important to remember that customer satisfaction is not an emotional state that always influences behaviour. Your customer could be satisfied, yet this doesn't automatically affect the actions they will ultimately take.

Regular, qualitative research supports the on-going identification of new areas to include in your quantitative research. Observations, in-depth interviews and focus groups comprised of existing and potential customers will help you to ascertain the factors that affect customer perceptions, such as product evolution, new market entrants and current trends. Feedback from potential customers will highlight what you need to do to encourage these customers to switch to using your products or services.

Research data should also not exist on its own without reference to the related transaction and interaction results that provide context and meaning. Both research and transaction sources should corroborate each other or provide insights into discrepancies. This information helps you to ascertain whether what customers tell you they do is actually how they behave, and this knowledge is critical when it comes to designing optimised and effective customer experiences.

It is also considered good practice that customer experience research includes questions that can highlight customer loyalty and potential future behaviour. Surveys should attempt to understand what the customers' expectations are as this too can be used to understand the results achieved. A high expectation and a mediocre experience will generate a poorer satisfaction level than a mediocre expectation and a mediocre experience would.

Mystery shopper research is another way to evaluate the customer experience. The value of this research tool depends entirely on the criteria used to assess the experience. Only evaluating adherence to organisational processes is not enough. What is missed in these instances is the emotional experience – the key differentiator in an excellent customer experience. Different questions are needed to what might typically be asked. How did I feel emotionally and how were my emotions engaged? What tone was used? How did they seek to understand my needs? What questions did they ask of me? What other options did they give me? Without this perspective, key clues will be missed. It is also advisable that an external provider conducts this research so that it delivers an objective perspective.

While good quality research is critical for understanding the voice of your customer, it is important not to fall into the trap of living and dying by your research findings. Instead, make sure you use your findings wisely to develop high-contrast signature experiences. The results should indicate a direction yet should not impose one. Henry Ford was known for saying that if he designed his organisation around what customers said they wanted we would have nothing other than faster horses today rather than motor cars. It is also important to temper research results with competitive analysis and, as Amazon.com does, to obsess over your customers, invent on their behalf and plan for the long term.

Your organisation has more than likely already made a significant time and money investment in improving your customers' experiences. Often this investment is wasted by focusing on improving the experience you deliver and not the experience your customer actually has. Frank Capek [67] named five culprits that might lead you astray in your quest for customer experience excellence: focusing too much on satisfaction and not the underlying behaviour change required; overreacting to VoC results; ignoring or failing to appreciate the significance of non-touch points; making only incremental service improvements and expecting them to influence customer behaviour; and viewing the training and development of frontline employees as the solution when improvements in experience require deep, organisational transformation.

Have your ear to the ground

Just as listening skills are a critical part of developing meaningful relationships with others, so too is listening a key part of really understanding the customer experience. Every touch point with the customer is an opportunity to understand their needs better, yet listening is often a competency poorly developed. As a fundamental component of a VoC programme, listening includes channelling and flagging relevant and pertinent information about the customer experience in a timely way that creates the opportunity for proactive solutions and contributes to a "dashboard" of customer measures. This necessitates that you provide your customers with easy-to-use feedback mechanisms at all customer interfaces to support the collection of useful, relevant and meaningful insights about the customer experience that you can use to improve that experience in the future.

An excellent way of really listening to the customer is for management to get involved with the customer experience at a basic level. This is often referred to as a "back-to-the-floor" scheme where management get a real feel for the customer experience at regular intervals and across a diverse range of customer touch points. This practice necessitates getting managers out of their offices and into the reality of the customer experience with enough depth that their learning can be used to improve the experience and provide new insights. This is especially important in organisations where employees are served by a different process to the one customers engage with. In this case, employees who use a company's products and services may tend to get special treatment, such as quick-swipe payment systems, specialised ordering and collection processes and fast-track queues. If managers do not know what it actually feels like to stand in the checkout line with other customers, how will they ever understand their customers' perspective?

Frontline employees are seldom given the opportunity to provide meaningful and contextual feedback. The same applies to suppliers and channel associates. It is much easier to commission a research project than it is to gather key nuggets of insight from your frontline employees that might otherwise be lost because the right listening mechanisms are not in place. Instead, employees and channel partners should be given structured and regular opportunities to discuss their learning, with the feedback from these encounters being delivered to those who can use it to improve the customer experience or even the design of that experience itself.

All feedback received from listening activities needs to be viewed from a balanced perspective. One piece of poor feedback should not unnecessarily lead to a "knee-jerk" reaction across your organisation. "Noise" filters help you to see the real themes and issues that enable you to implement the right solutions for your customers.

Listening also requires that you are able to mine comments from, and analyse the sentiments of, customers and non-customers through online and offline channels, thereby tracking what people are saying about your brand. This information should, therefore, help you to understand your customers' opinions and experiences from across different channels. The underlying tone in this sentiment can provide a wealth of insight into what people's experiences and perceptions are. This is challenging to complete successfully because it requires that your employees are able to identify the tone of the communication as well as detecting what the customer is not saying. How do you train your call centre agents to detect and document the meaning of a sarcastic remark made by your customer? How do you monitor what your customer is really implying in an e-mail or fax? What are you missing in the notes captured by call centre agents in frontline systems? Sentiment analysis can be conducted using text-based analytics systems that can be programmed with keywords and phrases that trigger analysis. Yet, identification of the right keywords and triggers can be extremely challenging and often data is generated that is not translated into meaningful knowledge.

There is a goldmine of information at your fingertips if you utilise the opportunity to really listen to the engagements taking place with your customers. This requires being very clear on the kind of information you are looking for and being able to ask questions that enquire after something important that you want to learn about your customers so that you can service them better.

"Surveys are important, but there are many opportunities to get close to customers and really 'listen' in on what they have to say about the experience you are delivering to them that is driving them to buy more or driving them away. If we wait for the survey results, or rely only on the data within them, we miss the simplest, most easily understood and passionate feedback that can help us understand the customer experience 'real time' – everyday" [19].

Customer experience requires proactive engineering

Earlier in this chapter I mentioned that the most effective approach for designing customer experiences was to adopt an "outside-in" view – it's about the experience the customer has rather than the experience you provide. The ultimate objective is to positively and profitably influence what customers think, feel and do in the pursuit of what they want. This means you must design the experience in order to influence the most valuable outcomes. Unfortunately, the customer experience is often allowed to develop organically over time, as opposed to being proactively designed. A proactive, design approach is essential in really ensuring your customers' experience reflects a true customer-centric philosophy and your business objectives.

Customer experience journey mapping is a tool used to engineer customer experiences and to represent those experiences in a visual format. The benefit of journey mapping is that you explore the ideal customer experience in detail over its entire lifecycle to define the kinds of experience they should be having at every touch point and non-touch point, including both rational and emotional factors, in order to deliver and achieve a desired outcome. Once your customer experience journey map has been benchmarked against other industries, reviewed and signed off by executives, then it is up to your organisation to optimise the people, processes and technology that will deliver that result.

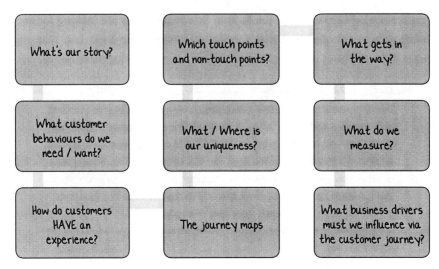

Figure 12: REAP Customer Journey Mapping Framework

There are nine steps in the framework to develop pragmatic journey maps [67].

Business Outcomes

It's important to begin with the end in mind. Be absolutely clear on the business outcomes you require based on the challenges your organisation faces and the particular REAP strategies you have defined to overcome them. Based upon these REAP principles, quantify exactly what it is that you wish to achieve via a specific customer journey. It may be that you want to increase your customer Retention rate in a certain customer segment by 10%, or you want to increase Acquisition of a certain segment by 2,000 customers per annum. Alternatively, you may want to increase your cross-sell rate in order to improve your product holding by customer from 1.1 products per customer to 1.7, a Penetration driver. Whatever your objective may be, be sure to quantify it.

Story

Once clear on the business outcomes you should then reflect on the "story" of your organisation. Great stories have a premise – an ideological centre that provides meaning. Your story conveys your message of uniqueness – the antithesis of "better sameness" that results in small incremental improvements that the customer fails to notice. Your story should be a powerful statement that creates a positive and emotional reaction in customers. There is no story without conflict. What struggle are you addressing? What are you looking to defend, regain or attain? Who is the hero? You, of course! Who then is the villain? If you want to create high-contrast, signature customer experiences, your story must be compelling. What do you stand for? What do you stand against? The conflict created by these questions creates tension, change and interest. For example, Metro Bank in the UK stands for "excellent customer service and customer experience". It stands against "stupid bank rules". Compelling? No doubt!

Behaviours

In order to achieve your business outcome, what specific set of customer behaviours do you need? How should customers behave? What do you need them to do? In order to positively influence their behaviour, you have to understand what people think and feel. What gets their attention? What preferences do they have? What do they remember? How do they feel about the experience? How do they feel about themselves? How do they feel about your products and services? How do they feel about your organisation? What choices do they make? What do they purchase? How do they adopt new offerings? How do they influence others? What are the influences on what customers think, feel and do? What are the most relevant drivers of behaviour per segment or audience? Research becomes a critical component of understanding behaviour and, without an in-depth understanding, your journey maps may not manage to influence the right behaviours to deliver the desired outcomes.

Current Experience

This is not about focusing on the experience you provide or deliver. It's about understanding the experience that the customer actually has. Consider your non-touch points – e.g. what the customer experiences after enquiring about your product or service and prior to making a decision to purchase or not. No doubt they'll have to identify, research and evaluate alternatives; consider their needs; reflect on their options; and make a choice, amongst many others actions. How does your organisation facilitate the decision-making process? What experiences generate and reinforce the required behaviours? What signature elements define what you're good and bad at?

Touch Points

Touch points are the events, connections and moments of truth that you need to consider for a group of customers. At each touch point an expectation is set with the customer, explicitly or implicitly, and you, therefore, need to understand the complexity of those points of engagement. You also have to consider the non-touch points that have an impact on the experience, or those experiences that the customers have when they are not engaging with you.

Uniqueness

One of the principles of customer-centricity is the delivery of differentiated experiences. In this aspect of the framework, therefore, you consider your uniqueness and where across the customer journey or lifecycle you will offer a high-contrast experience. If you are specific about this aspect you will focus your attention on delivering excellence in specific areas and spend less time and money developing a "little bit" of excellence across a wide range of experiences. Your focus should, therefore, be on the big, differentiated issues – those aspects that'll force the customer to take notice.

Journey Maps

The journey maps themselves are comprised of a number of levels: macro-journeys, micro-journeys and journey steps. In the case study at the end of this chapter, examples of these journey map levels have been provided from a journey mapping exercise conducted with General Motors Middle-East. Macro-journeys, collectively referred to as the journey "snake", define your high-level journeys across the customer lifecycle. Micro-journeys break down each macro-journey into a lower level of detail. Each micro-journey can then be further broken down into the detailed journey steps required. For each journey step you could ask: What do we do right? What can go wrong? What is the customer thinking when they come into this particular step on the journey? What is the organisational support that underpins that step? What do you want the customer to think, feel and do before, during and after that step?

Road Blocks

You need to consider the roadblocks that may get in the way of achieving customer experience excellence. These may be the unwritten rules within your organisation or the way of working that must be addressed if you are going to gain traction and build momentum. Be clear as to the motivators within your organisation. "What" and "who" is important to people? Is it more important to satisfy "the boss" than the customer? Unfortunately this happens far too often – anything and everything is dropped the minute "the boss" calls and is reflective of "inside-out" thinking, lack of respect and over-inflated egos. Other critical road blocks may be organisational politics or even cultural issues. Whatever your specific roadblocks are, identifying them will help you to resolve these issues and deliver the intended results.

Measures

Measurement is essentially your dashboard of quantitative and qualitative measures of business targets that each customer experience map aims to address. How in reality are people measured? While you may talk about customer-centricity, if no-one is measured on it and you must do whatever it takes to "make your numbers", you will not be able to design and deliver consistent, high-contrast signature experiences. Sometimes the measures in place are not in the best interests of your customers. Measures based on the performance of your function or department, and not the total experience, can lead people to getting into trouble for going beyond policy to satisfy the customer. Customer satisfaction and net promoter score measures alone are just not good enough.

While there are much deeper levels to this framework in practice, the framework illustrates that customer experience design is indeed a proactive and detailed process that innovates through the specific customer experiences that your organisation requires in order to deliver on its promise.

Deliver differentiated experiences for different values of customer

Customer experience management does not require that all customers have the same experience – quite the opposite. A customer-centric approach requires that you provide differentiated experiences for different values of customer.

This requires your delivery to be honed and targeted around your ability to differentiate the customer experience. Your frontline systems need to provide employees with the tools to understand the value of a customer so that they can become specific in how they manage that customer's experience. In addition, they need to be crystal clear on what that differentiated experience should be for the different customer value levels.

This does not mean that you treat low value customers below an appropriate standard. What it does mean is that the level of service all customers receive is at a baseline and you then build upon that level for higher levels of customer value. In a banking environment this would be tantamount to the different level of service between a basic savings plan, with servicing only through the call centre and general enquiries in the branch, and a high-end transaction account that includes a variety of value-adding services and a personal banker who meets you at your convenience. On a flight that might mean a smaller seat and less choice in meals in economy class while first class passengers enjoy a limousine drop-off at the airport, priority boarding and disembarkation, and privacy from the rest of the aircraft. For all these different levels of customer value there are different customer experiences that should be designed and delivered. Management and employees need to be committed to this principle in order for it to be successful.

Customer experience management is a critical part of driving the business case for customer-centricity. As there is a direct link between experience and loyalty, any improvement made in the experience of your customer will drive greater sustainability and superior results for your organisation. Journey maps support transforming the customer experience from one of accidental and inconsistent success to one of clear design, purposeful intent and consistency in delivering the results you planned.

Transformation questions

- Besides traditional sample based customer research, are you "listening" on an on-going basis to customers in order to understand the wider sentiment towards your organisation?
- Has your customer experience been designed, engineered and documented by experts with a focus on the customers' emotional needs as well as functional requirements?
- Do you have a clear picture of the process, by customer type, that customers go through when interacting with your company?
- Do you treat "different customers differently"?
- Do you know the customer pain points, what customers feel at these points, and whether you're addressing them?
- Do you know the moments of truth (the key interactions or areas) in which important brand impressions are formed?
- Is there a clear sense of purpose linked to customer management, and is the delivery of great customer experiences part of business-as-usual?
- Are you clear as to your most impactful opportunity for competitive advantage, and is it product, brand or customer experience?
- Does your customer experience support both the brand and the business strategy?
- Do you understand the link between customer experience and overall business results?
- Being constantly faced with situations that have multiple "right choices", do you explore each of these right choices in order to choose the "best right choice"?
- Do you pay attention to how customers experience your service/product?

Case study – General Motors Middle East drives experience excellence through journey maps

General Motors Middle East (GMME) identified customer journey mapping as a critical tool to support the development of customer-centricity within the organisation and to design the experience it needed to deliver to customers. To achieve this objective, the high-level customer experience map or journey "snake" was constructed to cover 95% of the interactions or steps that 95% of the customers go through (Figure 13). Each individual journey was then mapped in order to model in detail what the customers could be thinking as they went into the step, what could possibly go wrong and what GMME wanted them to be thinking when they had emerged from the step (Figure 14 and Figure 15). This process identified the keys steps or moments of truth where things could go wrong and where there were no prevention or mitigation mechanisms. Where this was the case, these mechanisms needed to be built as well as looking for opportunities to exceed expectations.

These detailed customer journey maps provided GMME with a way to increase the quality and value of the customer experience through more impactful and even mandatory standards that drove dealer behaviours, as well as the ability to monitor these on an on-going basis. In this way, GMME positioned itself to dramatically improve the customer experience, and in turn, increase their customers' commitment to GMME.

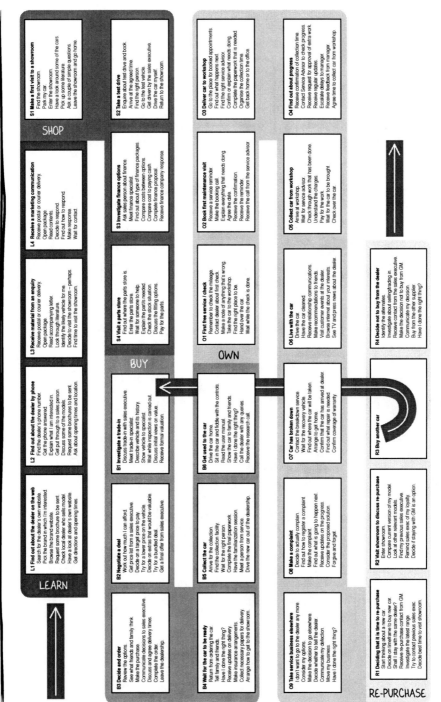

Figure 13: Customer Journey Map Snake for General Motors Middle-East

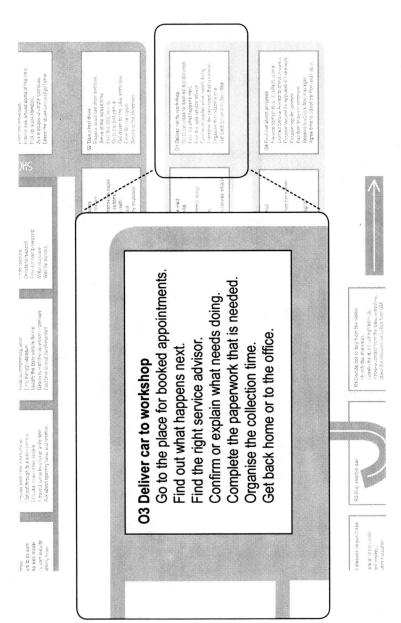

O3 Deliver car to workshop
Go to the place for booked appointments.
Find out what happens next.
Find the right service advisor.
Confirm or explain what needs doing.
Complete the paperwork that is needed.
Organise the collection time.
Get back home or to the office.

Figure 14: Macro- and Micro-Journeys for General Motors Middle East

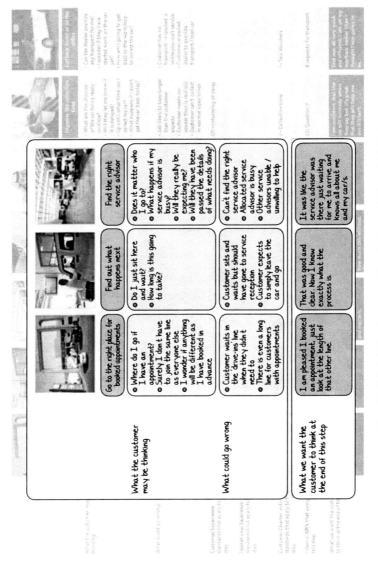

03 Deliver the car to the workshop

What the customer may be thinking

Go to the right place for booked appointments	Find out what happens next	Find the right service advisor	Organise the appropriate help	Collect my car at the dealer
• Where do I go if I have an appointment? • Surely I don't have to join the same line as everyone else. • I wonder if anything will be different as I have booked in advance	• Do I just sit here and wait? • How long is this going to take?	• Does it matter who I go to? • What happens if my service advisor is busy? • Will they really be expecting me? • Will they have been passed the details of what needs doing?	• What are the chances of the car being ready on time? • Will they let me know if it is delayed? • Up until what time can I collect my car? • What happens if I don't get the car back today?	• Can the dealer provide any transport for me? • I wonder if they have started work on the car yet. • How am I going to get back to the workshop to collect the car?

What could go wrong

| • Customer waits in the drive-ins line when they didn't need to
 • There is even a long line for customers with appointments | • Customer sits and waits but should have gone to service reception
 • Customer expects to simply leave the car and go | • Can't find the right service advisor
 • Allocated service advisor is busy
 • Other service advisors unable / unwilling to help | • Job likely to take longer than the customer expects
 • Customer needs car sooner than is realistic in normal expectation | • Customer has no transport – expected a while-you-wait service • Customer can't collect in normal opening hours • Customer expected dealer to provide transport / loan car |

What we want the customer to think at the end of this step

| I am pleased I booked an appointment, just look at the length of that other line | That was good and clear. Now I know exactly what the process is. | It was like the service advisor was there just waiting for me to arrive and knows all about me and my car/s. | | |

Figure 15: Detailed Micro-Journey and Steps for General Motors Middle East

CHAPTER 12:

AGILITY AND WORKFLOW

Transformation Intent

The ability to deliver a customer-centric experience is dependent on the speed at which your organisation can mobilise itself so that you can meet the changing needs of your customers and act on new opportunities as soon as they arise. In order to do this you need an agile decision-making infrastructure that is supported by efficient and technology-enabled processes that integrate teams and deliver on the opportunities for real-time responses.

Being quick off the mark

Time is one of the most precious resources of any organisation, yet it is often one of the most frequently abused resources. There is a multitude of ways that time can be wasted, including meandering strategies, process inefficiencies, poor data quality, ineffective and non-integrated technologies, limited or non-existent collaboration or having a culture where employees do not value each other's time. In a customer-centric business model, time takes on a new dimension — how you are using your customers' time and how quickly you are able to respond to their rapidly changing needs and expectations.

Economic, market and customer pressures are forcing organisations to speed up their time dimension, resulting in the drive to get to market quicker, respond to queries faster and invest heavily in all kinds of technologies to speed up the organisation's engagement with customers. Business process management and workflow technologies are used to optimise the time line in order to become efficient, focused and consistent.

Yet, there is a negative side to this process. As business processes and workflows become embedded and formalised through rigid constraints and systems, you run the risk of losing the capability to "leap-frog" restrictions, known as agility or the ability to be nimble and move quickly in response to changing conditions. This means that in order to create consistent and measurable delivery you need clear and detailed workflows, yet those very workflows can prevent your employees from seizing an opportunity to delight a customer or from solving a customer problem that falls outside the predefined flows of what they can do. You have no doubt had the experience that I have had many times of being told something cannot be done because "the system does not allow it". A different approach is clearly required.

Agility is not just about how you respond to your circumstances. It is also about being proactive to changing needs and, in particular, to the needs of your customer. Agility Consulting, an organisation which works to build this competency within organisations such as Coca-Cola, Dell and Disney, define agility as: "The dynamic capability to identify and exploit marketplace opportunities by building a superior capacity to sense and respond better and faster than competition at all levels in the organization" [68].

According to their methodology, known as The Agile Model®, developing agility competency requires five key components [68]:

- Anticipating change and, therefore, being ready for it when it arrives
- Generating confidence by aligning and engaging employees
- Initiating action through building a climate of urgency
- Liberating thinking by encouraging innovation, particularly in respect of the customer
- Evaluating results by closing the feedback loop

Nicholas Horney, a founding principal of Agility Consulting, cites Rice Toyota as an excellent example of how agility shows its true worth in the case of an emergency [69]. Rice Toyota, a large Toyota dealership, demonstrated their excellent agility in how they handled the recall of approximately 12,000 vehicles following Toyota's January 2010 recall. Their ability to anticipate the impact and action required, and their engagement with their customers through effective communication with the right information, did more than just handle a crisis. It increased their customer engagement positively as measured by a 1,500% increase in customer communications on its blog and a marked increase in the level of positive engagement through its Facebook page.

While agility, as defined by The Agile Model®, can be found across the REAP CCOB and in many of the SCHEMA® practises, the important insight from this model is that agility is not an outcome or about being reactionary. Instead, agility should be a fundamental part of your customer-centric business model, from end to end. This practice requires the right workflows to implement the operationalization of dynamic and proactive business processes that support the delivery of a superior customer experience.

Moving insight into action quickly

Being able to act quickly to changing circumstances is by no means equitable to being reckless. It requires instead the ability to find the balance point between responding swiftly to customers and their changing needs while consistently applying a set of criteria for risk-free decision making. This in itself implies a level of trust in your employees because you need to give them both the criteria they can use to make good, agile decisions and the freedom to do so.

If your customers complain, or have a query, they expect you to respond quickly and not to get bogged down in your own endless escalations and workflow loops. Decision points are often where processes fall down. Either too many decisions have to be made by too few supervisors or managers, or frontline staff are given the authority to make the decisions yet not the tools to support them doing so effectively. Either way, close scrutiny of your decision-making points and processes will help you to discover where you can improve the flow and timing of your customer-impacting processes. Time line studies of workflows quickly reveal where the bottlenecks are and, armed with this information, you can optimise the flow of these processes through improved decision frameworks and additional training.

By their very nature, legal and regulatory requirements can easily ensnare your processes in complexity as different departments bounce issues backwards and forwards. All the while your customer waits for a response, growing ever more frustrated with a process that blocks an excellent experience. If you reflect on the systems-thinking perspective used in this book, I am sure you will agree that a silo-based organisation will really show it limitations in the drive for agility. If your legal, regulatory and specialist departments operate in isolation, and without a collaborative approach with client-facing teams, it is obvious that the outcome will be negative.

There are, therefore, two approaches required in order to achieve an integrated approach. Firstly, look for ways to simplify the approvals processes that directly impact the customer, such as product and content development, propositions and customer management. And then find ways to bridge any gaps that may exist between the legal and specialist departments that are needed in order to respond to customers with agility. The solution may even be to have a specialist task team collaborating across those areas that has the mandate to address the kinds of processes and approvals that tend to trip up your efficient and prompt response to your customers.

Your customers' view of how agile you are is also critical and changes the way they engage with you. There are two aspects of their perception that require consideration — how quickly you are able to react to their changing needs and whether your organisation is so set in its ways that it cannot address real needs. Your customer research should help you to gauge your customers' view of how your organisation performs in this regard. As a customer, I find that I tend to refuse to lodge formal complaints or complete satisfaction surveys if I feel that nothing will come from my feedback. Why go to the effort of filling in all the details when the organisation will clearly do nothing about it.

The reverse is also true. Companies that demonstrate a culture and habit of making customer feedback count will engage their customers powerfully in sharing feedback and collaborating to solve problems. In this case, even a complaint is an opportunity to deepen the relationship with the customer and increase their loyalty.

Technology-enabled workflows

Workflow is a critical component in the creation of an agile customer-centric business model, and while closely related, is often incorrectly thought of as just another name for business processes. A business process is a set of one or more linked procedures or activities that may individually, or collectively, realise a business objective or policy goal. A workflow, on the other hand, is an automated flow across manual and system-driven tasks delivered upon a technology platform that drives the completion of those tasks, the movement of documents, the integration of functions and the rapid improvement in the speed and consistency of delivery.

The design of your workflow is especially important when considering customer-centricity. While workflow itself supports the direct improvement in efficiency and, therefore, the reduction in costs and risk, it will deliver much more efficiency if your customer processes are designed, developed and reviewed with workflow principles in mind. Some organisations develop their processes according to the standards set by methodologies such as Six Sigma [70], which in my view, with its origins in manufacturing, tends to bring a defect-based and mechanical world view into an organisation. In customer-centricity a much more human-centred and dynamic approach is required, which inspires the right behaviour, encourages innovation and engenders trust rather than being designed merely to handle failure.

Some of the key workflow design principles to consider in your customer-impacting processes are as follows [71,72]:

- Process design and review approach is centred around holistic, integrated processes rather than detailed tasks
- Performance is driven by customer contact and by what customers need and their relative value to the organisation
- Efficiency and effectiveness is increased and the turnaround times for processes are reduced
- Collaboration is improved across customer-facing teams, including access to, and the sharing of, information and resources
- Procedures can be escalated to specialist task teams to deliver quick and

effective responses, especially for exceptions
• Accountability and reporting is supported to enable effective decision making and continuous improvement

It is important for you to ensure that your workflow technology platform can drive the prompts and triggers required to ensure that workflow steps not only happen in the right sequence and at the right time, but also integrate a wealth of information into one central hub or access point. This information may include customer data across multiple systems, relevant resources and tools that can be used to provide the support, and specific next step workflows and actions as defined by the user's access rights. As a particular workflow moves through its cycle towards the point where it will be finalised, it must be possible to add relevant customer data to that flow to maximise the value of that contact and to ensure that nothing of value is dropped along the way. In principle this approach makes sense. Your challenge is to ensure that in practice this flexibility occurs.

At the same time you also need to ensure that you are still a humanistic business. Without a customer-centric mind-set it would be easy to turn your customer-facing processes into robotic experiences devoid of emotion. Never forget the powerful forces of collaboration and innovation as a means to empower your frontline to find new ways to solve your customers' problems.

"Efficient and effective service depends on the ability to implement process change in weeks if not hours. To make that possible your processes and IT systems have to be architected to support agility. A well-defined service oriented architecture for applications, defined integration strategy and model-driven process approach ensures that you can change service processes quickly — whether you are changing policies, SLAs or escalations. With agility you can do more than respond to changes in the market, you can exploit opportunities before your competition does. You can launch new products and offers quickly, rapidly impart knowledge to agents and have new processes up and running with minimal disruption to IT" [20].

Moving towards real time

In some cases, the drive to optimise your business processes and workflows goes beyond incremental improvement and into the realm of delivering real-time execution for your customers. Taking a customer-centric view would require you to have a very clear understanding of what real-time means to you and where real-time experiences would add the most value to your customers and your organisation.

The real-time update of customer data, and the preparation and assimilation of that data to make it ready for use, is a key consideration of the customer management team. How do you define what real-time means to your organisation and what information must be real-time versus information that does not? A batch process that updates your transaction database every 15 minutes may be as close to real-time as you need it, yet at eBay, if bids on an auction are only updated at 15 minute intervals they would have a major service experience issue on their hands. You will need to conduct your own research to ascertain your real-time needs and priorities, bearing in mind that every process and piece of data made available in real-time carries with it a cost that you have to justify in your business case.

Immense value can be found in improving the timing of processes that specifically derive customer insights from real-time data and then translate these insights into action. Can your organisation deliver feedback, input or prompts to a sales, marketing or service channel that is based on something that the customer has just said or done in near real-time? This might relate to a web page visit, an enquiry that they have made, a sales transaction or a social media comment. If your customer checked into one of your locations on Foursquare, how quickly could this trigger provide you with insights that you could act on instantly to engage with customers in an immediate and customer-centric way?

Any move towards real-time ways of working, for processes and data, may require new or upgraded technology along with new employee skills and behaviour. Standard project methodologies should, therefore, be used to ensure that such projects are implemented effectively, within budget and in ways that will deliver the agreed value.

"Anytime, anywhere access to real-time intelligence from remote machines or devices is changing the way that multinational businesses operate. Over the next five years we're going to see a dramatic breakthrough in new applications as organisations realise the unheralded potential M2M (machine to machine) represents — not just for increased efficiency and cost reduction, but also for revenue generation and improved customer satisfaction" [21].

Collaboration bridges silos

Collaboration is a critical success factor for the development and activation of organisational agility. While you have functional silos and teams not working together effectively for the benefit of the customer, you cannot deliver the kind of response times required for a superior customer experience. You, therefore, need to become aware of which specific barriers may be preventing collaboration and then work to remove those obstacles, which may include anything from cultural mismatches to technical challenges.

One of the ways of removing barriers to collaboration is the establishment of a specific forum or council focused on customer experience. This forum must be comprised of employees with cross-functional skills and experience that specifically address the need to bridge your end-to-end processes, while creating consistency of the customer experience across your organisation.

Most organisations will invariably have some form of technology platform that could and should facilitate greater levels of collaboration. Social and online technologies, therefore, should be widely accessible and used across your organisation to support collaboration. Video-conferencing, discussion boards and chat rooms are great tools you can use to increase collaboration. The challenge often lies in how these platforms have been operationalized. Without the necessary accountability, measures, KPIs and collaborative culture, these technologies can quickly fall into disuse.

An excellent tool to support collaboration is a peer-to-peer knowledge base that collates relevant content to support improvements in the service offered to customers. A knowledge base is particularly useful for areas that would benefit from the repeated application of that knowledge across different business units. This means that your employees do not need to reinvent how they are dealing with certain problems and queries. They then learn with every contact and this increases their ability to resolve problems and address client issues promptly the first time around.

Having a knowledge base, and being able to use it effectively, is a different matter entirely. A collaborative culture will go a long way in overcoming this challenge because it will naturally encourage employees to refer to it for help and also to contribute their own knowledge to it. Usability is also a very important consideration and includes user experience, access, search functionality and content currency. As soon as employees conclude that the content is outdated they will stop using the knowledge base and look for other ways to manage their knowledge, creating more silos of learning along the way.

Microsoft is well known for their enterprise applications that deliver, amongst other things, workflow and collaboration platforms. As you would expect, they use their own technologies to deliver the business and productivity benefits of collaboration. Tony Scott, CIO of Microsoft, shares his perspective on collaboration and productivity [73]: "For us today, it's about better collaboration across all of the business groups, geographies and markets that we serve. I have teams all over the world and with these tool sets that we have we communicate and collaborate with our teams all over the world every day as though we were in the same city, which we're not. As we look out into the future a couple of things become very apparent. This world of high powered devices that increasingly are much more relevant to what we do and understand the context of the work we are engaged in, coupled with the cloud and putting to work all that compute power in a way that is easily accessible, means that I think there is a bright future for productivity going forward".

Sustainable centres of excellence

If in working to understand your customer-centricity and business agility you identify a gap in capability that you need to address, a highly effective approach is to establish a centre of excellence. A centre of excellence is a specialised and formalised unit within the organisation that focuses on accelerating the development of operational capability across the organisation while developing business understanding for a particular focus area.

There are a few key outcomes that a centre of excellence should deliver:

- Thought leadership that inspires the business on the specialisation area of the centre
- Hands-on support for specific initiatives within the focus area, particularly through communication and collaboration
- The building of capability through knowledge and training, thereby providing tools, methodologies, models, support and infrastructure development
- Clear sponsorship from a very senior division or stakeholders in order for it to be effective

Sometimes there is confusion between a project and a centre of excellence. A project has a finite end point. When the project is finished it's switched off, and, very often, the outcomes of the project do not become embedded within the organisation. A centre of excellence is more sustainable and, while not always permanent, it specifically focuses on the operationalization of that capability until it is part of "business-as-usual". The positive benefits of a centre of excellence are often long lasting, creating real and meaningful change.

A centre of excellence requires a clear road map and operational processes that structure and define how its mandate will be delivered, from initiation through to the phasing in of defined deliverables. A managed approach also requires that its activities and deliverables are monitored, measured, reviewed and reported on across the organisation. This method can provide crucial learning experience, particularly around the reasons for initiative success and failure.

The success of a centre of excellence is determined by the extent to which the learning and best practice capability, defined by the centre, is fully embedded into your organisation. Depending on the extent of change required, extensive communication and lobbying across your organisation may be needed. In some cases this may result in large communication projects that tap into the myriad of communication and training tools available throughout your organisation. One of my clients planned for a news channel that could engage employees in a new and fun way so that new learning could be effectively implemented. A centre of excellence would, therefore, explore using a broad set of internal marketing programmes to achieve buy-in and, more importantly, deliver the intended results.

A customer-centric business model will demand many changes in your organisation. It may just be that becoming agile and responsive to customers in a rapidly changing world is a real challenge for you to achieve. At the heart of overcoming this challenge is the need to integrate and interconnect the people, processes and technologies in your organisation so that your overall "system" is mobilised to move quickly, while doing so responsibly.

Transformation questions

- Is your organisation set up to take customer insight and feedback through to new or amended processes/propositions quickly and can customers perceive this agility?
- Do your customer-impacting employees collaborate effectively, enabled by relevant technology, both on an overall basis and focussed at specific areas of need?
- Do you recognise and understand that the main obstacles to improved business responsiveness include slow decision making, conflicting departmental goals and priorities, risk-averse cultures and silo-based information?
- Are you able to transform information into insight in response to market movements, with this process being core to sustainability?
- Do you acknowledge that the better you know your customer the better you are able to gauge what matters most in defining a positive customer

experience? Do you understand that this knowledge is core to competitiveness in today's market because it helps to direct innovation, create value and ensure flexibility and nimbleness in decision-making?

- Is your business able to adapt rapidly and cost efficiently to both market and environmental changes?
- Do you and the senior management team recognise that change is something that comes from the external world of customer demands, competitor influences, technical progress, legislative changes as well as internal drivers?
- Have you been able to make change a routine part of organisational life to reduce or eliminate the trauma that paralyses many businesses attempting to adapt to new markets and environments?
- Is responding to concerns, critique or needs expressed by your customers a priority for you?

Case study - Coca-Cola engages consumers in real time

The Coca-Cola Company is a global organisation known for its ability to keep its finger on the pulse of the consumer heartbeat, especially through their associations with music and sport. Their ability to respond quickly to changing conditions, while continuing to actively engage consumers, is a key part of their success. As a global organisation it is critical that their global culture and marketing activities are able to move quickly as consumer needs change.

Joe Tripodi, Coca-Cola's chief marketing and commercial officer, shares his view on the new dynamics of business which demand that companies are agile and quick to move [74]: "The world, brands and consumers are evolving at such a fast pace. The opportunities and challenges are quite dramatic. The new world order of consumer engagement and change that's occurring gives a unique opportunity to really understand the motives that people are using and how they are behaving. Instead of looking in the past to predict the future, we are using real-time now to say how we are going to engage with those consumers in a more effective way and ultimately to get them to buy our products." Tripodi adds that Coca-Cola especially uses their speed and agility when it comes to the innovation of their products.

In 2009, Coca-Cola Freestyle was launched to connect Coca-Cola with real-time information about its consumers. The Freestyle is a soda fountain that provides over 125 different drinks and custom flavours, and consumers can mix their own flavours from the range. The choices that consumers make provide real-time information to Coca-Cola about their consumers' flavour preferences. This information is used directly by the product development team to innovate future flavours.

Coca-Cola's ability to use real-time information to understand their consumers, and then take appropriate action quickly to seize opportunities, extends into their use of mobile phones to issue mobile coupons to drive traffic into their retail partners' stores. As Tripodi says, the mobile phone is now "the remote control for people's lives". Using mobile coupons incites consumers to take action with urgency and try something new. In addition, the way in which consumers redeem their coupons provides further information into how they are behaving and responding to special offers or new products.

Social media plays a big role in Coca-Cola's quest for agility and a high responsiveness to consumer behaviour. Coca-Cola has an enterprise-wide social media strategy and monitoring social sentiment helps them to understand the extent to which people are engaged with them, their brands and their campaigns. This provides real-time feedback, whereas, historically, this kind of campaign feedback would take months to obtain.

Coca-Cola also invested in an online, real-time messaging system called The Coke Digital Network. This is an electronic billboard system backed by complex content management that allows Coca-Cola to ensure their message to the consumer is relevant all the time. It gives them the capacity to adjust that message as they learn more about local consumer behaviour. As Coca-Cola has exclusivity to their electronic billboards they can control their flow of communication better and develop extensive insights from consumer behaviour. One example of the real-time nature of this system is that messages displayed early in the day would likely include products such as Minute Maid, whereas afternoon messages would include Coke, and after hours, Vitamin Water would be more appropriate to target the work-out market [75].

In order to turn this kind of strategy into reality it requires a company to have the organisational capability to innovate with agility while supporting its real-time and dynamic consumer engagement with integrated end-to-end processes and a global culture that seeks to become more responsive to consumer needs.

○ CHAPTER 13:

○ MEASUREMENT

Transformation Intent

While customer-centricity does not change the importance of organisational performance measurement, it does change what, when and how you measure business performance. In order to measure the right information about your customers at the right time you need to create "line of sight" measurement that connects your customer measures and the profitability improvements, driven by a clear focus on your customer value drivers.

The "line of sight"

As explored in Chapter 3, one of the challenges faced by the 21st century organisation is that measuring success on profit and financial measures alone can no longer deliver a complete picture of how sustainable an organisation really is. Instead, new measures are needed that can more accurately depict how an organisation is faring in meeting its strategic outcomes and delivering the future capability required to fully express the principles of customer-centricity. Demonstrating that your organisation has what it takes to beat the competition requires the development of a superior ability to deliver on one or more key measures that drive sustained profitability in your business. Creating and managing new key measures is particularly important for those who want to revitalize their organisations and is also a signal that the business model has changed, which can be critical both within the organisation and for its outside constituencies.

"Line of sight" is a business philosophy and measurement approach in which everyone understands and aligns with the overall purpose and aspirations of the business [24]. It's a systemic approach to business, and its measurement is underpinned by a set of principles as illustrated in Figure 16 below. These principles demonstrate that sustainable business performance is achieved by developing the capability to influence customer behaviour through relevance and value in order to optimise Acquisition, encourage Retention and increase customer spend through Penetration. The ability to influence customer behaviour is achieved through gaining commitment and sales from those customers who are, or can become, heavy spenders and/or influencers. Commitment is gained through delivering a distinct and appropriate customer experience for these customers with the right blend of functional, rational, sensory and emotional elements. Delivering high-contrast signature experiences effectively requires engaged and motivated employees and partners. Employees and partners work within the context that the company sets, which encourages the appropriate customer-centric approach including: structure, culture, capability, budgets, policies, products and services, pricing, propositions, environment, processes, IT infrastructure, and measures. Although each element of the "line of sight" correlates with business performance independently, the overall effect is to focus on optimising the system as a whole. This system must work in harmony in order to ensure that the organisation is aligned to deliver sustainable business performance.

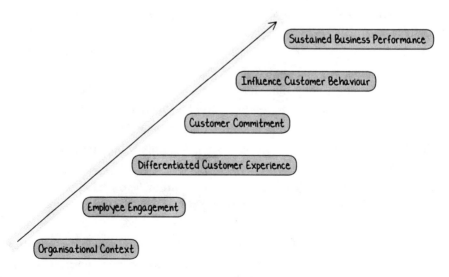

Figure 16: Line of Sight (QCi)

Every single employee, from executives to frontline staff, needs to understand how the end result of a superior customer experience and sustainable business performance is connected through every action of every person across the entire organisation. If your employees can understand how their individual efforts are contributing directly to the customer experience and to the bottom line, you can create a level of employee engagement that will drive a much greater financial return.

There are many facets of customer-centricity that are drawn together through measurement, including the absolute clarity of your purpose and end goal, a unified culture that places your customer at its centre, an integrated business model that bridges organisational silos, and an explicitly defined understanding of what success means to your organisation. Measurement is no longer just about financial success but covers a wide range of complex layers that all need due consideration and an understanding of how all these aspects are interconnected.

While this different approach to measurement may seem daunting, there are many examples of large organisations that have transformed their approach to measurement by putting their customers at the centre of their overall measurement framework, and coupled with employee engagement, have driven exponential financial results as a by-product of this customer- and employee-centric focus.

"No one's connecting the mess of company metrics. Does anyone even know what the metrics should be? Who is the point person for all of these metrics? No one knows. Each area has its own spin on what it owns, what's important, and how to measure it. Everyone's got a version of success that they trumpet to leadership. Each silo creates an annual plan and metrics for its own operating area. When these are presented separately they make sense. But if you tried to connect them, the metrics most likely wouldn't connect. The sum of the parts wouldn't add up to managing and end-to-end customer experience" [22].

The customer dimension

At its core, a customer-centric approach to measurement requires that there is a very clear customer dimension within your overall measurement framework. Having only a customer satisfaction measure is not enough, as by itself, it is not an indication of customer loyalty and your long-term value growth potential. While some practitioners advocate that a measure such as the net promoter score is the only customer measure you need, in reality, a balanced and holistic set of measures across your customer dimensions is preferential. This balance should embrace all the stages of the "line of sight" as well as your REAP strategies.

Satisfaction and loyalty measures are lagging indicators of the success of your customer-centric efforts. They are unable to provide deep insight regarding the extent of your overall customer-centric capability development, or whether these capabilities are being developed at the pace you require. It is, therefore, imperative to incorporate a leading measure of this capability development, such as the comprehensive SCHEMA® measure, which also provides benchmark standards against which you can assess your position compared to "best-in-class".

Your high-level strategic customer measures are then translated into top-level value drivers for each of your REAP strategies. Value drivers at a macro-level or by customer value group or segment may include: "attrition rate" for your Retention strategy; "cost to acquire" and/or "cost to serve" for your Efficiency strategy; "new customers per year" for your Acquisition strategy; and "cross-sell ratio" for your Penetration strategy. These value drivers are directly linked to the business case you have defined for your customer-centric transformation. Refer to the case study in Chapter 3 for more information on the SCHEMA Value Estimator™ used for this purpose.

The principle of treating different customers differently, and the REAP levers to specify the customer strategy for each customer segment, are fundamental to the mind-set you need when implementing customer measures. This is because it forces you into being specific on your strategy for each customer segment while recognising that there are going to be customers who are worth more to you today, and in the future, than others. Not taking cognisance of measuring this differentiated value, and not planning accordingly, is an opportunity for growth and efficiency that is lost.

Those strategic level value drivers should be cascaded down into the business units that will operationally deliver on those measures. This gives you a clear perspective on the specific REAP strategies and value drivers to be measured for each customer segment. For example, perhaps for your high value segment your key focus is going to be Retention and Penetration. Keeping your existing customers and selling more to them is a sound strategy, based upon their value to you and their capacity to spend more. In your low value segment, your primary focus may be Efficiency because you need to find a way to service these customers profitably – at a lower cost due to their lower value. With the right set of consistent and specific value driver measures in place across all business units and all segments, and the data to support accurate and meaningful reporting, it is possible to optimise development of value effectively in your customer base.

The customer-centric approach to measurement would not be complete without connecting those specific operational measures to employee engagement which, in turn, creates customer engagement and ultimately profitability through your key value drivers. Each employee's measures are then linked to how he/she influences customer engagement and, through the "line of sight", how he/she directly affects customer experience. Consider a call centre environment as an example, in which an agent is measured on the number of calls handled and average handling time. In this reality, the agent isn't encouraged to consider, or be sensitive to, a situation in which the customer requires more talk time. This may be nothing other than an emotional requirement on the part of the customer. By establishing a connection between operational measures, including both rational and emotional dimensions, and customer and employee engagement measures, you can demonstrate how each employee's actions affect the entire system.

A measure that is gaining an increasing amount of attention is the "customer effort score". Customer effort is reputed to be significantly superior to traditional measures, such as customer satisfaction and the net promoter score, in terms of the predictive power of re-purchase and increasing spend. The customer effort score is based upon how much effort, as a customer, you personally have to invest to have your request handled, to make a purchase or to secure the resolution of your issue.

"We surveyed more than 200 large organizations and found out that customer experience (CX) metrics are important and many companies are already getting value from using them. Firms use a wide range of metrics with varied results. They track customer service, satisfaction, and phone experiences fairly well. On the other hand, they're not very effective at measuring customers across the lifecycle, the emotional response of customers, or cross-channel interactions. When it comes to how they run their businesses, companies haven't integrated CX metrics into their decision-making or operational processes. In only 41% of firms, for instance, do execs look at CX metrics more frequently than once per quarter. Using Temkin Group's CX metrics assessment, we found that only 10% of firms have good CX metrics programs, and those that do, deliver better customer experience. Companies need to develop metrics in four areas: interactions, reactions, attitudes and behaviors" [23].

Channels and media

Channel performance measurement should include a customer dimension, for example segments, customer types or value groups. A channel may, in isolation, only deal with one or two customer groupings, yet different channels may deal with the same customer groupings. It's important to ensure that where different and separate channels are reporting on the same group of customers that they are reporting on exactly the same type of customer. I have seen companies where high value customers are defined differently across the organisation and this has the effect of rendering most channel and segment data meaningless.

With customer-focused channel and media measures in place you can begin to compare the performance across channels and media types that are used for the same function (Retention, Acquisition and Penetration) even if they're not addressing the same group of customers. New and emerging channels and media may require a different measurement framework than the more traditional channels do. Digital, social and mobile approaches may be designed to drive different behaviours – influence being an example – than the typical measures such as purchases or sales.

Furthermore, earned media measures such as "likes", "comments" and "shares" should be measured, thereby enabling you to understand where customers are amplifying your brand message or content for free. Your customer advocacy on digital and social channels should be measured in a way that is meaningful and useful. So many organisations only use easy-to-measure "vanity" criteria, such as the number of "likes", "followers" and "fans", but what does that really mean in terms of business performance and return on investment? Is that a true reflection of the value of your earned media? Perhaps the number of shares, re-tweets and unsolicited mentions is more appropriate. Is your organisation in a position to track these interactions with meaningful insight? Can you compare earned media to your owned and paid-for media?

Just as we understand that every aspect of an organisation is interconnected with every other part, so do we need to recognise that a channel may play a role in supporting the revenue reported by another channel. It is not possible to definitively determine which channel a particular customer segment will always use. They may switch between channels, between transactions or even during them. Your channel measurements must, therefore, assess this support role that channels provide to each other, with a clear understanding of the typical paths-to-purchase of customers who buy from a particular channel, based upon the interactions they have with another channel. How does your online channel support your direct sales channel? Does your web site, for example, reduce the number of calls into your call centre due to the good information available, or does your web site increase the work in a more expensive channel because it is confusing or just not up to date? A customer experience view of your channels will, therefore, help you to identify how the interdependencies of channels should be measured and managed.

Employee engagement

According to Gallup's research [76], employee engagement directly influences customer engagement, which in turn, directly impacts on an organisation's financial performance. The findings of Gallup's research show that companies that score above the 50th percentile for either employee or customer engagement, experience a 70% higher financial result than those companies who score poorly on both those measures. This result jumps to 240% for companies who score above the 50th percentile for both employee and customer engagement. These statistics are compelling and drive home the fact that employee and customer engagement are critical measures for superior business performance.

It is obvious, therefore, that any employees who have a degree of customer-facing responsibility, or impact the customer in any way, should have customer-specific measures built into their individual performance measures. These measures must be directly linked through the "line of sight" principle to the key strategic outcomes of your organisation to make sure that the measures drive the right employee behaviours. This will require an explicit process to check that the employee performance measures are indeed appropriate and relevant in light of customer objectives and the defined customer experience. For example, if your strategy with a particular customer segment is Retention, what kind of behaviour would you need to see from an employee servicing that segment? How would you measure that behaviour? What rewards could encourage excellence in Retention?

In a classic case of the wrong reward stimulating the wrong behaviour, one company set a complaint threshold as part of their measurement dashboard. It is not surprising that once the threshold was reached, frontline employees began classifying complaints differently. The company was happy because complaints were reducing but, before long, customer dissatisfaction began to escalate. When it became apparent why, the management reversed the process and began to encourage complaints. Complaints increased, yet so did customer satisfaction.

You see this same phenomenon so often when companies incentivise employees to reduce costs even when revenue and sales targets are being met. While efficiency and cost optimisation is critical, it's important to consider the impact of cost reduction on the customer experience, both today and in the future. There must be a balance between measures that assess internal business benefit and those that assess customer benefit.

With employee engagement being so critical, part of the employee performance measurement process should focus on ensuring that employees and their managers have a full understanding of their performance measures and that they accept those measurement criteria as fair, relevant and appropriate. However, a customer-centric organisation wants more — the employee should be excited and totally committed to meeting and exceeding their measurement criteria.

Campaign activity and effectiveness

In Chapter 8, *Insight and Planning*, the case study on Harrah's introduced their very successful closed loop marketing approach through which they could run a quick, test sample of a particular campaign with almost immediate feedback that allowed them to refine the offer and re-test. This idea is one to bear in mind for your campaign measurement — as close to real time is the ideal. The measures and feedback received as the campaign is unfolding should allow you to adjust and optimise that campaign and, in some cases, even end it. There isn't time to waste conducting reviews of campaign results after the fact. This is particularly important with any digital and social campaigns. The next day can be simply too late.

The measures you use to ascertain campaign results should cover a broad range of dimensions to provide a more holistic perspective. Traditional measures, such as the number of responses, leads and conversions, should be supplemented with "softer" measures, such as referrals, emotional commitment and attitude. The short-term perspective on a campaign's return on investment also needs to be assessed with reference to the potential long-term benefit and even the long-term negative impact of the campaign. As an example of this practice is should be noted that some Acquisition campaigns actually penalise existing customers. While the campaign may be incredibly successful in the short term, over a longer time period the negative impact on existing customers may produce a very different result. Measurement of your campaigns must be able to provide the information required to ascertain what the financial return was in light of the marketing investment made in that campaign.

Once the campaign has been completed, the learning should not end. Instead, the marketing activity should be reviewed against a consistent set of criteria, storing the facts, insights and learning from those campaign reviews in a library that is easily accessible for future campaign planning and design. In so doing, you speed up your learning cycles and tap into the wealth of knowledge that each campaign generates.

Customer engagement

Every organisation may define "customer engagement" differently, and it is thus critical that you have defined what it means to you holistically and what the differing levels of engagement actually mean. The trick is to ensure that your engagement levels are relevant to the way your organisation functions and for the goal you are trying to achieve. Perhaps your levels of customer engagement are similar to the Gallup indicators [76] — from fully engaged, engaged, disengaged to actively disengaged. If so, what does each of these levels mean to you? How do you ascertain a customer's level of engagement? Is emotional engagement considered alongside contractual, obligatory or monopolistic engagement? Whatever definition framework you choose, you must ensure that you apply those definitions consistently so that the level of engagement can be measured.

The level of customer engagement also changes over time and as customers move through their life cycle with you, from earliest involvement to last involvement and customer loss. In the early stages of the relationship, customers are not that likely to be "committed for life". Ideally, customers should become more engaged over their life cycle. Research and analysis of your customer behaviours at each stage in your life cycle will determine the overall pattern in engagement and whether there are any particular trends that are insightful and warrant action. This awareness would include understanding the factors that decrease and increase customers' level of engagement over time.

Advocacy is often considered the highest level of engagement success. It arises when prospects and customers feel strongly enough about your brand, organisation and products to promote your company through their networks. While impressions are directly linked to the efforts you have made to put content in front of people, expressions are a much more powerful measure of the extent of your customer engagement. Pinterest is a digital platform that for marketers has become "expression gold". Every time a user pins an image of your product and others share it, a wave of expressions is created that you can measure and track. While initially organisations thought of Pinterest as a scrapbook site, the understanding of its true potential is rapidly getting the attention of marketers. As with other social platforms, the rules are different. You don't get expressions by selling yourself. You get it through engaging in new, powerful and sensory ways.

As your understanding of customer-centricity and the new world order deepens, so will the means of measuring your success become more complex and refined. In creating "line of sight" measurement between your customer and the bottom line, you will enable employees to fully understand how critical their commitment and engagement is to your vision in delivering sustainable business performance.

Transformation questions

- Is a top-level (executive team) set of measures in place that cover the key value drivers of REAP (Retention, Efficiency, Acquisition and Penetration)?
- Have a relevant set of metrics that measure the degree of customer engagement been developed in a way that is consistently understood across your organisation?
- Do you have a balanced set of cross-functional customer metrics in

place?

- Are your measures a combination of both leading and lagging customer metrics?
- Have you introduced a customer management dashboard that links service, experience and impact on company business results?
- Are your customer management metrics reflective of your customer management strategy and are they implemented at the overall company level as well as at an operational level?
- What are the big and critical driving objectives and goals of the operation and are divisional and functional goals aligned to support the business ambition?
- Does the board ensure that the company's ethics performance is assessed, monitored, reported and disclosed?
- Is the ethical treatment of customers included in your metrics?

Case study - Ritz-Carlton measures its mystique

The Ritz-Carlton Hotel Company is a luxury hotel group steeped in history and known for their dedication to the highest standard of quality and service. With over 80 properties in 27 countries and 38,000 employees worldwide, The Ritz-Carlton is an organisation dedicated to both its customers and employees. They refer to their "The Ritz-Carlton Mystique", which aims to encapsulate the meaning of their brand promise — elegant, enigmatic and memorable experiences of exceptional quality. Employees are even referred to as "ladies and gentlemen" and so are their customers [76].

A review of The Ritz-Carlton's Gold Standards — their values and philosophy — quickly reveals the depth of their customer-centric values and culture. The following key phrases from their service values epitomise this culture: relationships, responsiveness, experiences, innovation, accountability, ownership, teamwork, growth, planning, professionalism, confidentiality and high standards.

While their recruitment and training approach plays a large part in their success, their extensive use of measurement to continuously improve and deliver beyond expectation is world class. What makes The Ritz-Carlton measurement system so effective is that it connects the entire organisation, from top leadership right down to the frontline staff, while creating a closed loop feedback system that engages the entire organisation with focused direction.

The foundation of their measurement system is what they refer to as "key success factors", which are outcome measures for their strategic objectives and business priority factors that positively affect their brand and customers. These factors include: mystique, employee engagement, customer engagement, product service excellence, community involvement and financial performance. In true customer-centric fashion, The Ritz-Carlton believes that financial results are the by-product of all their other achievements, and so their measures are largely focused on employees and customers, with engagement at the centre of those measures. The priorities of the key success factors are defined as actionable achievements and are drafted by a cross-functional team comprised of a diversity of levels and responsibility. This active participation in defining measures, targets and actions helps to make employees feel actively involved.

Masses of data are generated by staff, which is fed through filters as defined by the key success factors. Everything is reported on in great detail and this provides a real-time view which in turn supports generating insights that adjust the key success factors themselves. Priorities define what measurements are needed from that data and those results, in turn, amend the priorities when new insights become available. This is a dynamic process that keeps The Ritz-Carlton learning and improving. Everyone can see how the entire organisation is connected and what their role is in supporting that picture. Their daily team rituals serve to continuously keep those success factors as a high priority issue that is constantly reviewed in order to ascertain whether or not they are being met and what can be done to improve performance. These learning and feedback processes have taught employees how to listen for and observe the subtle clues customers give about their experience, which is also fed into the measurement system.

In developing the measurement system in use today, The Ritz-Carlton referred to the principles of Gallup's [76] well-known research into the factors that influence employee engagement and the role that it plays in customer engagement and organisational performance. Since 2006 The Ritz-Carlton chain of hotels has used the Gallup Q_{12} employee engagement metric as one of its critical focus areas. Through this approach the management teams have been able to tie together employee and customer engagement, creating awareness in employees of the direct impact that their actions have on their customer and overall organisational performance. By focusing on the employee experience, they have been able to raise their employee and customer engagement to legendary levels.

The success of The Ritz-Carlton measurement system is testimony to how it has approached customer-centric measurement in its organisation. Instead of adding a few customer-focused measures to its balanced scorecard, and filtering in data from a few customer initiatives, it has built customer-centric measurement into the very DNA of its business model.

Joseph Michelli, in his book about The Ritz-Carlton entitled *The New Gold Standard* [77], summarised this achievement: "Ritz-Carlton leadership has, in essence, produced a company of inquiry — one that is always looking for the best metrics to ensure that their employees find their work meaningful, that their customers are engaged, and that their business continues to stay relevant as they aspire to fulfil the lasting needs of all those who they serve."

PART FOUR:
EXECUTION

● CHAPTER 14:

● RETENTION

Transformation Intent

Retention is all about understanding your customer base and the drivers that create and maintain loyalty as well as the factors that destroy it. Coupled with this is the need to consistently deliver on your promise while ensuring that over-delivery is balanced against the overriding goal of doing just enough to ensure repurchase. A retention strategy also demands that you are pro-active with your customers, monitoring them for signs of defection and implementing constructive plans to generate customer commitment to repurchase. Should customers become dissatisfied, the right flows of communication alert you so that the issues can be addressed promptly and consistently, whilst solving the problem at a root cause level.

Where the rubber hits the road

Customer-centric strategies cannot remain purely theoretical. They need to be translated into practical interventions which deliver real results. Experience has shown that by applying customer-centric thinking, improvements in business performance are achievable at the point at which it really matters – the bottom line. If the basic purpose of a customer-centric strategy is accepted to be an improvement of the value created by the organisation for the customer – hence driving profit – then there are just four interventions necessary to achieve that goal.

Customer-centric strategies have as their core the principles of Retention, Efficiency (understanding cost to serve), Acquisition and Penetration (customer development, cross-sell and up-sell). These principles can be considered as "levers" which, if managed properly, create improved business performance. Focusing on planning for these levers is intended to support rather than replace current business planning activities. This process encourages organisations to build an understanding of where their business comes from in terms of contribution from new customers, contribution from existing customers and contribution from increased sales and/or service to existing customers. Once organisations understand where their business actually comes from they are able to model and develop different REAP strategies for different groups or segments of customers.

In the last part of this book, *Execution*, I share with you the practical aspects of operationalizing your customer strategy through your REAP levers. The intention is to provide you with a broad range of considerations that need to be taken into account to address the goals you have for your REAP levers and the change in value drivers that justify your business case. In this chapter, *Retention*, I explore techniques to manage your existing customer relationships. One of the most cost-efficient ways of driving profit in any organisation is to examine the means of retaining good customers.

According to a report by the CMO Council [78]: "Profitable customer relationships are the very lifeblood of commercial organisations." Yet most companies under perform in terms of nurturing, cultivating or re-activating customers to drive sustained revenue growth, advocacy and bottom line performance. Retention is an elusive goal for companies worldwide.

Retention's goal is the development of long-term, sustainable and profitable relationships that continue to grow in value over time. Retained revenue as a result of lower churn has a significant impact on profitability. Research conducted in the hotel and wireless service industries indicated that small shifts in customer loyalty can translate into billions of dollars of incremental revenue per year. Even the least effected industries, such as retailers and Internet service providers, can gain tens of millions of dollars in revenue benefits. For the hotel industry, if you are a regular traveller, you will know that a hotel runs the risk of driving customers away when it delivers a sub-par experience — there is no switching cost for taking individual business elsewhere, and many people have numerous options when looking for accommodation. To what extent are you at risk of losing your customers?

In order to increase customer retention, affinity and loyalty, whilst improving advocacy and word-of-mouth, greater customisation of your customer communication is required. This demonstrates your strong commitment to your customer and a sincere desire to retain and develop the relationship for the long term [78].

Understanding Retention

Understanding Retention, and what it means in your organisation, requires you to have a deep appreciation for the dimensions of loyalty, the nature and reasons that your customers leave, and why their value may decay over time.

To understand loyalty, you need to research the nature of your long tenure customers. Tenure is the time between your customer's first transaction and their last known transaction. Understanding the nature of long tenure for current, lapsed and lost customers provides insight into why they remained or still remain with you and, therefore, which of your approaches to build Retention have been the most successful.

You also need to be clear on the factors that impact the development of loyalty. Research, and possibly even analytical testing, will reveal the extent to which emotional factors affect your loyalty compared to physical factors, such as pricing, packing, location or even availability. How far would your customer drive to overcome the closure of a store in their local vicinity in order to get your brand? How much of a price differential would they tolerate before choosing to buy something else?

While we know that customer satisfaction does not necessarily lead to loyalty, it is insightful to use correlation analysis to understand what your organisation-specific link is between your overall satisfaction score and a behavioural measure of loyalty, such as repurchase rate, length of tenure or even purchase value. In this way you can turn your satisfaction research into something more meaningful through understanding its correlation with customer behaviour.

Having a deep insight into why customers are lost is critical for Retention. In order to understand customer loss you need to have clear definition of what loss means, while bearing in mind that a customer-centric perspective is that a lost customer is not one who has terminated only one of the products in their portfolio with you. A silo-based and product-centric organisation will find it very challenging to have this perspective. Do you have a consistent way of categorising lost customers versus a lost product sale? How do you report that fact within your organisation and how do you manage such a situation?

Understanding the reasons for loss requires regular and in-depth analysis, using a substantial sample that evaluates data across different customer types, segments, channels, geographies, needs and product holdings. This process allows you to compare the reasons for loss across customer categories so that you can understand the trends better and make positive changes as a result. Of course, the value of such research is dependent on the quality of the data captured by your customer-facing employees and whether you capture the real reasons for the loss along with what the final trigger was for the customer making the decision to terminate.

Another dimension to customer loss relates to the changes that occur across life cycles and life stages. A life cycle is the set of steps that customers progress through as they evaluate, purchase, utilise, maintain loyalty to or even end their use of your products or services. Life stages relate to the stages of life that a customer goes through as an individual. "Loss" research into those life cycles and stages can indicate what you need to do to prevent a loss from occurring. This could be relevant for customers who never actually become active, as is the case when they receive a credit card or a SIM card for a mobile phone that they never activate. Understanding loss in light of life stages also provides useful context regarding natural changes that you are not in control of, such as an "empty nester" moving into a smaller home.

Value decay refers to the reduction in the value of customers over time, resulting ultimately in dormancy, where the relationship has not been formally ended yet there is no customer value left. Defining decay requires that you recognise that there are levels of value reduction for certain customers that may fall outside any pattern of normal variation, such as seasonality or budget cycles. As such, defining value decay should take cognisance of the reduction in the number of transactions or reduced values of those transactions.

You also need to understand why customers decay in value, or become dormant, yet do not leave. Analysis of research in this area may yield interesting trends that could be used to prevent decay. If the customer has not terminated because of the effort involved, perhaps it is better to support them to a place of decision, be that termination or getting them engaged once again.

In order for the senior leadership team to have an accurate picture of the size of the customer base, it is important to make sure that reporting clearly denotes those customers who are active versus those who are dormant. This transparency will encourage the dormant customers to be actively managed out or back in, while ensuring that you don't over-inflate the significance of the customer base and, thereby, making incorrect assessments from it.

Retaining through business-as-usual

One of the most powerful ways of developing your customer relationships is through building a Retention focus into your everyday activities – your "business-as-usual". It requires that any new customer relationship begins on the right footing and that you consistently deliver the basic service that customers expect. On-going contact management serves to deepen that relationship yet you need to ensure that customers are in control of how they engage with you. Customer-facing employees play a critical role, as do pricing and exit barriers, in encouraging customers to stay.

It is crucial that you get the customer relationship right from the outset. This process begins with collecting basic information about the customer through mechanisms you should have in place for this purpose. The type of data obtained extends beyond basic regulatory information, with just enough relevant information so that you can get to know a little more about the customer. This initial information starts to build a customer picture without overwhelming the customer with a request for too much personal information too soon in the relationship.

As customer experience includes both emotional and physical factors, it is essential to understand a new customer's attitude to your organisation, market and industry at the beginning of the relationship so that you can track changes in attitude over the customer life cycle. Research of this change over time will help you to mitigate the risk of the customers' disappointment, while understanding why their expectations may be set too high or too low in the beginning stage.

This early phase in the customer relationship can be reciprocal in nature. You want to learn more about them, and so too is there an opportunity for them to learn more about you. While some customers may not necessarily want a relationship with your organisation, you can potentially develop a deeper understanding of them by offering them useful and relevant information about you while obtaining information about them in return. Perhaps you could provide them with back issues of your customer newsletters or copies of your social responsibility reports on their completion of registration information. At this early stage you are really looking for ways to start establishing a reciprocally beneficial and long-standing connection.

Your definition of the basic service you deliver is critical as a guiding principle for employees to deliver against and for customers to evaluate the quality of their experience against. It is, therefore, important that your organisation has a widely agreed definition of your basic service delivery and the interactions it does and does not include, such as payment conditions, exchanges, repairs and refunds. In addition, you need to publish the agreed time frames or service levels for any scheduled or regular interactions, such as billing, maintenance visits, complaints and general enquiries. This definition should take cognisance of the time frames that may differ for different customer types or segments.

It is also important to understand how the performance levels achieved in each of your defined basic service commitments affects your customers' behaviour. For example, is there a relationship that might exist between increased billing accuracy and reduced attrition, or between answering enquiries more slowly and a reduced cross sale rate? This analysis of performance levels includes both under-delivery and over-delivery. To what extent does delivering more than expected influence your customer behaviour?

Your on-going customer contact must be geared for relevant and strategically-aligned communication. This should be done in a structured way driven by defined contact strategies that may be applied to specific customer groups, segments, types or even to individual customers based on relevance and requirement. One contact strategy may relate to targeting a particular group because of its value and another may relate to a particular life cycle or stage. Your specific industry or market may even have regulatory requirements that enforce rules about customer contact that you need to factor into your contact strategies. The issue really becomes how you manage your contact strategies recognising that there may be multiple and different contact strategies that are applicable to the same customer.

Besides any specific regulatory requirements, your customer should also have a choice in how you contact them, which means being able to record their preferences and then making sure you honour those preferences. At the same time you need to keep the volume of communication at the right level to prevent over-contact with individual customers. What is deemed to be acceptable levels of communication can either be determined by the customer's specific preferences or by a common sense view of what is just too much. Your customer may not necessarily even want a relationship with you. As such, you need to recognise that the control of that relationship needs to move towards the customer. You will need mechanisms in place so that customers can self-select the type of relationship that they require, which may include what information they are prepared to exchange and what products and services interest them.

Your customer-facing employees are critical in developing long-term, successful relationships with your customers. You need to give these employees the requisite training, tools and support systems so that, wherever possible, they can resolve customer requests correctly the first time. While this concept may seem straightforward for a call centre environment, are you able to deliver this same result in your online channels? Best Buy's Twelpforce [79] is a great example of using social media to do just that.

In order to retain customers, your customer-facing staff should demonstrate empathy, accuracy and adherence to standards. Quality controls should be in place to listen to the tone of these engagements, through video or live observation or recorded audio. There is also advanced context analysis software and text analytical software that can automate the monitoring of the tone of conversations and the trends in sentiment being captured in the text based fields of systems.

When customer-facing employees deliver great customer experiences, managers and supervisors should be able to celebrate the moment through recognition of the employee and through appropriate rewards, recognising that this does not necessarily mean financial rewards. The default "employee of the month" approach just does not do enough. It's more about rewarding quickly and visibly.

As Sears did with their Employee-Customer-Profit Chain [37], so do you need to define what your correlation is between employee engagement, as demonstrated by attitude, satisfaction and commitment, and your levels of customer engagement. Gallup's research [76] provides hard evidence of that correlation, yet you need to define the details that are relevant to your organisation and share those widely to ensure they are given due consideration by all employees. The results of your research should then be compared to customer satisfaction research or any other customer related surveys in order to understand whether there is a correlation between the two.

Using exit barrier techniques to develop Retention is a tricky one to do well. Certain regulatory issues create opportunities to exploit an exit barrier and can be useful if managed effectively. However, complex and entangling contracts that restrict the customer from leaving may result in negative feelings and expressions. Apple's use of proprietary technology barriers is another example of how you can create a negative response. While there are positives and negatives of such an approach, just be very clear on what the unintended negative consequences might be.

Inertia techniques are another way to increase Retention and are especially useful if there is a renewal process involved. It brings into play the critical role of timing in how you manage renewals and contract renegotiations. Your data should provide insights into how you can get the timing of the renewal engagement just right so that you stimulate your customer to remain with you.

Pricing is a well-used technique to retain customers, and is especially useful when a stage in life cycle or a life stage itself indicates that attrition is an issue, such as someone becoming a pensioner and cutting back on their expenses. The key consideration is whether the price reduction is warranted for the value of that customer. If you have an in-depth understanding of your pricing and costing then you can make these kinds of decisions with intelligence. Sometimes these price reductions are introduced merely to show appreciation for loyalty.

Proactive Retention activity

Developing Retention capability requires a proactive strategy that looks ahead and plans for how best to keep customers and support those who wish to leave. For those customers who want to have a relationship with you, creating levels of engagement opportunity and implementing Retention programmes can support the development of those relationships. Being proactive also requires that you both recognise and reward those customers who are loyal while implementing special care for those who are at a high risk of loss. Wherever possible, customers who wish to leave should be convinced to stay if they're profitable or potentially profitable, and those who still wish to depart should exit on a positive note.

While some customers will not want to become involved with you, other customers may very well want to and doing so adds immense value to your organisation and deepens their relationship with you. You, therefore, need to understand customers' perceptions regarding engagement with your organisation. This will ascertain what their needs and expectations are, where they want to pro-actively contribute, and how involved they want to be.

Using the content created through your campaign and communication activity to drive customer involvement can be a powerful approach in proactive Retention. It requires that the content produced is consistently designed to encourage customers to become more involved, or alternatively, that communications are designed to deliver specific, persuasive and engaging messages. This principle then needs to be included in briefs for creative agencies and partners and the selection thereof.

In some cases, customers have a need for even deeper levels of involvement. As this is an opportunity that would add immense value to your organisation, it is worthwhile to have developed a range of experiences that enable greater levels of participation. This could include subscribing to an information feed, signing up to a group or a community, posting reviews, participating in product innovation and becoming a brand ambassador.

Developing specific communication messages designed to retain your customers can be used to communicate why they should stay with you. You would, therefore, hone in on your strengths and promote the reasons to stay. In some cases, I have seen these Retention messages being used to communicate the "hassle factor" of changing their provider compared with the ease of staying where they are. Testimonials are particularly powerful and could feature customers who've had a great experience or who are still with the organisation after many years.

There are points in the customer life cycle where attrition is higher than normal, as is the case when your mobile phone contract is due for renewal. The same applies to life stages, for example, when your customer starts a family or a business customer moves into bigger premises. These transition points might make your customer reflect and consider whether there is an opportunity to try something else. While quite likely not visible to the customer, you could have Retention programmes in place to mitigate the risk of the customer defecting. In the case in which your product is indeed renewal-based, being proactive means that you have planned, designed and prepared those special offers and incentives that would streamline the renewal process and dramatically increase the likelihood of that renewal taking place.

As may happen from time to time, you may have a product line that is discontinued. If there is no direct replacement within the portfolio, you need to consider what the next best alternative would be for your customers. This indicates that you're at least addressing the characteristics of the original product that were understood to be important to the customer and could even sell additional functionality that may have been introduced. Your frontline employees should be briefed with a specific message for those wanting the explanation as to how the next best alternative meets the customers' needs. You could even use incentives to encourage customers to use the best alternative product.

In order to reward loyalty you have to first understand the ways in which your customers, both loyal and lapsed, prefer to be rewarded. Your research in this regard should explore what your customers expect or what they would appreciate as a means of recognising their continued business. You could even approach customers who have left, asking them what they would have wanted as a means of recognising their loyalty. So often, customers move because there is no recognition of their value.

If you do not have your own proprietary loyalty programme, it may be worth exploring a third party programme. Typically, such a programme has a variety of sponsors, brands and retailers through which loyalty points can be earned and redeemed. The value to the customer is the broader applicability, and for your organisation, it would save you having to create your own. The proviso is that you have done enough research on the third party programme to feel assured that it will deliver both on its promise and on your brand promise too.

If you do offer a loyalty programme it is useful to provide customer-facing employees with visibility of the rewards used and the rewards that are available so that communication of this information to the customer can take place, if relevant, during engagement. As it is valuable to the customer, being reminded of benefits not claimed builds your relationship with them. They feel that someone is now paying attention and cares about them.

Managing Retention requires that you manage the risk of customers leaving. This means that you score all customers using a propensity model that predicts the likelihood of customers being lost within a defined time period. The development of this model requires an understanding of what the triggers indicating loss may be. These triggers may be really simple, such as the customer phoning to cancel an insurance policy. Many insurers have no "save team" in place to try to stop customers from cancelling. Often, the only interaction the customer receives is an e-mail confirming the policy has been cancelled.

Mitigating customer loss also requires that you have identified the behaviour indicators that may indicate a risk of loss. Customers considered at risk should be closely monitored across all channels to ensure that action is initiated to save that customer, should that risk be escalated. This information should then be provided through your systems to customer-facing employees to clearly flag for them when a customer they are dealing with is a high loss risk. Employees can then behave accordingly, going beyond the normal basic service. In this way you could change the mind-set of the customer and mitigate the risk of loss. In such cases, customer-impacting employees should be empowered through information and guidance on how to "go the extra mile" to try and retain those higher value customers who have been flagged as high risk. This might include the authorisation to bend rules, exceed limits and give free upgrades and add-ons to such customers.

You also need a formally constructed "save team" with the right processes and training to specifically deal with customers who want to leave. At a minimum you need such a team for your high value customers, whose loss will have the greatest impact on your organisation. It is clear that your "save team" should be staffed by capable and empathetic people. Within the team there is also room to consider levels of skills and expertise, with the most highly skilled staff allocated to your high value customers. The "save team" needs to have a realistic budget that it can spend in an appropriate way. Incentives offered to customers wanting to leave, such as an offer or gift, should be matched to the needs of the customer and to the reason for their wanting to leave. These incentives must have a real impact otherwise they might just infuriate the customer further.

Should a customer still choose to leave, the opportunity to win them back remains. "Sorry you're leaving" communications can be used to create an appropriate and impactful last message of farewell with the hope that they might return. O_2, a mobile service provider in the United Kingdom, did this very successfully [80]. This company purchased and mailed unbranded farewell cards containing personalised, hand-written messages with tactful reminders of the benefits customers would miss out on in the event of removing their custom.

There are of course many risks that exist when a customer exits. Research should be conducted with customers who have left and through other channels, such as social media, to understand the level and nature of any negative communication that is coming from existing customers prior, during and after them leaving. The depth of risk you face is also largely dependent on how you manage the exit. Even though your customer has chosen to leave it is in some ways even more important to consider the emotional dimension of the customer experience at that point in the life cycle. In reality, it does not take a lot of effort to ensure the relationship ends well, or as well as can be expected.

In planning ahead for a potential win-back opportunity, you need to maintain some level of information as to why customers left so you can address these issues prior to sending them win-back messages. Although they may have left, you should not delete information you have about them. It's important that when you approach these customers in the future, you have accurate historical information readily available to you so that you can demonstrate knowledge of the past relationship.

Managing dissatisfaction

Dissatisfaction requires active management and includes understanding the indicators and triggers for it occurring. Complaint management should be encouraged and even celebrated, integrating your own complaint process with any regulatory bodies that may lodge complaints with you on behalf of customers. Listening to and responding to wider dissatisfaction may require new approaches using digital channels, while customer relationships that have experienced challenges should be closely managed through and out of the danger zone.

Being able to manage dissatisfaction is dependent upon being able to identify it in the first place. Having defined indicators of dissatisfaction in place will support you to flag issues that may not have been communicated by the customer as a formal complaint. These indicators may be certain words or phrases used in communications or, even more subtly, certain behaviours that indicate dissatisfaction, such as not opening important e-mails. Customers' behaviour should be monitored for these indicators so that remedial action can be initiated.

While some organisations shy away from complaints, my view is that "complaints discovery" is free consulting. If you encourage your customers to complain, and you provide an easy and effective process to manage complaints through to resolution, you can unlock the valuable insights that your customers can contribute. This active encouragement of complaints should extend to your employees, who should be encouraged to record all instances of dissatisfaction, including issues not formally lodged yet consciously or subconsciously expressed. Your systems and processes should support this, even if it is a simple notes field that can be used to capture sentiment. Morning team huddles are another avenue to share employee insights about dissatisfaction that can either be addressed individually or systemically for wider issues.

Listening in on social media platforms using digital media tools and technologies is another way to monitor expressions that indicate dissatisfaction. Even though a complaint may have been made in a Facebook post or via a tweet, it is important that you manage this grievance in the same way that you would a formally lodged complaint. This process requires that you have very clearly defined categories, triggers and criteria that would determine when follow up is required.

Most organisations have some form of regulatory body that oversees their industry or governs certain quality criteria, such as a banking ombudsman or a consumer protection council. It is a dangerous trap to fall into the mind-set that the regulatory body is there to impede your progress. Instead, you should view their involvement as an opportunity to improve through their complaint process that they feed into yours. It simply represents another feed of insight that you can use to improve your customer relationships.

Part of this customer-centric mind-set is that the minimum standards set by the regulatory body should not become your standards. Instead, your organisation should move above and beyond those minimum standards. This indicates that your organisation is authentically committed to doing the right thing for customers, rather than being whipped into place to perform the bare minimum by a regulator. A successful and constructive relationship with your regulatory body will support the close cohesion between their complaints process and yours, resulting in the swift and effective resolution of customer complaints lodged through those regulatory bodies. While the regulatory bodies may have their own complaint management time frames and processes, you must make sure your service standards are higher, within commercially viable boundaries, to ensure that your company easily meets and exceeds the minimum regulatory requirements. It is also useful to review the reports from appropriate regulators to monitor the trends in specific customer complaints. Even if these complaints do not necessarily apply to you, they will certainly provide input that can help you refine your processes so that those very issues do not arise in your organisation.

Your own complaints process should be a well-defined, formal system that applies to all parts of your organisation with clear standards and visibility of its effective functioning. Regardless of who submits the complaint, it should follow the same process that all complaints do. It is also essential you have a very clear definition of what a complaint is compared to an enquiry or contact. The standards that apply to the complaint management process should be easily and readily available so that your customers and your customer-facing employees are clear on what can be expected. For example, your customer must know exactly when they can expect a response at each stage in the process.

Wherever possible, the complaint should be resolved immediately and by the person who has taken the complaint. The longer you leave the complaint unresolved, the more annoyed the customer is likely to become. This requires good training, the right information and clear guidelines on what can be done to meet this objective of immediacy and urgency. You may find that you need to implement process optimisation to shorten the time and activity distance between the complaint being lodged and resolved.

In conjunction, you need to analyse your complaints at a root cause level, which should not halt the process of resolving the issues promptly. Your processes should enable you to do both activities at the same time — resolve the issue and understand its root cause. Some form of reporting should then be made available to customers so that they understand that you have taken the issue seriously and that it is going to create meaningful change. If you cannot settle the issue in the short term, create the awareness and transparency with your customers so that they understand what is required to resolve the problem and they can rest assured that your company is committed to taking action.

At a wider level there is also a need to keep your finger on the pulse of any relevant dissatisfaction or trends on social media that you need to pay attention to. This is beyond the individual expressions of dissatisfaction and refers more to patterns in changing sentiment. Perhaps it makes more sense for your organisation to outsource this function if you do not have the expertise required. Certainly, listening analytics tools would partly support the automation of this process.

Sometimes your "fans" are a powerful tool to help you address dissatisfaction, yet your ability to leverage this is directly related to the relationship you have formed with your "fan base". Committed "fans" may counter negative sentiment and defend your brand on your behalf. They could also support you by solving problems. You, therefore, need to find ways to both encourage this positive behaviour and even reward your supporters for their efforts.

The hallmark of a customer-centric organisation is the ability to bridge the silos within an organisation and to demonstrate an agile and integrated approach to solving problems. In the event of a major service issue or an emerging service pressure point, you need to have the ability to respond quickly. This will be enabled by monitoring all interaction points across your organisation, having clear escalation processes and ensuring all insights derived and actions required are disseminated to the right team for speedy resolution.

For customers who have been flagged as dissatisfied, it is important that the visibility of that dissatisfaction continues for a period long enough that the relationship can be recovered to a large extent. This action involves supporting customer-facing employees to continue to serve these customers with a conscious awareness of their potentially fragile state and taking particular care to serve them well. Once the flag has been removed, you still need to be able to see the history of that dissatisfaction. While it would be a positive achievement that an issue with a customer had been resolved, there might still be damage to the relationship that requires careful management. You, therefore, need clear criteria to govern the extent to which that relationship is being actively managed back into health. Activity such as communication, compensation and genuine remorse needs to be explicitly planned for and applied. In order for learning to take place, you need to research the extent to which the complaints and dissatisfaction processes were effective in dealing with the issues raised and how the customer felt going through these processes. It is ideal that this occurs quite soon after the resolution process so that the experience is still fresh in the customers' minds while still giving them enough time to reflect fully on the outcome.

While it may be tempting to acquire new customers at the expense of existing ones, there is a wealth of value sitting within your existing customer base that should be protected. A Retention strategy focuses on developing this value through specific, targeted initiatives aimed at deepening the relationship with existing customers even further.

Transformation questions

- Has the relationship and correlation (if any) between stated customer satisfaction (from research) and measured loyalty (from behavioural analysis) been examined and documented?
- Has a clear definition of "customer loss", as opposed to product line loss, been agreed to and is this monitored and reported on?
- Even though they may vary by customer type or value, are service levels for all basic service delivery interactions formally documented and published?
- Are customers given the capability to manage their relationship with you by choosing elements such as products of interest, type of dialogue and frequency of contact?
- Have loyal and lapsed customers been researched in terms of the way they want or would have wanted their loyalty recognised and rewarded?
- Are customers who are identified as being "at risk" flagged in a prominent way on all systems used to interact with customers?
- Is explicit relationship recovery activity (communication, compensation, apology, etc.) applied to individual customers?
- Is Retention viewed as an important driver of customer value?
- Are you clear as to how you will retain your most profitable customers?
- Does your organisation have a specific focus on Retention?
- Do you understand the business impact of improvements in your customer Retention strategies?
- Is there clarity as to the required behavioural changes that will enhance customer Retention?
- Have you identified the most important two or three customer-related value and behaviour metrics that specifically relate to customer Retention strategies within your industry or company?
- Are service standards and targets developed to deliver what is best for the customer rather than to meet any specific regulatory requirements?
- Do you make sure that existing clients aren't prejudiced through special offers that are compiled in an effort to acquire new customers?
- Do you ensure that you do not alienate customers through unethical behaviour?
- Do you mourn the loss of a customer?

Case study – USAA leads from the front

USAA is an American bank and insurance company. Even though it is a private company, it serves a very specific market — the United States military and their families [81]. With over $68.3 billion in assets and an extremely niche market, USAA has managed to achieve excellence in customer service and is a world leading example of a highly effective retention strategy. USAA has held the first or second spot in the annual Customer Service Champs ranking for *Bloomberg BusinessWeek* for fours year in a row, yet what is even more startling is their retention rate — 97.8%.

Their ability to deliver this exceptional level of retention is due to the depth of their understanding of the niche market that they serve. It allows them to anticipate their customers' needs, resulting is service offerings that directly deliver on those needs. For example, when a military member wants to deposit a check, they do not need to post it or get to a bank. If you are stationed in Afghanistan this is indeed impossible. Instead, you can take a picture of your cheque with your mobile phone and send it to USAA through a mobile app. Within minutes the cheque is deposited into your account. Other services include sending text balances to your mobile phone and reducing car premiums while you are stationed away from home. There is also a personal touch that would be difficult to find anywhere else. As Staff Sergeant Corey Mason says: "It's not every day I get addressed 'sergeant' by a customer service agent."

As USAA broadens its customer base, it will be challenged to maintain this level of understanding and intimacy that has driven the company's outstanding success to date. Bruce Temkin, a leading customer-centricity specialist, studied USAA and concurs [81]: "The real trick for USAA will be how they continue to serve their core military customer while serving this broader set. It can get really messy if they grow too fast."

CHAPTER 15:

EFFICIENCY

Transformation Intent

In treating different customers differently, your organisation needs to develop the capability to optimise customer profitability through the efficient calculation, allocation and control of customer costs in retaining, acquiring and developing your customers across all segments and channels. This enables you to perform value analysis in a way that supports your customer engagement within the defined profit bands per customer and per segment, and if need be, influencing their behaviour to reduce the cost-to-serve or even terminating them as customers if necessary.

The cost-to-serve

Efficiency is the second REAP lever and seeks to manage customer costs from a customer profitability perspective. This approach evaluates costs in light of the value of the customer those costs are incurred for. The cost-to-serve is relative to the type of customer and his or her behaviour. The acceptability of these costs is based on what that customer or the overall segment is currently and potentially worth to your organisation, not only in direct monetary terms but also in advocacy and influence. In treating different customers differently, you can determine where you should spend less and where you could potentially spend more.

A customer-centric approach to Efficiency requires that you are able to define what costs are customer-related, allocate those costs effectively and manage those costs according to your customer profitability guidelines. Once customer costs have been identified, calculated and allocated, optimising these customer costs becomes a task that requires careful attention. There are a variety of approaches that can be adopted, depending on your company strategy. These tactics include matching customers to the right channel, controlling the costs of acquisition, reducing marketing costs and the cost-to-serve overall, reducing customer process failure costs and exiting those customers too expensive to serve.

For most organisations this is a hugely challenging process to get right, principally because of the mind-set change required as well as the traditional, functional or silo-based organisational structures in place. Each product or business unit is often required to be profitable in its own right and this, in turn, influences how that unit makes its decisions in an attempt to fulfil the expectations held of it. Organisations functioning in such a manner will struggle to develop the systems-thinking and holistic perspective that customer profitability demands, as opposed to the perspective that product or business unit profitability requires. Perhaps a good litmus test would be to ask yourself the following question: "Would it be acceptable within your organisation to have an unprofitable product if that product was associated with a profitable customer?"

"First Union is but one example of a company that has adopted new strategies to increase shareholder value. Although exceeding customer expectations is a worthy goal, companies recognise that exceeding those expectations profitably is necessary for long term corporate viability. To improve corporate profitability and shareholder value, companies must have a more complete understanding of the drivers of value in their organisations. To do this, companies increasingly focus on the value drivers and on the causal relationships among employee satisfaction, customer satisfaction, customer profitability and corporate profitability. Improved corporate profitability requires a deeper understanding of ways to increase customer revenues and decrease customer costs. Essential components of improved customer profitability include: the analysis of the cost of customer service through ABC (activity-based costing); the measurement of the lifetime value of a customer; and the development of long-term customer relationships for increased revenues and profits" [17].

Calculating and allocating costs

In order to calculate customer costs, you have to determine which costs are directly related to the customer. It is not often that you see organisations doing this computation well, especially as it requires a detailed, activity-based approach. What are the key activities involved in managing your customers? Have you been able to identify the cost of an inbound service call, a sales visit, a sales lunch, processing a refund, sending a direct communication, handling a complaint or an executive visit? For each of your customer activities you need to have allocated a cost that is agreed upon with the finance division. This calculation forms the foundation of your customer level activity-based costing.

Your financial systems must enable you to extract the transactions and associated costs per customer. You may find that this data needs to be automatically streamed from multiple systems in order to provide this view. Where your systems are not able to specifically allocate costs, some kind of proxy or estimate should be used. This requires that your company has in place an agreed methodology for estimating specific costs and allocating these at a customer level.

In an ideal world, your actual and estimated direct customer costs would be updated against your customer's profile in real-time, giving you a truly dynamic view of what each customer's cost-to-serve is. In reality this is not always possible. You should, however, at least have a defined, regular update that takes place with sufficient frequency that it does not inhibit accurate decision-making. For direct customer costs that span separate divisions you need to allocate these costs accordingly, with at least your Acquisition costs separated from management and servicing costs. Costs can typically be higher during the Acquisition stage of new customers, compared to the on-going management costs required to retain those customers. Being able to discern between these two categories is important in that it provides a clearer picture of what Acquisition per customer really costs as opposed to an average Acquisition cost.

When you are able to integrate customer costs in a way that can facilitate analysis of the true value of a customer, then you have the makings of customer-centric Efficiency. Customers using the same product may have different costs depending on how they behave. Customer A may prefer e-mail contact and may hardly ever require support, while Customer B may contact the call centre frequently with copious complaints that need to be managed. The cost-to-serve of Customer B is significantly greater than Customer A for the same product and, therefore, Customer B has a significantly lower profitability, all other things being equal. Understanding this level of financial detail and providing it to frontline employees then allows for a very conscious approach to what offers are provided to Customer B. That being said, even if you just have a cost-to-serve understanding at a segment level, you are already significantly ahead of many other organisations.

Key customers are those large customers that typically require multiple points of contact and, quite likely, need a team to manage them. This is usually more relevant for business-to-business relationships. Due to the complexity and importance of managing key customers well and efficiently, it is particularly relevant to use a customer profitability approach in the management of their accounts. This approach includes calculating profitability and then monitoring that profitability on an on-going basis, using real cost data that has been accurately allocated for the majority of the customer's direct costs. All of the team involved in engaging with that customer, including sales, service, marketing and technical support, should have access to the cost and profitability data of that customer. With specific objectives set regarding those costs, it is then possible to set and issue rewards and incentives for reaching longer term profitability objectives, rather than more simplistic targets such as revenue or volume.

Bearing in mind the complexity of customer-based profitability, it is best that you have a specific team responsible for understanding, monitoring and managing customer costs. Managing costs also requires the broad-based support of employees so that everyone can make a positive impact on managing customer-related costs. Company-wide communication needs to create clarity on the importance of understanding and controlling these costs. This requires a balanced view that does not focus on generic cost reduction but rather explains the importance of matching costs to customer value. This approach raises the level of awareness that most, if not all, customer activities have an associated cost and, although individually those costs may be small, they can become substantial when put together for an individual customer or for a group of customers.

Controlling costs

Your channels are a critical part of your capability to deliver, and you should have a cost perspective for each channel across the three dimensions of Retention, Acquisition and Penetration. As an example, the Acquisition cost of a customer through an online channel is likely to be much lower than the Acquisition cost through a direct sales force. If you can understand the relative differences in costs between these levers and channels, then the channel management function can optimise profitability by matching customers and channels more effectively. This procedure requires that channel management do, in fact, have the influence to optimise the channels used for Retention, Acquisition and Penetration initiatives across different types of customers, if those costs become too high. At the same time, customers should have the right to engage with you using their channel of preference and you should, therefore, be able to support them accordingly without discrimination.

Once you have a clear idea of the cost of each channel for your Retention, Acquisition and Penetration levers, you may want to exercise some control over which channels customers use, factoring in the added complexity of the customer segments. Ultimately, the choice in channel is your customers' to make. However, if you understand your customers' needs and their profitability, you can find ways that your lower cost channels can possibly support these needs. You can also factor this understanding into your channel strategy and planning so that you create compelling reasons for customers to use the channel you would like them to.

Controlling the costs of Acquisition is a challenging task as you need to break the mind-set that "a sale is a sale" and that it is unnecessary to consider the cost of securing that sale. This requires calculating and, possibly, setting the maximum acceptable cost of Acquisition relative to the value of a customer in each customer segment. This action is tied directly to the need to prevent "Acquisition at any cost". At an individual customer level, there needs to be some indication for direct sales employees of where the threshold is beyond which there is no point acquiring that customer due to their poor projected profitability. While this may be frustrating for sales agents who want to close deals to earn commission, continuing to do so erodes overall profitability. This same principle also applies in cases where a high Acquisition cost is justified due to the high lifetime value of the customer – the cost of acquiring that customer relative to their long-term value is the most critical consideration.

One of the key costs incurred in Acquisition is the commission generated for sales agents. I have seen call centre environments in which the moment the customer agrees to the sale, the agent earns his or her commission. A few weeks later, when that sale is either not fully activated or lapses, there is already a loss that has been incurred. Agents' commissions should, therefore, only be paid once customers are "active". You need to define carefully what "active" means. In your organisation it may refer to the date the customer starts paying and in another organisation it may be after a three-month period of payments being made.

Almost all marketing campaigns are created to drive sales. While marketers may claim that they specifically design campaigns for Acquisition, Retention and Penetration (cross-sell and up-sell), I have yet to experience a Retention campaign through outdoor or above-the-line advertising, or even through a direct communication, that just simply says "thank you for being a customer". While it is challenging to quantify the return from a Retention campaign, it is equally important not to ignore the value it can create in light of its cost to deliver.

In many organisations the business case justification for a marketing campaign normally has to be very thorough in order to get it signed off. However, from the moment that campaign goes "live", the controls are often very slack. What is needed is the ability to evaluate how that campaign is performing once it is live and adjusting the campaign factors in line with this information or, perhaps, even cancelling that campaign if it is not delivering. This kind of optimisation process, and the software that supports it, will provide greater campaign cost efficiency compared to a campaign poorly targeted and not monitored while in progress. Once the campaign has been completed, post-campaign reviews provide invaluable insight that supports the optimisation of the next campaign.

Controlling costs is all about getting the most value out of the budget that you have. When it comes to your marketing budget, if you have clear segment information, understand your customers' needs and have effective propensity modelling, you are able to allocate your budget across segments and according to your Retention, Acquisition and Penetration priorities. Even if you had exactly the same budget as you had the previous year, and you deployed it differently across your customer segments, you could see a marked improvement in your return on spend.

Part of working with your marketing budget effectively includes looking for ways to maximise the marketing opportunity in every contact with your customer, thereby reducing your marketing costs. If your customer is contacting you with a service request or an enquiry, be it online or offline, this is an excellent opportunity to leverage this engagement by including a specific and relevant offer to your customer if appropriate. You save on the cost of the outbound communication and, if done right, the customers do not feel that they have been targeted through a direct campaign. This approach requires a high level of integration between your systems and channels, so that the same campaign data that outbound communications may use to sell are accessible and ready to be used in the other direction. It is critical that you make sure this data is appropriate to the situation. The last thing an irate customer needs to hear on a complaint call is the latest offer being sold to them.

Within a customer segment there will always be variations in the cost-to-serve by virtue of the fact that customers ultimately behave differently. In the quest for continuous improvement, if there are any particular cost-to-serve differences across a segment, these differences should be analysed to determine whether they are significant enough to warrant attention and what their cause may be. One way to reduce the cost-to-serve is by influencing customers' buying behaviours in a way that reduces their cost-to-serve, whilst still recognising their needs and, hopefully, delivering a superior experience. If you can see from your analyses that encouraging customers to purchase from you in a slightly different way would reduce your cost-to-serve, you could offer financial incentives such as a discount to encourage them to change their behaviour. This may relate to transaction-related costs in processes such as ordering and delivery. If you know the baseline number then you can potentially reduce costs while still serving customers effectively. Providing customer self-service options can also be used to reduce the cost-to-serve and, in the new climate of digital and social channels, many customers prefer self-service. You should, therefore, embark upon a process that will help you to understand what the opportunities may be and what cost benefits may accrue through self-service activities. The same applies to providing customers with the ability to easily update their own information. There is a direct benefit to you and your customer in doing so.

A customer process failure is any process that has not delivered according to standard and, as a result, incurs further costs to correct it. As that additional cost has not been planned for in cost-to-serve, careful management of such failures is critical for cost efficiency. For example, you may have run an extensive campaign that generated new sales, yet those sales required accurate address details in order to deliver your products. If the address data was captured incorrectly, you would need to follow up on each order to obtain the correct address and repeat the process all over again. That failure would have a financial and reputational cost associated with it. You, therefore, need to identify what the most common types of failure are in your organisation, along with identifying what the cost of such failures would be.

If you considered the process failure cost in relation to the customer experience degradation that required remedial action, you could prioritise which action gets priority because you can now understand the cost impact of each alternative. It is obviously not enough just to understand your cost of failure and the reasons for process failure. You also need to pro-actively look for points of failure before they materialise. An analysis of inbound contacts, including social media, will reveal areas of potential failure that can be corrected before too much damage occurs.

In some cases, the only way to control unprofitable customers is to exit them from your organisation or reduce your level of engagement with them. You could reduce the level of service or marketing provided to them when the unavoidable costs of transacting with them are too high to justify the level of revenue that they generate. Their higher costs may relate to the mix of products that they buy, the specific support they require, or perhaps even due to a remote location or specialised requirements. This reduction does not mean that their quality of service is in any way changed, rather just the scope of it.

If the right level of profitability cannot be achieved irrespective of a change in engagement then you may need to exit that customer altogether. To do so you would need to have the right measures and processes in place to explicitly manage them out while ensuring that you manage that process carefully to minimise any damage. Some companies openly incentivise such customers to exit. Sprint Nextel, the third largest US wireless provider, terminated the contracts of 1,000 of its subscribers due to the high costs of servicing them. These customers called with enquiries and complaints an average of 25 times a month — 40 times higher than the average customer [82]. You have to find the balance though. You don't want customers to feel singled out or that they've done something wrong, while at the same time, you also have to be direct about your reasons for termination. The absolute clarity of your message, process and justification is essential.

The customer-centric approach to Efficiency requires a different mind-set and view on profitability measurement — an in-depth understanding of customers and a cost-to-serve approach to driving customer profitability, while continuing to meet customers' needs. The conscious, deliberate calculation and allocation of accurate direct and indirect customer costs creates a solid foundation upon which you can then control these costs and deliver upon your strategic objectives.

Transformation questions

- Have all identifiable costs been allocated to individual customers and are they being included in value analysis activity?
- Do all staff understand the critical importance of effective customer cost management and is there clear responsibility for achieving this for all types of customers?
- Are the relative costs of acquiring, retaining and developing customers by each channel understood and do they have an influence on your customers' allocation or entitlement to each channel?
- Are the drivers of cost-to-serve variation understood and is the overall level being reduced by changing buying behaviours and maximizing the use of self-service wherever possible?
- Does your organisation fully value the importance of customer experience and customer service?
- Does your organisation see customer experience and customer service as a source of positive value rather than as a cost function?
- Do you understand which customers you can afford to spend more on?
- Have you investigated the correlation between the provision of unique and differentiated customer experience and revenue generation?
- Are ethics compromised in your quest for efficiency?

Case study - RBC invests in their future

The Royal Bank of Canada Financial Group (RBC) is the largest financial institution in Canada and operates in 30 countries around the world. RBC is also one of the largest banks in the world, based on its market capitalisation.

Even though this organisation had focused on delivering great service for many years, the real "wakeup call" came for RBC in the mid-2000s when they realised that they were not differentiated in their market, finding themselves in the middle of the pack amongst competitors. Even more startlingly, they discovered that within one year, 26% of their high value clients had defected. This desertion translated into $165 million net income before tax lost in the personal side of the business and another $30 million lost in their business markets [83]. For the board of directors and the senior team this loss was the catalyst for doing things differently.

RBC introduced a new vision that still guides them today — "always earning the right to be our customers' first choice" — and a new strategic priority entitled "superior client experience" in order to communicate the importance of this focus and ignite the organisation into action. Even though delivering a superior customer experience is fraught with complexity, such as multiple channels, products and segments, RBC has shown that if there is real commitment to customer-centricity then results will be visible in a very short time frame.

One of the many ways in which RBC has subsequently demonstrated customer-centric excellence is the calculation and management of its customer costs. This is driven by a customer profitability view of the organisation. As a result of identifying that 17% of their customers in their retail division earned 93% of their profits for that division, RBC concentrated its efforts on the 17% while looking for ways to discourage non-profitable or low profit customers [84]. RBC implemented activity-based costing to allocate costs to specific customer activities while monitoring its cost-to-serve through a variety of its channels. As a result, RBC understands which customers are profitable and which ones are not. With this insight the management can take action to address non-profitable customers and segments. RBC has also been able to link customer profitability to shareholder value, using a price/earnings (P/E) multiple that, when compared to the market average, helps the bank to evaluate the investment value of a particular customer segment.

This kind of sophistication in customer profitability modelling and customer-centricity is rare to find and challenging to implement and maintain. RBC's achievements mean that it is possible for other organisations to do the same, as long as the will and commitment is there to do it. The evidence demonstrated by RBC shows the tangible result of doing so. On the 3 March 2011, RBC announced that its first quarter results were 23% higher than the previous quarter and 64% higher than the same quarter of the previous year.

● CHAPTER 16:

● ACQUISITION

Transformation Intent

A customer-centric Acquisition approach begins with a clear and intimate understanding of your customer universe and the factors that impact your ability to sell to them. Acquiring your share of this customer universe is achieved through appropriate targeted marketing activity across a broad range of relevant channels and media, and interest generated is managed effectively so that prospects are kept warm until the sale is closed. While the sales process itself should focus on closing the sale, it should also take into account effective lead management, specific sales targets and rewards and careful controls over pricing. Customer-centricity also recognises that new clients have not been secured until you have taken them through an experience-based initiation process, where they are made to feel welcome and are well informed.

Colonizing your customer universe

Acquisition is the third REAP lever and focuses on the specific, practical activities that will support you to increase both the volume and quality of new customers. Whereas Retention ensures that the customers you have stay with you and Penetration deals with customer development (cross-selling and up-selling), Acquisition explores ways in which you can increase the size of your customer universe and your share of it.

Your customer universe is the total size of the market within which your organisation operates or could operate. Underlying this whole principle of the customer universe is an understanding of whether your growth means that you now have a greater share of the existing overall universe or whether you are in fact growing the size of this overall universe or both. In order to colonise this overall universe and increase your share of it, you need to understand the different facets of Acquisition, including how big your share could be in the future, how effective you are at selling to both current and potential customers and what the ideal, perfect current and potential customer would be for your organisation. In sourcing new prospects, you have to be effective at finding prospects in the right places, leveraging the influencers and referrers, ensuring your propositions are relevant, and potentially even winning back lost customers. In the early stages of prospect interest there is also much to do to keep prospective customers engaged, while leveraging communities of interest and managing prospects that seem likely to convert to sales. In converting sales, managed lead processes will help you to close those sales whilst making sure, if possible, that you minimise the number of customers you acquire who do not meet your minimum requirements. Lastly, new customers should be made to feel welcome, informed and confident with the start of their new relationship with you.

Acquisition can, in certain cases, be a very costly process for an organisation and, if not effective, can be unprofitable. A customer-centric approach, therefore, requires a specific and purposeful strategy that embraces the bigger picture of what the future customer universe could look like and what you need to do to capture a greater share, while matching that vision with detailed action.

Understanding your universe

Developing a deep understanding of the Acquisition lever requires that you understand your customer universe. You need to research it to determine as accurately as possible what the size of that universe is for each of your markets, including its current size and its future potential. This research process requires more than just using existing statistics that may have been produced by governmental or official bodies. This approach serves to counter the negative practise of just adding a percentage onto your last year's sales figures to determine a future target.

Within the overall customer universe you also have to determine what proportion of that universe, current and future, you may be able to realistically capture and retain. In taking this insight to another level, you could then estimate how the current customer universe may be divided between providers. This estimation requires you to explore a lot deeper than simply using market share, value and volume estimates, or even assuming that the average customer values are the same across all providers.

Another aspect of developing a deep understanding of your Acquisition capability is the effectiveness of your sales. If you can understand the reasons why your sales process fails to convert a prospect into a customer, you can then implement the necessary changes to improve your Acquisition results through a better proposition with greater relevance. You might also find that there are specific failure points in your sales cycle. You need to identify what these failure points may be so that you can correct them.

As an example of the above situation, you might have a very strong promotional campaign that creates much "hype" and interest, yet when prospective customers see the detail of the proposition and realise that it does not deliver the expectation that the promotions created, you might have a sudden drop off right at the end of the sales cycle. In this example you would, therefore, need to analyse why those prospective customers did not buy at the last minute. In many cases, the failure points that are of the greatest concern are those that occur right at the end of the sales cycle or even the cancellation of sales just after the perceived completion of the sale if your process provides for a cooling off period. The reason that these failed processes need such critical attention is due to the accumulated Acquisition cost that has been incurred up to that point. Understanding the real reasons that someone did not become a customer will be very insightful in improving future sales processes and value propositions. Perhaps you should also bear in mind that, while it is natural to consider the reasons for someone saying "no", it is also useful to include research into why someone said "yes".

As an organisation you would have both internal and external factors that affect your sales effectiveness. Your internal or controllable factors, such as pricing, advertising and incentives, should be regularly analysed to understand the impact they have on sales. The external, or uncontrollable factors, include seasonality and competitive action. While these kinds of factors may be beyond your control, you can, nevertheless, understand what their impact may be in reducing the effectiveness of your sales. By understanding the factors that have the greatest impact on your financial sustainability you can work to mitigate the risk of these impacts.

In a perfect world, every customer would be a "good" customer. In reality this is not the case. However, it is within your grasp to understand what makes a "good" new customer. If you can understand the profile or persona of such a "good" customer and where you might find such customers, you can specifically focus on increasing the number of these customers. There is an inherent challenge in defining what "good" means. While your ideal characteristics may include hassle-free, loyal and profitable, your proposition and purpose for existence may need to accommodate a different scenario. Consider health insurance for example. Is it fair to define a "good" customer as one who doesn't claim? I don't think so!

Once you have defined what "good" means, you can analyse how good customers of the past had been acquired and from where. Are there any distinctive characteristics in the Acquisition process that would help to attract more customers of this kind? What channels were used? Were there any other behavioural or attitudinal factors during the Acquisition process that would be useful to understand? How long did it take for these customers to make a decision? What was the reason for their choice? Were there any other influences that are relevant?

In understanding new customers in general, geo-demographics information can prove very insightful, especially if it sheds some light on "good" customers as you have defined them. This includes age, gender, location, social group and nationality for individual customers and size and sector for business customers. Socio-graphic information on new customers provides insights into the social behaviour of these customers. This can directly improve the Acquisition process by leveraging the positive social influences that support successful Acquisition.

Identifying good new customers

By using the profile of "good" customers already identified, you can then define the specific characteristics of these "good" customers and clearly articulate those characteristics into a cohesive description that can be widely distributed to employees and channel partners. In creating awareness of the early indicators for the so called "good" customers, you can increase the percentage of such customers obtained through Acquisition initiatives.

It is best practice to be really clear on where you might find good customers within your customer universe. This means understanding which part of that universe will hold the highest number or proportion of customers that exhibit the indicators of good customers. You can now be much more effective in the quality of Acquisition and the efficiency of the costs incurred, by understanding the pain points and offering the best solution and experience. This requires that you look across your organisation for those people, teams or groups that have the best access to your defined "good" customers. By using this access you can provide specific support to maximise the potential to reach those target customers.

In identifying new prospects, do not ignore the importance of harnessing those influencers and referrers most likely to direct good prospects to your organisation, such as trade associations and online communities. You need to develop appropriate relationships with these groups, bodies and individuals to fully harness their potential.

One such influencer may be aggregators and comparators, which tend to provide price comparisons across a market that may both positively and negatively influence a purchase decision with you. You need a mechanism in place to review the presence and activity of such providers in order to understand what their likely impact may be and to determine your extent of direct involvement. So often these types of tools are driven by price. If your proposition is not about lowest price, you could be at a distinct disadvantage through your actual proposition not being visible and your message, therefore, not coming across.

Another source of new prospects is your customers themselves. Ensure that you maximise this potential through specific processes that encourage customer referrals and reviews, and that you make it easy for them to do so, perhaps even through a specific and dedicated channel. While you can use referral incentives and paid referrals, the real value lays in impartial referrals, such as customer testimonials and positive expressions that encourage others to purchase. You then need to build these customer messages into your existing communication activity to make it easy for prospects to access referrals.

Within your base of active referrers, you may have certain individuals who are ready to be moved to a higher level of referral activity for you. This next level may include being a spokesperson, hosting an event or talking to a focus group. Identify who these people are and provide them with support to do so. Perhaps this would involve providing them with access to new products in advance of those products being made available to the market, or even providing them with tools they can use for promoting your products or services. Ford have done this very successfully with the Fiesta Movement, a non-traditional social media campaign where 100 powerful social media influencers were given a Fiesta to drive so they could tweet about the experience. At the time this resulted in 6,000 pre-orders of the Fiesta and the development of interest in 100,000 prospects — all without a single vehicle in a showroom.

Marketing plays a critical role in driving your Acquisition strategy. You, therefore, need a specific Acquisition marketing strategy for each target group that is matched to the type of prospect that group contains as well as the type of customers these prospects are likely to become. The type of prospect then defines the marketing message, value proposition, product features and benefits focus. You need to connect with these target customers as directly as possible, be that through online or offline mechanisms. If you engage through intermediaries you should support these partners to create this close connection themselves, whilst ensuring that your proposition, as the originator, is understood. This direct-to-prospect Acquisition approach should be applied cost effectively in relation to the value of the target customers.

The other Acquisition resource at your disposal is your online and owned sources that can be specifically optimised to make sure the right prospects are connected with and drawn into the Acquisition process. This includes ensuring that your online content has been optimised for relevant search engines using the tagging and keywords that are most appropriate.

Your Acquisition processes should also involve an assessment of what the likely impact may be of an Acquisition offer on existing customers, making sure that they are not penalised or feel worse off than newly acquired customers. O_2, a mobile phone provider in the United Kingdom, sought to do just that through its "Fair Deal" practice. In this business practice, O_2 commits that a customer will never be penalised through an offer made to new customers. This approach significantly differentiates O_2 in a market well-known for prejudicing existing customers in the quest to rapidly acquire new ones.

For Acquisition campaigns involving the winning-back of previous customers, there are a few particular facets that should be taken into account. Lost customers should be scored according to clear criteria, or a model or methodology, to ascertain which customers you want back and which you may not. Using the reasons why certain customers left in the first place, you can then match them to propositions that address the exact issues that drove them away. The message you then share with them in a win-back Acquisition campaign will be different from a message in a brand new Acquisition, because your customers expect you to know that there's a history. They expect you to remember them. A specific example is a win-back campaign launched by Vodafone. Win-back letters sent to its business customers were creatively formatted as a CV with a covering letter, which both recognises the history with the customers and brings to their attention the reasons they should come back. This creative approach should certainly capture the attention of lost customers, especially because it frames the new start as a collaborative business partnership.

A win-back customer experience journey map would likely focus on recognising the reason for their loss, encouraging re-engagement, introducing the win-back proposition and then communicating about what has been fixed so that they don't experience the same problem upon return. When they do return, they should be recognised as returning customers with an appropriate win-back welcoming phase. It goes without saying that those people involved in win-back campaigns should have access to the reasons why these customers left. This information will support the win-back team to ensure their communications are relevant, appropriate and considerate in light of the customers' history.

Engaging customer interest

For more complex and higher value sales, you may need to specifically manage a prospect in the early phase of engagement to ensure that they are carried from prospect through to a sale. If the nature of your Acquisition process is one where the prospect has to wait for a time period before the sale can be concluded, you can offer increasing levels of engagement as the prospect gets closer to formally buying. This serves to build up excitement while encouraging customers to share more information with you along the way. Mini Cooper is an excellent example of building customer enthusiasm. Not only do buyers customise their car, but once they place their order, they receive notifications as their car goes through its creation and delivery processes. This creates excitement and reinforces in the prospect's mind that they have made the right decision.

You can also use above-the-line (ATL) marketing activity to encourage prospects to stay engaged with you and learn more in the process. You could use a variety of channels, such as online, video, QR codes to access information via mobile channels, or social media. The objective would be to keep the conversation and the experience in the forefront of the prospect's mind. The content you use for Acquisition is equally important. It should be designed in a way that it can be used across a variety of channels and even devices, such as mobile phones and tablets. This creates flexibility in how you effectively reach your prospects while recognising their media consumption preferences.

Communities of interest are another way that you can keep the fires of interest burning. Through having depth in your understanding of your target customers you should be able to identify formal and informal networks or communities of interest through which it is possible to engage with prospective customers. This requires careful management to demonstrate your support of those communities rather than your attempt to manage, control and sell. You have to demonstrate your interaction and participation in those communities, in which you share in an open way. As an example, Amazon.com, through its publishing divisions, have been encouraging some of their staff to become actively and visibly involved in popular writing networks, where a wealth of future authors looking to be published can be found. The manner in which Amazon.com has established these networks makes it an exciting and participative process and not a way to sell at every opportunity.

The content that you provide to these communities of interest should be engaging, valuable and aimed at building trust. Reworked propositions and blatant sales messages would only serve to close off these communities from you. You will also typically find that within these communities there are particular members who are more influential than others. It's worth identifying who these influential people are so that you can ensure they stay engaged with you and that you are aware of the kind of expressions they make.

Detecting sales interest will help you ascertain the extent to which you are managing to create and grow interest. There are a variety of approaches that will give you this feedback. Your digital and social channels are one such avenue. You should be able to monitor your web site, social media accounts and corporate blogs to determine whether or not the nature of conversations that are taking place around your content is indicative that the content is generating interest.

Developing an understanding of the behaviours that indicate interest and defining those criteria helps you to identify those prospects that are in the category of "probably interested". The indicators of their interest could include becoming a "follower" or "fan", contacting the call centre, downloading a brochure, forwarding and sharing your content, and web page views. This area is in itself quite tricky because there is so much distrust for unsolicited marketing pitches that you have to be careful and conscious of how you take those prospects that you deem to be "probably interested" to the next level. If the right processes are in place and your front line employees are well trained, it should be possible to identify those prospective customers that meet the interest criteria even from general enquiries made.

Once an interested prospect is ready to take the next step on the journey with you, they need to be able to make sales enquiries with you using any format or medium in the market that they choose to use. Technology in many ways makes the path to purchase less linear and more dynamic. With multiple contact points available, you need to monitor all the channels that prospective customers may simultaneously use for their enquiries.

The sales enquiry is also a critical point to gather "first interest" data about the prospect if possible. The set of data to be collected should be clearly defined as well as consistently applied across your entire organisation. There is a direct link in this area with your customer information plan, which prioritises what data you might want to collect at the point of first contact and sets the criteria for data quality. This is often a bare minimum set of data that takes cognisance of the early stage in the relationship and, therefore, should not be perceived as invasive.

When it comes to determining whether a prospect has become a lead, a set of consistent and carefully designed qualification questions can provide the clues that would allow any customer-facing employee to determine this. You don't always need complicated models and analytics – a set of relevant questions, training on how to ask the questions and intelligent interpretations of the answers should provide the required insight.

Once prospects have been formalised as a qualified lead, they need to enter a specific lead management process, through which, regardless of which channel the information originated from, the lead can be captured into a system to be tracked, disseminated, actioned and monitored. There should be standards in place for tracking leads to ensure that none of them are overlooked and, when necessary, leads not followed up can be escalated and reallocated if need be.

For those prospects that are not yet ready to take that last step and buy, yet seem likely to do so at some point in the future, it is useful to have what is called a "warming" programme to keep them engaged until they are ready to buy. This warming process can involve regular communication at an appropriate level, such as newsletters, an update or a care message. It necessitates having a holistic mechanism to keep these prospects updated and interested while demonstrating, in a professional manner, that you care. At a certain future point, these prospects will be moved from the "warming state" into the sales process because of an indicator that demonstrates that they are ready.

Closing the deal

Your approach to sales planning and targeting should be supported by analytical thinking. Instead of idealistic sales targets and the sincere hope that they can be met, the numbers should be driven by both an in-depth analysis of past data and potential in the customer universe, tempered by market and external factors. In this way you can prevent the limited mind-set of simply adding a percentage increase on top of your previous year's results without due consideration of the real forces that may impact the result. Within your sales planning, targeting and measurement processes you should also recognise the difference between selling a product or a unit of revenue, and acquiring a customer. This distinction is a fundamental mind-set required for customer-centricity.

Selling an additional product to an existing customer is not the same as acquiring a new customer, which is the backbone of Acquisition. There is also a difference between acquiring new customers and winning back customers who no longer deal with you, yet have done so in the past. Your planning and targeting should take these categories into account, enabling you to discern the different revenue and profit contributions between them.

In managing sales leads, it is important to build on the information that has already been provided through the enquiry process and to honour the prospect's selection of preferred media for follow-up contact. At this critical stage in the sale you cannot afford to irritate the prospect.

In deciding when and how often to follow up on sales leads, some form of formal investigation and analysis, thereof, would be very useful. This would provide insight on the optimum time frames for lead follow-up in order to maximise the conversion rate. So many organisational timing standards are set without reference to any kind of formalised analysis or, even worse, are set by the limitations of the process itself and not by the customers' need. As with prospects, sales leads should be actively monitored by the team or individual with the allocated responsibility to ensure that the agreed sales and escalation processes do occur. Other useful information includes the time taken to close the deal, the number of contacts that may have needed to be made to close the deal, and the success of your channels in closing deals.

The correct use of Acquisition pricing requires that for every new customer there is always a consistent start point price that can be quoted. While there might be a level of individual negotiation around that price, your systems should enable frontline employees to see both this base start price and any special pricing agreed for that customer. There should be some form of flexibility around pricing that accommodates future customer value, if appropriate. Any discounts that are applied should be done so only to the extent that it is likely that you recover that discount at a later date. While some sales agents may be reluctant to give that discount away, others give it away at the outset without any thought of whether it can be recovered or not.

Another aspect to Acquisition pricing relates to understanding the pricing of "first purchase items", which are those items that lead to the purchase of other items. It is important to understand what your customers' first purchase items are per segment and what pricing your competitors are offering for those items or for substitutes. One example is the new Wii brought out by Nintendo, which they openly claimed to have sold at a loss because they made their profit from the games bought for the Wii. The Amazon Kindle is another example: Amazon announced that no profit was made on selling a Kindle because the real profit resided in the books the company would sell as a result. The Wii and Kindle are both examples of first purchase items. As a competitor, you would need to have a clear idea of how others' pricing matched yours.

In supporting the closing of sales you could perhaps use pre-approval techniques to speed up the process and prevent a deal from being cancelled in the last hour. You want to minimise the risk that a barrier unnecessarily delays the conclusion of the sale or renders it void altogether. Pre-approved home loans are such an example, as are some of the credit check services that can pre-vet the customer's level of financial fitness.

You might well find that useful insights on the last minute sales barriers can be gleaned from your own sales and channel data. Research into the reasons a purchase was negated at the last minute will help you to identify barriers and how you can remove them. In some cases it may be that customers change their mind or that there is a lack of sufficient closure from a process perspective by your organisation itself.

When the sale does occur you should have the mechanisms in place so that your sales channels can share in that excitement with the customer. This is particularly relevant for larger purchases or for business customers. This may require an acknowledgement or a thank you from a senior manager, an appropriate and relevant gift, or even introducing a new customer to the service team or to other employees. This recognises the significance of that purchase for the customer. Internal celebration is just as important. In a customer-centric context this takes on a new dimension. Instead of only celebrating a sales target being reached, you might celebrate the Acquisition of a specific customer, which for example, may represent a new revenue stream or a strategic win that deserves attention.

It is also advisable that you review your Acquisition approach to identify instances of poor Acquisition. Detailed analysis may reveal if free gifts and Acquisition promotions have translated into the sales needed to justify the expenditure, or whether those campaigns may have attracted the wrong kind of customer. This action is related to making sure you get a positive return on your Acquisition investment.

If there are any specific types of customers who would not deliver the necessary level of profitability, it will be necessary to define what the criteria are for being "not wanted". With those criteria clearly communicated to all Acquisition touch points, you can reduce the risk of that type of customer being acquired. It is a bold stance to take as most organisations would not consider turning away a sale. Another aspect to this customer selection process is having the mechanisms in place that enable you to halt the Acquisition of a "not wanted" new customer or customer type, as opposed to realising too late that they are on your books.

Getting your customer on board

The process of setting up a new customer requires a formalised process for welcoming them so that their experience of becoming a customer is positive. This makes these customers feel at home and creates a whole different level of interaction when this practice is conducted effectively. Explicit monitoring of this process will ensure that all the required steps take place in the right sequence. As soon as a prospect becomes a customer, this set up and welcoming process should be activated. It is also important that the welcoming activity is cognisant of whether the customer is completely new or is a returning customer. Not being able to show your customer that you recognise them makes your welcoming message seem unauthentic.

Specifically designed welcoming materials and perhaps even fit-for-purpose engagement activity should, therefore, demonstrate an authentic appreciation and excitement. Any attempt to send a sales message at this point would be inappropriate. It must feel real to the customer, unlike the ubiquitous, automated birthday greetings organisations send their customers believing it builds relationships. Of course, any welcoming material and activity should be appropriate for the level of the customer's value. Go Daddy, a large United States domain registration and hosting company, have such a welcoming process. They welcome each new customer with a personal call irrespective of the value of the purchase. Through this call they ensure that any questions a new customer has have been answered and they gather additional information about their customer as a result.

In some cases, the final transition from a prospect to a customer requires some form of activation. Using the example of a credit card, that activation may only occur when the customer uses the card for the first time or calls into the call centre to specifically activate it. You would, of course, need to have a clear definition of what activation means for each of your products or services, with the welcoming activity being linked to activation and not when they receive their credit card.

If you have products or services that require activation, then you need to have specific contact messages that are triggered if there is delay in the activation. This might involve a simple communication, a reminder, or a set of steps to show customers how to initiate activation. As an example, if your organisation was a credit card company, you would want to incentivise your customers to use their credit cards because you only start earning when they start using them. Those customers that have not activated should be thoroughly analysed and reported on, so that you can understand the reasons for non-activation. Does it relate to demographics? Is it as a result of a particular channel? These insights will help you to address those issues and stimulate activation in a shorter time period. You could certainly address activation as part of a welcoming process.

Depending on what products and service you deliver, there may be varying lengths of time for a new customer to settle in. You would need to define the relevant time periods for your "early experience" process with specific activities defined. This is not the same as the welcoming activity. For example, your welcoming activity may be an e-mail and your early experience intervention a call from the service manager.

If you have not been able to realistically and accurately allocate new customers to the right segment at this point, you could create a "new customer" segment that they are allocated to until you can re-allocate them accurately. If you take this approach it would be wise to treat this "new customer" segment as a high value segment — giving new customers the best treatment at the outset will build advocacy and loyalty.

In some cases, the nature of your business may warrant having a formal programme in place for customers once the welcoming process has been completed. This "nursery" programme may send customers informational content, past newsletters, or useful and valuable media that translates into them becoming better customers. The goal of such a programme is to immerse the customer into your organisation and provide organisational context.

A customer-centric approach to Acquisition requires a deep understanding of who your ideal customers are, where you can find them and how you can attract them into to buying from you. In being relevant, specific and focused in managing this process and making sure that you take the long-range and strategic view, you can create immense value through new, sustainable and successful customer relationships. The mantra of the past "sell, sell, sell" becomes the now of "focus, attract, engage".

Transformation questions

- Are sales processes understood in terms of why they succeed or fail and are they regularly adjusted based on this understanding?
- Are the sources and nature of new customers understood and used to improve targeting and proposition development?
- Is the nature of target customers defined and are the potential sources of these types of customers identified so that the chances of winning poor quality customers are reduced?
- Are targeted Acquisition offers across all media delivering good quality new prospects (as opposed to any new prospects) and are they having a minimal negative impact on existing customers?
- Are individual prospects engaging with the organisation from early in their purchase process in a way that they feel comfortable and that deepens as they get closer to purchase?
- Are sales enquiries being captured by all of the media that prospective customers want to use, in a way that collects consistent information from them and ensures the right nature and priority of follow-up activity?
- Are sales targets and rewards driving the Acquisition of the "right" types of customers and do they recognise that not all sales are the same?
- Are sales leads distributed, followed up and monitored in a way that delivers against the researched needs of prospects as well as the organisation's need to drive sales?
- Are new customers set up quickly and welcomed effectively in a way that is appropriate to their potential value?
- Are customers who have not settled into an active transactional relationship with the organisation detected and given additional support or encouragement to do so?

- Is your business fully aware of ethical danger points through selective marketing, invasion of privacy, targeting the vulnerable, unsolicited approaches and puffery (false advertising)?
- Do your ethics give you a competitive edge in acquiring new customers?
- Do you avoid ethically questionable (corrupt) customers?

Case study - Tesco gets on the move in South Korea

Tesco, a retail chain that originated in the United Kingdom, has been growing successfully in South Korea under the name Tesco Homeplus. Ranked the second largest grocery store chain in South Korea, it faced the challenge that it had fewer physical stores than its first position rival E-Mart. Tesco Homeplus wanted to find a way to take that first position without increasing the number of its stores.

In searching for a solution, Tesco Homeplus conducted an in-depth study into the Korean market in an attempt to understand what their target customers may need that they could provide. Their research uncovered that Koreans are the second most hardworking people in the world and that they consider grocery shopping to be a dreaded chore, especially being so tired and busy.

The solution was ingenious — a virtual store in subways and bus stations. Starting with a test site in a Seoul subway, Tesco Homeplus used virtual displays to mimic what shelves and produce would actually look like in a physical store. Using a mobile phone, customers could scan the QR code for the item on the "shelf" and it would be automatically added to their shopping cart through a mobile app. You could then select the time for same day delivery and your shopping would be done. In so doing, waiting time at the subway became an opportunity to shop.

As a direct result of this campaign, the online store saw a sharp increase in registered shoppers, with a total 76% increase over a two-year period and a 130% increase in online sales over the same period. Tesco Homeplus then took the top online store spot in South Korea and is now in a very close second position for the offline market.

SH Lee, the CEO of Tesco Homeplus, shared his views on its popularity [85]: "The growing trend in smartphones in South Korea means that virtual grocery shopping is even more accessible and convenient than ever before. The first virtual store in the Seoul Subway was a great success with customers and has paved the way for the opening of these new stores at bus stops. We've found it most popular amongst 20 to 30 year olds, so the new stores will be opening close to a local university and other pedestrian areas."

The success of this initiative stems from Tesco Homeplus understanding its target market with sufficient detail that it could pinpoint specific needs in its customer universe that were not being addressed. Through innovation and technology Tesco Homeplus was able to capture a new segment of that universe with a compelling business case that justified the continued expansion into bus stops. This new channel has also created an exciting opportunity for customers to solve a real need while having fun doing so.

CHAPTER 17:

PENETRATION

Transformation Intent

Delivering sustainable and superior business performance requires the on-going development and growth in the value of your customer base. To do this you need to have an in-depth understanding of your customer value so that you can identify opportunities to increase this value. This potential uplift is then supported through relevant propositions, cross-selling, up-selling, indirect value creation and expansion of existing product usage. In treating different customers differently, high value customers should also be given special attention so that the right team equipped with the necessary budget can deliver on their specific needs.

Sustainable, superior value development

Penetration is the last and final REAP lever and relates to the ability to develop more value from existing customers through cross-sell and up-sell activities to improve return on customer investment. Formal management of high value customers and key accounts is a critical part of this. It also requires clarity as to how you deal with low value customers from a development perspective, if at all.

Understanding customer value

In order to understand value development, the starting point is to define what you mean by current value and how you calculate it. While revenue is probably the most well used method and easiest to calculate, there are other contributors such as influence, advocacy, fast payment and duration of custom. Whatever method of calculation you choose it should have a rationale behind it that is relevant for your organisation and is, in some way, correlated to your industry. More importantly, it should be applied consistently. Creating this consistent definition and calculation is important, as without it, it can be interpreted in so many different ways. In the case where accurate figures or real data is not available to calculate value, value proxies and indices can be used. For example, if you are not able to ascertain the specific price that a customer has paid for a product, you could determine an average across the customer base for that product and use that in calculating a customer's value.

Understanding customer value also requires that you are able to calculate the potential value of customers. While it would be easy to use extrapolation to estimate future value, that really does not give you a sufficiently realistic picture. An example of extrapolation would be assuming that because a customer has spent $X per year with you over the last four years that they will do so in the coming year. Perhaps over a ten year period that annual average drops to a third. Perhaps your data indicates that the majority of customers that remain with you for four years rapidly increase their spend in year five. In factoring in this complexity, you need to define your method of calculating future value so that it too can be consistently applied. This level of understanding assists in decision-making in areas such as allowable cost of sale and Acquisition pricing.

Your customer life time value is the net present value of all the revenue earned from that customer over their life time. Your definition and calculation of customer lifetime value must be meaningful and relevant for your organisation. In your organisation, for example, a 10-year calculation period may be relevant, whereas in another organisation five years may be appropriate. It's important to understand how value is distributed across your customer base, including revenue from all products and services bought from your organisation. An analysis of the distribution of value across your customer base will yield insights into where the real value is sitting within your base. The Pareto principle, also known as the 80-20 rule, is often used as a means of understanding this distribution. According to this principle, 80% of your value would be created by 20% of your customer base. Alternately, you could use decile analysis (refer to the case study in Chapter 3) to categorise your customer value across ten deciles or bands in order to understand this distribution from a different angle.

Your in-depth customer value analysis will also reveal the variations in value between customers in a high value category and those in a low value category. In the process you would define the key variables that influence variations in customer value the most. In your analysis, the value drivers might be based upon products that have been purchased, number of products per purchase, frequency of purchase or portfolio spread. This would help determine the extent to which each of the variables influences the difference in value across different customer groups or segments. For example, the main difference between high value customers and very high value customers could be in the value of each product that was bought, whereas the difference between low and medium value customers may be explained by a combination of how often they buy products and their portfolio spread. Your customers' value will likely evolve over their life cycle. Analysis into the customer value evolution over a typical customer life cycle will reveal patterns of growth and decay, and when their value may reach a maximum.

It's also important to understand and estimate your share-of-spend by customer segment. The objective is to understand which characteristics cause variation in share-of-spend and how much additional revenue might be available. Equipped with these insights you can then take action in terms of those characteristics that are within your control.

IBM has used customer value analysis to drive significant results. A pilot study [86] was conducted for about 35,000 customers where the evaluation of the defined customer lifetime value resulted in a reallocation of resources for approximately 14% of the customer sample. The previous valuation method was based on past spending history. This led to a revenue increase of approximately $20 million, the equivalent of a ten-fold increase, with no adjustments to IBM's marketing investment for these customers.

With an in-depth understanding of your customer value, you can then look to predicting development opportunities. Research into patterns of purchase behaviour will reveal common purchase sequences, or the likely sequence of purchases made from different parts of your portfolio. A purchase sequence may be that, if a customer purchases Product A, the next purchase is likely to be Product C. There might be no logical correlation between the two products other than a reliable history that this sequence is a likely pattern. This kind of research, along with implemented predictive models, can support your cross-selling and up-selling efforts to be more effective. You can also mine your data repository to determine the link between a wide set of variables and changes in customer behaviour. Variables within your control may include price and target group, while external variables may include market conditions, economic factors, competitor offerings and regulators. Insights gleaned from this multivariate analysis will guide you as to the factors in offers that would stimulate the desired customer behaviour.

Developing customer value

In order to optimise customer value development there needs to be specific responsibility allocated to an individual or team with the requisite skills to do so. Just as you need a sales team and a Retention team, so too does your customer value development require special attention. While in some cases it may be the same people across all such teams, it is important to bear in mind the fundamentally different skills that are required for Retention, Acquisition and Penetration. At the very least, value uplift needs its own targets and performance indicators.

Customer value development activity should be supported by a very specific value proposition. In your organisation, what propositions exist to persuade customers to buy more of the product that they currently buy, or to buy additional products to those that they already buy? Even without different products and services, propositions can still be tailored in a way that they generate additional revenue. These propositions may include new packaging, special editions of a product or even additional service features.

One of the dangers to consider is that of existing revenue "cannibalisation". The objective of value development is incremental revenue across the entire business, not only for a specific business unit. If you do not have formal processes and checks in place to analyse the consequences of new offers, you run the risk of "cannibalising" the customer value developed in other parts of your organisation. Increasing incremental revenue is the goal and when reviewing the impact of new offers you should evaluate their impact carefully.

Even if you did not develop any new products, you could still create new offers by bundling certain products together for increased value. When developing bundled offers it is important to remember that the selection of products in the offer should be based on analytical insights derived from the patterns of customers' purchases or what they tend to purchase together. A bundle should provide more than just a price advantage for customers — it should have its own customer value proposition because of the particular need it fulfils.

One way to increase customer value is to encourage your customers to use their core products more often, thereby increasing usage or requiring faster replacement. In order to do this you need to think in the broadest sense of additional applications or uses that could encourage this change in behaviour and how you could then stimulate customers to embrace new ways of using the product or using the product more often. Obviously, there is an ethical consideration to this notion. If you have a gambling, alcohol or tobacco related business, then this approach would not be appropriate. Yet for most other types of business there should be room to increase usage. Step-up opportunities can also be used to increase customer value. You could use bulk purchasing offers to increase revenue and, at the same time, offer the customer a price reduction as an incentive.

For any product that will soon be obsolete or for end-of-line products, you can promote the sale of those items to existing customers through special offers. Such a promotion provides a powerful opportunity if you can target it at those specific customers that regularly use that product as opposed to a more general offer. To support these kinds of opportunities, you would need some kind of structure in place to facilitate the special offers while ensuring that the frequency and nature of such promotions does not encourage habitual end-of-line purchases. For example, if you have too many end-of-season sales you could land up encouraging customers to delay their purchase until the sale starts.

Up-selling is the process whereby you increase customer value by selling the customer "up the range" or upgrading the product or package they currently have. Much careful consideration is required in planning for what that step up might be. On the one hand, you have to make sure that whatever is being offered at the next level is worth that additional spend for your customer. To create traction, the customer must perceive that the additional value is actually more than the additional cost. At the same time, you also have to make sure that the step-up offer does not suddenly make the customer feel that the lower cost product is no longer attractive. It is, therefore, worthwhile to invest time in analysing and clearly specifying the next step up for each product so that it will be something that customers will desire and not a reason to dislike what you offered them in the first place.

If you have developed a level of understanding about the profitability of your customer transactions, you can then determine the profitability thresholds upon which incremental up-selling purchases for a customer can occur at a lower cost. Using mobile phone contracts as an example, a customer's profitability on a certain post-paid package or tariff plan might be relatively low because they use all their "air time" and do not make many "out of bundle" calls that are typically charged at a much higher rate per minute than the "in-bundle" calls. Up-selling the customer to the next level package, via an incentive that may require greater subsidisation on a handset, may increase profitability through the guarantee of an increased monthly spend without the concomitant increase in call volume.

Through loyalty programmes and effective analytics you can also encourage increased spend that is triggered by a customer's behaviour and is delivered at the point-of-sale, online and offline. Safeway, a United States grocery chain, has implemented just such a programme that discounts customers at the till point depending upon their behaviour [87]. In one example, a customer who routinely purchased other items of a brand from Safeway received a greater discount on a new product with the same brand name compared to the same product for another shopper who would typically not buy that brand at all.

In this way, Safeway rewarded the customer for purchasing a product from a brand because that customer was more likely to purchase more of that brand in the future.

Cross-selling increases customer value through selling more products from the overall portfolio to the same customer. In developing cross-selling offers, you need to make sure you target those customers who have a higher likelihood of purchasing and that you do not try to sell these products to customers who have already purchased them or have already been offered them. This practice requires customer knowledge and understanding to deliver these insights and achieve effective results from cross-selling outbound campaigns.

For any inbound contact with a customer, you should also be in a position to provide the customer with appropriate cross-selling offers. Care must be taken with how this is done in order to prevent customers becoming irritated as a result of feeling that every time they contact you someone is trying to sell them something. To counter this problem you should have clear rules of engagement that define when it would be inappropriate to cross-sell, such as when contact volumes are high and basic service standards are likely to drop.

Another way to increase value is by having customer-specific, prompted "next best thing" offers that can be presented to the customer, once the customer has been successfully dealt with. These prompts should be provided at both inbound and outbound interfaces and aim to guide the employee with what the next best action is to increase the value of that customer. These "next best thing" activities may be sales or non-sales related, such as collecting a missing piece of data or validating that data records are all correct. The rules of engagement apply to ensure that the action is appropriate and that the customer is not oversold. A technical solution that supports the implementation of such business rules is essential.

An important part of customer value development is to determine how best to deal with low value or loss-making customers. This is important in developing your pricing strategies to ensure that low value or loss offerings are not offered to low value customers, thereby dropping already low profitability levels below the threshold. There may also be the opportunity to define ways that specific lower cost offerings address the needs of these low value customers and, therefore, increase the value they contribute. Sometimes low value or loss offers make sense if sold to a high value customer, yet if you do not have the necessary mechanisms in place to control this, these offers may dramatically reduce customer value overall.

Best Buy is one of the largest consumer electronics chains in the United States. They identified that at least 25% of their annual customer visits were from undesirable, low value customers [88]. Best Buy did not want to be perceived as trying to get rid of these customers, so they had to find a way to discourage what they termed "devils" and encourage high-profit "angels". Through focused offers directed at their key segments, reduced numbers of clearance sales, product return fees and staff education on how to identify "angels", Best Buy have been able shift their profitability while attracting more customers of the kind they do want.

Besides the increase in direct customer value that a Penetration strategy aims to achieve, there are also indirect elements of customer value that do add financial value, such as willingness to recommend, length of tenure and exceptional payment record. What is the value of a customer who has been with you for 20 years versus one who has been with you for 6 months? What is the value of advocacy, word-of-mouth marketing and social media influence? You need to define the specific elements that offer indirect value to your company so that you can quantify customer value and assess the return on investment.

When it comes to advocacy you need to define a scale or levels of advocacy that are relevant for your organisation and ensure that you are clear as to what each of them involves. As an example, these levels could include reactive (reacting positively), pro-active (actively share by word-of-mouth) and ambassador (championing your cause), with a variety of options in between. You need to understand what these levels are worth and, if possible, record the advocacy level per customer so that there is a deeper level of understanding of how to increase the value of your customers. With your levels and their values defined and matched to customer advocacy levels, it should be possible to calculate a financial value for advocacy using a consistent methodology. Using single-click customer forwarding on offers through online channels is one way that you can tap into customer advocacy, thereby, increasing value. By making it easy for customers to share special offers and promotions with others, you provide them with the tools and good reasons to do so.

High value customers

High value customers are critical sources of value by virtue of the large proportion of value that they provide. Using the Pareto principle, you can expect that while your high value customers may comprise 20% of your customer base, it is quite likely that they contribute 80% of the value. While the close management of high value customers is more applicable in business-to-business environments rather than business-to-consumer environments, the principles are nevertheless critical for any type of organisation. Do you know what constitutes high value customers? Even if you don't manage them all that differently from the other segments within your organisation, do you allocate the care of these high value customers to certain higher skilled individuals?

Managing high value customers involves monitoring and researching these customers to make sure they are not encountering any problems that might lead to their diminishing spend, reducing purchase volumes or, the worst case scenario, contemplating a decision to leave. If you review your ordering processes, delivery patterns and payment terms, do these encourage high value customers to stay and increase their value? One way to mitigate the risk of value reduction is by allocating higher than average resources to high value customers, with perhaps even a higher concentration of resources. Specific responsibility to define and develop high value customers should also be allocated to appropriate staff members. Additional resources can also entail additional budget to provide the necessary support. In the process, management of high value customers would require that you specifically define their needs and address these accordingly through customised changes. An example of these changes can be found in some call centres in which high value customers are provided with a fast track service when they call, thus avoiding wait times. If you are able to reliably determine the potential for customers to become high value customers, you could also provide a formalised care-taking process that eventually manages them into their "high value" status.

Key accounts are few in number yet large in significance and size for any organisation. In order to effectively manage such accounts you need to have a robust methodology in place for key account management planning. Central to this approach is the ability to understand the group of individuals who are critical to decision making for that customer, including influencers, gatekeepers, advocates and detractors. If these role players are mapped out and understood by your account team you can plan how you will manage them effectively.

Your account plans for key accounts should have relationship-building and engagement objectives alongside any sales and profit objectives. The account team should be able to clearly articulate these objectives with an understanding of the investment and time needed to build that level of engagement with key account customers because there is a direct relationship between this level of engagement and sales volume. Budget and resource allocations should be appropriate for those objectives and in alignment with the size and the potential size of that key account. The account plans themselves should be living documents that everyone on the account team can readily access. In some cases it may be possible to develop your account plan in conjunction with the customer, yet this is very challenging to do well. It requires a deep level of maturity from both the customer and the account team to make it work.

Due to the critical nature of key accounts, it is necessary for account stakeholders to regularly review key accounts, including the defined objectives, the execution of the plan and the results achieved from the account team's efforts. Account stakeholders include anyone with a vested interest in the account, such as the account manager, senior management, sales management, finance and the customer. This joint review from both your team and your customer's team, ideally at least annually, will support assessing the effectiveness of your approach and identifying any possible barriers, personality conflicts and potential issues. The account plan should then be updated accordingly.

It is also extremely beneficial to have an independent party conduct periodic, formal reviews with the customer. The objective of this process would be to build an in-depth understanding on a variety of fronts: how your customers judge your organisation, what they judge you on, how well you measure up against those criteria, how your competitors perform in each of those areas, what you are good at, what you could do differently and where and how you could improve.

Although it seems obvious that an account team, if business is reciprocal, should have access to the value of purchases placed by your organisation with your customer, this is not something I have witnessed many organisations do well. This data is valuable information for negotiating purposes. A silo-based organisation will naturally struggle to understand reciprocity due to the disconnection between the finance team and the customer-facing departments. Ideally, at least one person in the account team should have direct or indirect access to the sales and purchasing systems. In a perfect world your purchasing systems would be integrated with the account management systems so that you've got a real time understanding that can become a point of reference in on-going account planning and reviewing.

Collaboration is a powerful way to deepen an engagement with a key account customer and requires an account manager and team with enough vision to seek opportunities to do so. For example, an engagement may involve working on a marketing campaign or managing a programme together. The important issue here is that the collaboration process is not a random idea that originates from an account manager or a customer, but is part of the initial planning process.

The REAP levers are powerful drivers of specific, targeted actions and initiatives aimed at delivering tangible results while supporting your organisation on its transformation journey. There is a wealth of tools, techniques and examples to be explored beyond what has been provided in this book. It's important to remember that a REAP strategy begins with your strategic outcomes and the specific objectives you have set. Everything else exists to support that vision. A prioritised action plan that addresses the areas of highest value first is the place to start. Step by step, these REAP initiatives can create exponential growth for all your stakeholders.

Transformation questions

- Is the distribution of value across your customer base understood, along with what drives value and how it develops over time, at the absolute level and at the share-of-spend level?
- Is customer value development activity based on deep analysis and predictive modelling of how to change behaviour?
- Is value development managed as a business discipline, such as Retention, with clear responsibility, specific propositions and checks that development is generating incremental value?
- Does cross-selling happen at both outbound and inbound levels, based on clear rules-of-engagement and prompts to ensure appropriate offers from the organisation's whole portfolio?
- Do you treat all your customers with equal respect, regardless of the size of their business with you?
- Are current and potential high value customers identified and managed as a distinct group even if there is no formal concept of key accounts, or even if they do not fall into the definition of key accounts?
- Are key accounts managed at deeper and more pro-active levels than other customers' accounts, with regular reviews and active seeking of opportunities for collaboration?

Case study - Exostar engineers a global supply chain

Exostar was founded in 2000 with the vision of creating an integrated global supply chain and security solution for the global aerospace and defence industry. Its founders identified that large organisations in this industry wanted and needed to move towards a global, collaborative and distributed supplier model, leveraging an international network of expertise in the wake of globalisation. Exostar provides its own suite of products and services that service this industry through a secure network of over 70,000 companies globally [89].

Kevin Lowdermilk, the CEO of Exostar elaborates [89]: "Exostar was created nine years ago really as the central aerospace and defence hub for multi-enterprise collaboration. We were formed by BAE Systems, Boeing, Lockheed Martin, Raytheon and Rolls-Royce. Technology is really at the core of everything that Exostar does. We take technology platforms and create them in a multi-tenant environment."

Exostar understood that this collaborative and technology-enabled approach to supply chain management would create a compelling platform for their customers. Some of the benefits to customers include: leveraging world class suppliers; minimising waste in production; managing on-time delivery to the end customer; ensuring continuity of supply through synchronised demand and supply information; improving cash flow for all participating partners; being able to identify issues early in the process; and reducing manual processes.

Tim Opitz, the Director of 787 Production and Support Tools for Boeing Commercial Airplanes, shares how Exostar has created value for Boeing [90]: "By helping us proactively flag any business process exceptions as they occur among our network of partners, and providing a consolidated view of all material movements across the supply chain, the Exostar solution is expected to tighten our efficiency in the way airplanes are manufactured. In addition, the ability to have a common view with our partners of real-time, supply chain performance will reduce risk, improve cycle times and ensure compliance with agreed processes."

Once an organisation like Boeing commits to using Exostar's secure and collaborative platform, which effectively integrates the supply chain and delivers direct value and cost savings, that company would be hard pressed to move somewhere else. The value offered is clear, tangible and directly relevant to their needs. The exit cost is high. As Exostar continues to introduce new offerings to customers through their portal, so will they have a captive market looking to find ways to expand the value from Exostar's offerings [89].

● CHAPTER 18:

● BUILDING AND LEADING THE 21ST CENTURY ORGANISATION

There is no doubt that organisations of the 21st century operate within a whole new world, with new dimensions of consideration, complexity and relevance to consider. The world is changing, people are changing and the customer is changing. In the midst of all this change, together with the challenges it brings, most organisations are still playing it safe, making marginal improvements to the way they work today in order to continue the fight with competitors for market share. They mistakenly think that this archaic approach will translate into meaningful competitive advantage and sustainable financial performance.

A new breed of organisation is required – one that passionately embraces ethics; one that clearly understands the links between stakeholders, strategy, risk, sustainability and performance; and one that places the customer at the centre of everything that it does. Most organisations that claim to be customer-centric are not. The few that are truly customer-centric are a rare breed. Some of the organisations that recognise the criticality of the customer are often blinkered in their understanding of what customer-centricity really means. Customer-centricity is not about customer-focused projects and trickle-feed, incremental improvements. It is about reinventing the business model to find new ways to create, deliver and capture value [14]. It's about making the radical, transformative leaps necessary to move from the current reality to becoming the defined "business of tomorrow".

Customer-centricity is also about surmounting the deeply-entrenched habit of perpetual mediocrity and "better sameness". It's about overcoming the trap of believing that the design and structure of the 20th century organisation will suffice in today's world. A leading organisation of the 21st century, therefore, has to embrace and commit to the transformative journey required through bold leadership and adjusting the genetic code that defines the organisation's DNA.

A disparate and disconnected organisation will be unable to achieve the transformation required. Short-term and quick-fix repairs to the fractures in the business model will not solve the problem. Instead, leaders must embrace the idea that everything is interconnected, and that their organisation and all the parts within it are systemic – connected and interdependent. They should strive to build links and inspire a culture of collaboration, innovation and interconnection, with the customer at the heart of their ecosystem.

The REAP Customer-Centric Organisation Blueprint®, or REAP CCOB, is a customer-centric business model that supports and enables your organisation to strategize, plan and operationalize the future in order to create, deliver and capture value, whilst delivering sustainable, superior business performance. At the centre of this business model is SCHEMA®, a customer-centric framework that is the most sophisticated and integrated customer management model currently available and provides a practical and focused approach in the implementation of customer-centric capability. This book has explored all the interconnected components of a truly customer-centric business model and how you can apply its principles practically within your company and achieve tangibly significant business results.

It may just be that, having walked this journey of customer-centricity with me, you feel a little daunted as to the amount of work and transformation required to become customer-centric and to sustain it. Remember, however, that customer-centric capability development and the operationalization of a customer-centric business model is a journey. I don't believe that there is ever a final destination to this journey, but I do know that there is a starting point. The scale of transformational change required is dependent on your level of current customer management maturity. After all, if building and leading a customer-centric organisation was easy, everyone would do it. So I urge you to think about the unbelievable opportunity that customer-centricity provides your organisation. It is an opportunity to leapfrog your competition and build sustainable competitive advantage by knowing and understanding your customers better than everybody else and having the operating platform that allows you to turn that learning into action faster than anybody else.

For the majority of organisations the question is no longer about whether they should embark on this transformative journey of customer-centricity, but about when they should start.

● APPENDIX A:

● SEE THE SCHEMA® MODEL AT WORK

An offer to readers of this book

The developers of the SCHEMA® model, which plays such a central role in the structure and content of this book, have developed a 'lite' version of the SCHEMA Assessor Benchmarker™ for you. This offer entitles you to experience some of the more detailed content of the world-leading diagnostic and benchmarking capability that SCHEMA® delivers to its clients across the globe. The offer provides access to an online version of the assessment tool and the provision to you of a set of benchmarked results, based on your inputs and matched to your organisation type.

Fascinating insight in return for considered input

The SCHEMA Assessor Benchmarker™ is the core of the SCHEMA® approach and is based on some of the most highly-developed intellectual property that exists in this field. In its full form, the SCHEMA Assessor Benchmarker™ is deployed by trained and accredited practitioners to examine the degree to which almost 400 practices are consistently implemented in client organisations, each practice being supported by a description of "What Good Looks Like" to ensure consistency and challenge.

SCHEMA Lite™, a scaled down version of the SCHEMA Assessor Benchmarker™, has been specially developed for you, comprising 50 of the practices from the full assessment. It is available for you to complete online for your own organisation by following the simple process below. It cannot, of course, provide anywhere near as full and accurate a picture of your current level of customer-centricity as the full assessment can. Care has, however, been taken to select practices that both illustrate some of the concepts covered by SCHEMA® and to drive stimulating thought processes and/or discussions with colleagues.

In order for this collective understanding to contribute value to others in the future, it requires that you complete the assessment in sincerity and with as much accuracy as is possible.

Your results will be compared with and reported against benchmark data from previous full assessments and other SCHEMA Lite™ assessments. Due to the fact that SCHEMA Assessor Benchmarker™ engagements are evidence-based and practitioners have to be trained and accredited before assessing any client company, we reserve the right to contact you to discuss any of your responses that may seem unrealistic based upon benchmark data and the knowledge base, before sending your report to you. Once validated, your answers will be added to a separate section of the main benchmark database and will be used to refine the benchmarks of future SCHEMA Lite™ participants.

Here is how it works

Visit http://www.schemacustomersolutions.com/content/reap.

Enter the details requested and submit these to complete your application.

You will receive an email with a personalised link to the SCHEMA Lite™ online software where you will have been set up as a guest user. The email will also contain a password to access the site.

Once on the SCHEMA Lite™ website, you can access all the practices from a single screen that has clear instructions on what you need to do. Review each of the practices across the main areas of the model in any order that you wish. You can complete as many practices at a time that you wish and can return to complete the rest in the future. This process enables you to collate input from colleagues or partners.

When you have provided your input for as many of the practices as you are able to, you can submit your results for benchmarking and reporting.

You will then be emailed your scores at an overall level and also for each of the main areas of the model (Retention, Efficiency, Acquisition, Penetration, Enablers and Foundations), along with a benchmark comparison to organisations similar to your own from the SCHEMA® database.

─● APPENDIX B:

─◎ SCHEMA® MODULES

SCHEMA® has a number of modules that support the effective use and operationalization of its practices.

SCHEMA Assessor Benchmarker™

The SCHEMA Assessor Benchmarker™ is used to understand and quantify an organisation's current customer management capability against the 399 practices of the SCHEMA® model and provides a benchmark, either against other organisations or between different parts of your organisation.

Through the carefully planned and highly structured interviewing of approximately 30 people in a broad mix of customer-impacting positions (depending on organisational size) – from the CEO and directors down to the frontline – the SCHEMA® Practitioner rates performance in each practice against a clear definition of what "excellent but commercially sensible" looks like in the best and most customer-focussed organisations. This rating is supported by evidence collected from the organisation. The interviewing process takes into account key customer-facing staff, such as call centre agents, but also those whose actions can have an indirect impact on customer interactions and experiences, such as IT and Finance. The process embraces the degree to which strategy and plans drive customer-centricity, how the culture and leaders encourage it, and whether people are skilled and empowered to manage customers well. It also explores whether people have effective systems in place and access to the data they need.

The process looks for the enablers of good customer management, such as how insight is generated and used to plan activities; the way propositions are created to reflect the brand; and how they are delivered across channels to deliver the desired customer experience. It looks at the workflows that exist; the agility of the organisation; and whether the right things are being measured through to the actual execution that enables the organisation to acquire, retain and develop (penetrate) the right customers and control the efficiency of doing so. Evidence is collected throughout the process to allow the SCHEMA® Practitioner to credit good practice as well as identify poor, missing or broken practices. This results in insightful and often surprising clarity about the organisation's "as is" capability.

SCHEMA Vision Shaper™

The SCHEMA Vision Shaper™ identifies misalignment and then generates alignment around a vision of the way the organisation wants to manage its customers in the future. It explores 20 carefully designed "Customer Dimensions" with the leaders of the business individually and then collectively in a workshop setting. Each of these 20 dimensions links directly to the capabilities needed to deliver it. By comparing the vision requirements with the current capability the scale of change required is identified.

The Vision Shaper stimulates and drives the thinking of senior stakeholders in defining the nature of customer-centricity that is required for the organisation. It addresses the gap that often exists between the inevitable, but very broad, "customer" imperative in the organisation's top five focus areas and the detailed plans needed to change processes, behaviours and systems.

The dimensions of customer-centricity used in the Vision Shaper drive relevant and meaningful input and debate. The combination of individual input and leadership team alignment activity builds ownership of the outcomes and minimizes any time or money spent on areas where alignment already exists. The outputs provide a clear "next-level-down" definition of customer-centricity for the organisation based on its own start point and overall strategies. This is supported by a textual and graphical illustration of the scale and nature of the change required to deliver the vision state.

SCHEMA Value Estimator™

The SCHEMA Value Estimator™ takes current key customer-related value and behaviour metrics to produce a segmented view of where value currently comes from. It shows the value of customers acquired and those being lost; how customer value grows; and how much is spent on customers of differing values. It is built up from information provided by the organisation about its current REAP (Retention, Efficiency (cost to serve understanding), Acquisition and Penetration (customer development, cross-sell and up-sell)) activities with briefing and support being given in sourcing this data.

The Value Estimator then drives the development of a realistic, precedent-based estimate of the potential value uplift from adopting various types of customer strategies, including or even challenging the strategy that is being constructed using the other SCHEMA® modules. It enables the fast and robust testing of a wide range of "what-if" scenarios against a set of industry-specific value drivers under the Retention, Efficiency, Acquisition and Penetration dimensions upon which the module is based.

The testing is made even faster by the provision of a series of start-point strategies, based on approaches known to have worked in other organisations and supported by statistics and precedents from the SCHEMA Knowledge Base™. The results can be extended to cover periods of up to five years taking into account the build-up and decay patterns of different type of benefits. Cost data can also be added if a full ROI view is required to support a business case.

SCHEMA Action Prioritiser™

The SCHEMA® process delivers the organisation a robust and transparent recommendation of the key capability areas that should be addressed to improve customer management capability, drive customer-centricity and increase financial performance. The finely-calibrated SCHEMA Action Prioritiser™ is based on all of the inputs provided by other modules and takes into account the gaps that exist between the SCHEMA Assessor Benchmarker™

score and best practices in the industry; the gaps between the "as is" situation and the required "to be" vision; and the customer strategies that the company is currently following or wishes to follow in the future.

SCHEMA Activity Planner™

The SCHEMA Activity Planner™ is used as a follow on to the SCHEMA Action Prioritiser™ to produce a detailed plan of the activity needed to deliver against the vision, strategy and prioritization developed in the other modules. A high degree of in-built content is incorporated that covers the activities that are likely to be needed to address all of the core capability areas, typical activity durations and the dependencies between them. It combines this with complete flexibility to include any number of client-specific activities and to tailor all of the proposed activities to suit the available resources and any particular needs to deliver quick-wins.

The plan can be as focused or exhaustive as needed to match the organisation's own planning and programme management approach. It can be structured into the areas of the model underlying SCHEMA®, by a set of default work streams or by a set of work streams created specifically for the client. The final plan can be delivered as a simple spreadsheet for ultimate portability or easily exported into Microsoft® Project for a more visual look and easy adoption by programme managers. The emphasis is on producing a realistic plan that very specifically addresses the capability uplifts that the organisation most needs.

APPENDIX C:

ABOUT REAP CONSULTING

REAP Consulting is a business advisory firm that specialises in leading-edge customer management thinking, and in the design and operationalization of 21st century customer-centric business models. Using proprietary methodologies and tools, REAP Consulting walks the transformational journey with its clients, providing support to organisations requiring major customer-centric change programmes. REAP Consulting partners with its clients to:

- Increase profit sustainably, by developing the organisational foundations and enabling organisational capacity to achieve this transformation profitably and consistently.
- Solve challenges on how to become more profitable and customer-centric with logic frameworks and mechanisms to force comprehensive thinking, thereby making better decisions.
- Operationalize customer-centric business models and integrate creative thinking with execution in order to create sustainable competitive advantage.
- Design and execute customer experience strategies.
- Share knowledge gained from being at the forefront of emerging trends and evolving techniques and showing how these practices can be harnessed to deliver customer engagement and profit.
- Develop prioritised 100-day customer-centric programmes that are designed to engage the whole organisation and achieve significant returns within short time frames, while methods of planning and ways of working are designed to build long-term capability.

reapconsulting.com

○── ● ACKNOWLEDGMENTS

Writing a book has always been on my "bucket list". Whilst I knew writing a book would be a fairly mammoth task, I'm not sure that I'd managed to quantify the actual scale of that task. It's been a great journey though, and I hope you have enjoyed reading this book as much as I have been inspired writing it.

My underlying intent for my work and this book in particular, is based upon a dream to change the world – to change the experiences we as customers receive and to embed sound, empathetic and world class experiences into individual and organisational DNA. In so doing, organisations can move beyond mediocrity and, in turn, society benefits through better customer experiences. I have been blessed with the opportunity of working in many different countries and have met many interesting people over the years, all of whom have in some way influenced my thinking and informed what you find in this book.

My entry into the consulting field was driven largely by my involvement with the Peppers & Rogers Group in 2001. Whilst always fiercely cognisant of organisations that "went the extra mile" to provide a superior experience, I was impressed with the thoughts and approach of Dr Martha Rogers and Don Peppers.

Soon after that, while working as CEO for a marketing services company, I discovered and licensed a methodology called CMAT™ (Customer Management Assessment Tool). That process introduced me to Neil Woodcock and Paul Weston of QCi – a small consulting business that had been sold to Ogilvy. Paul and I have collaborated together over a number of years and his support, contribution and friendship means the world to me. Paul is also the architect of SCHEMA®.

Through the QCi network I met many extremely capable individuals who have contributed in so many positive ways to my journey, some of whom have worked with me on various client engagements. I would especially like to thank Merlin Stone, David Williams, Mark Say, Ian Henderson, Bill George, Andy Green, and my good friend and colleague, Peter Lavers.

I am also most grateful for the contacts and connections formed as a result of my association with CustomerThink Corp, previously CRMGuru.com. My thanks to Bob Thompson for the annual retreats he used to host on the Californian coast.

A special mention to Belinda Doveston, whose commitment to the writing and publishing of this book deserves an "Oscar". Without her this book wouldn't be in your hands.

Others, whose insight, encouragement, support and contributions have been invaluable include John Caswell and Hazel Tiffany from Group Partners, who have really helped me to think and work differently; Sifiso Dabengwa of MTN Group who engaged our business in the early days and through the breadth of work across the MTN Group allowed us to build our foundation; the team at Nedbank Limited, particularly Doug Hardie, who has been a consistent and staunch supporter of our approach over many years; Professor Deon Rossouw from the Ethics Institute of South Africa; Professor Ian MacMillan from The Wharton Business School; and Ica van Eerden, Cathy Burrows, Rob Shuter, Jeanne Bliss, Dick Lee, Larry Hochman, Alan Price MBIDA and Naveed Syed.

The list of individual thanks is too long. There are many others who have influenced my thinking. I am as grateful to you as I am to those whom I've named. You know who you are.

Thank you.

REFERENCES

1. Alvarez, G. & Thompson, E. Gartner Opening Keynote: Top Trends for 2020. in *Gartner Customer 360* (Gartner, Inc, 2012).

2. Columbia Business School. *BRITE '10 Conference.* (Columbia Business School, 2010).

3. RightNow Technologies. *2011 Customer Experience Impact Report.* (2012).

4. Strativity Group. *2010 Consumer Experience Study.* (2010).

5. Searls, D. *The Intention Economy: When Customers Take Charge.* (Harvard Business Review Press, 2012).

6. Group Partners. *The 21ˢᵗ Century Organization.* (2009).

7. Fader, P. *Customer Centricity: Focus on the Right Customers for Strategic Advantage.* (Wharton Digital Press, 2012).

8. Kumar, V. *Managing Customers for Profit.* (Wharton School Publishing, 2008).

9. Pine, J. & Gilmore, J. H. *The Experience Economy, Updated Edition.* (Harvard Business Review Press, 2011).

10. Gulati, R. Silo Busting: How to Execute on the Promise of Customer Focus. *Harvard Business Review* (2007).

11. Peppers, D. & Rogers, M. *Managing Customer Relationships: A Strategic Framework.* (Wiley, 2011).

12. Booz Allen Hamilton. *The Customer-Centric Organization: From Pushing Products to Winning Customers.* (2004).

13. Fader, P. Sifting Through the Ashes: The Kindle Fire and Customer Centricity. *Forbes* (2012). at <http://www.forbes.com/sites/wharton/2012/02/03/sifting-through-the-ashes-the-kindle-fire-and-customer-centricity/>

14. Kaplan, S. *The Business Model Innovation Factory: How to Stay Relevant When The World is Changing.* (Wiley, 2012).

15. Institute of Directors in Southern Africa. *King Code of Governance Principles for South Africa 2009.* (2009).

16. Sustainable Business Forum. *Implementing Sustainable Development as a Strategic Business Model.* (2009).

17. Institute of Directors in Southern Africa. *Practice Notes King III Chapter 2 - Improving Board Functioning through the Performance of the Sustainability, Risk and Audit Committees.* (2011).

18. Eccles, R. G., Miller Perkins, K. & Serafeim, G. How to Become a Sustainable Company. *Sloan Management Review* **53**, 43–50 (2012).

19. Bellingham, R. *Ethical Leadership.* 93–94 (HRD Press, Inc, 2003).

20. Woodcock, N. *Aligning Stakeholders to Achieve Business Performance.* (2008).

21. The American Customer Satisfaction Index. The American Customer Satisfaction Index. (2012). at <http://www.theacsi.org>

22. QCi Assessment Ltd. *State of the Nation III: 2003.* (2003).

23. Gulati, R. *Reorganize for Resilience: Putting Customers at the Center of Your Business.* (Harvard Business Press, 2010).

24. QCi Assessment Ltd. *State of the Nation IV: 2005.* (2005).

25. Sisodia, R. S., Wolfe, D. B. & Sheth, J. N. *Firms of Endearment.* (Pearson Prentice Hall, 2007).

26. Bliss, J. *Chief Customer Officer.* p.116 (Jossey-Bass, 2006).

27. Peppers, D. Make Room At The Meeting Table--For Your Customer. *FastCompany* (2012). at <http://www.fastcompany.com/1811671/make-room-meeting-table-your-customer>

28. Weston, P. *We will be more customer-centric. Now remind me what that means!* (2011).

29. Kosdrosky, T. The Emperor's Used Clothes. (2012). at <http://www.bus.umich.edu/NewsRoom/ArticleDisplay.asp?news_id=24177>

30. Hsieh, T. *Delivering Happiness.* (Business Plus, 2010).

31. Nayar, V. *Employees First, Customers Second.* (Harvard Business Review Press, 2010).

32. Temkin, B. Leadership Principles for Changing Corporate Culture. (2012). at <http://experiencematters.wordpress.com/2012/08/02/leadership-principles-for-changing-corporate-culture>

33. Temkin, B. 6 C's Of Customer-Centric DNA. (2009). at <http://experiencematters.wordpress.com/2009/04/10/6-cs-of-customer-centric-dna/>

34. Booz & Company. *Achieving Cultural Change that Sticks.* (2012). at <http://www.youtube.com/watch?v=OF9F5D3qXgs&list=UUUpeC56j0S2LNqOTAvT_wXQ&index=4&feature=plcp>

35. Lowenstein, M. *Satisfaction vs. Engagement vs. Commitment: Which Framework Best Explains the Linkage of Employee Attitudes and Beliefs to Their Propensity to Act in Loyal Ways?* (2007).

36. Gallup Inc. *The State of the Global Workplace.* (2010).

37. Rucci, A. J., Kirn, S. P. & Quinn, R. T. The Employee-Customer-Profit Chain at Sears. *Harvard Business Review* **76**, (1998).

38. Duhigg, C. How Companies Learn Your Secrets. *The New York Times* (2012). at <http://www.nytimes.com/2012/02/19/magazine/shopping-habits.html?page wanted=1&_r=3&>

39. Thompson, B. Solving the Digital Experience Conundrum: Three Roles for Technology in Customer Delight. *CustomerThink* (2012). at <http://www.customerthink.com/article/solving_digital_experience_conundrum_three_roles_for_technology_in_customer_delight>

40. ISO 9241-11. *Ergonomic Requirements for Office Work with Visual Display Terminals (VDTs) - Part 11: Guidance on Usability.* (1998).

41. ISO 9241-210. *Ergonomics of human system interaction - Part 210: Human-centred design for interactive systems.* (2010).

42. User Vision. Emirates Airline. (2012). at <http://www.uservision.co.uk/resources/case-studies/ema/>

43. DiNucci, D. Fragmented Future. *Print* **53**, 32 (1999).

44. Applegate, L. M., Piccoli, G. & Dev, C. *Hilton Hotels: Brand Differentiation through Customer Relationship Management.* (2008).

45. Lee, L. & Sobol, D. What Data Can't Tell You About Customers. *Harvard Business Review* (2012). at <http://blogs.hbr.org/cs/2012/08/what_data_cant_tell_you_about.html>

46. REAP Consulting. *Rolls-Royce and Bentley Motor Cars.* (2008).

47. Schehr, D. *The IT Implications of Customer Driven Segmentation — An Investment Services Perspective.* (2012).

48. Godin, S. *Tribes.* (Portfolio Hardcover, 2008).

49. Watson, H. J. & Volonino, L. *Harrah's High Payoff from Customer Information.* (2001). at <http://www.terry.uga.edu/~hwatson/Harrahs.doc>

50. Lawrence, A. Nothing left to chance. *Information Age* (2007). at <http://www.information-age.com/channels/information-management/features/272256/nothing-left-to-chance.thtml>

51. Iezzi, T. Red Bull Stratos Shatters Records—and Traditional Notions of Marketing. *FastCompany* (2012). at <http://www.fastcocreate.com/1681748/red-bull-stratos-shatters-records-and-traditional-notions-of-marketing#1>

52. Aaker, D. A. & Joachimsthaler, E. *Brand Leadership*. p.17 (Pocket Books, 2000).

53. Ritchie, C. Marketing. (Pearson Prentice Hall, 2009).

54. Altitude Volvo. Safety First. (2013). at <http://www.altitudevolvocars.com.au/safety-first-volvo.html>

55. AAMI. AAMI Customer Charter. (2013). at <http://www.aami.com.au/insurance-services/customer-charter>

56. Parker, S. Building a model for customer co-creation. *MyCustomer.com* (2010). at <http://www.mycustomer.com/topic/customer-experience/co-creation/111040>

57. Wong, V. Co-Creation: Not Just Another Focus Group. *Bloomberg Businessweek* (2010). at <http://www.businessweek.com/stories/2010-04-01/co-creation-not-just-another-focus-groupbusinessweek-business-news-stock-market-and-financial-advice>

58. firstdirect. Why co-creation is the way forward for first direct. (2011). at <http://www.newsroom.firstdirect.com/articles/why_co-creation_is_the_way_for>

59. Fera, R. A. General Mills Wants Your Ideas For Its Next Cereal Game And Cake App. *FastCompany* (2011). at <http://www.fastcompany.com/1799413/general-mills-wants-your-ideas-its-next-cereal-game-and-cake-app>

60. Israel, S. Dell Modernizes Ideastorm. *Forbes* (2012). at <http://www.forbes.com/sites/shelisrael/2012/03/27/dell-modernizes-ideastorm/>

61. CInergy International. *Vodafone improves customer acquisition and retention with Accelerated Intelligence*. (2009).

62. Cunard Line. Cunard Weddings. (2013). at <http://www.cunard.com/cunard-experience/why-cunard/special-occasions/>

63. Communispace. Sweet Success: Godiva Gems and Communispace. (2010). at <http://www.communispace.com/godiva-gems-customer-co-creation-case-study/>

64. Corcoran, S. Defining Earned, Owned and Paid Media. *Forrester* (2009). at <http://blogs.forrester.com/interactive_marketing/2009/12/defining-earned-owned-and-paid-media.html>

65. Peveto, A. KLM Surprise: How a Little Research Earned 1,000,000 Impressions on Twitter. *Digett* (2011). at <http://www.digett.com/2011/01/11/klm-surprise-how-little-research-earned-1000000-impressions-twitter>

66. Goldman, S. M. Trialogue: The Intersection of Social Media and Loyalty. *Colloquy* **19**, 13–20 (2011).

67. Capek, F. Customer Experience Beyond Better Sameness. in *European Customer Experience World 2011* (Customer Innovations, 2011).

68. Agility Consulting. The Agile Model®. (2012).

69. Horney, N. F. Successful companies respond to challenges with agility. *Agility Consulting* (2010). at <http://www.agilityconsulting.com/uploads/Toyota Article Trends April 2010.pdf>

70. General Electric Company. What is Six Sigma. (2013). at <http://www.ge.com/en/company/companyinfo/quality/whatis.htm>

71. Anand, N. & Daft, R. L. What is the Right Organization Design? *Organizational Dynamics* **36**, 329–344 (2007).

72. Pieterse, J. Everybody know what is workflow? *Toolbox.com* (2006). at <http://it.toolbox.com/blogs/enterprise-design/everybody-know-what-is-workflow-8750>

73. Microsoft. Tony Scott on Productivity today and tomorrow. *Showcase* (2011). at <http://www.microsoft.com/en-us/showcase/details.aspx?uuid=08a0ef64-7cf9-43e1-bb27-75718438c337>

74. Scribe Media. Joseph Tripodi, CMO, Coca-Cola. (2011). at <http://www.youtube.com/watch?v=BVj_tyInYDw>

75. Zmuda, N. Coca-Cola Gets Hands-on With Its Own Digital Billboards. *Ad Age* (2010). at <http://adage.com/article/media/coca-cola-hands-digital-billboards/142179/>

76. Robison, J. *How The Ritz-Carlton Manages the Mystique.* (2008). at <http://businessjournal.gallup.com/content/112906/How-RitzCarlton-Manages-Mystique.aspx>

77. Michelli, J. *The New Gold Standard.* p.256 (McGraw-Hill, 2008).

78. CMO Council. *Business Gain From How You Retain: Addressing the Challenge of Customer Churn and Marketing Burn.* (2008).

79. Neisser, D. Twelpforce: Marketing that Isn't Marketing. *FastCompany* (2010). at <http://www.fastcompany.com/1648739/twelpforce-marketing-isn't-marketing>

80. Xtreme Directory. O2 retention direct mail case study. *Mail Media Centre* (2008). at <http://www.mmc.co.uk/Knowledge-centre/Case-Studies/O2-direct-mail-case-study/>

81. McGregor, J. USAA's Battle Plan. *Bloomberg Businessweek* (2010). at <http://www.businessweek.com/magazine/content/10_09/b4168040782858.htm>

82. Srivastava, S. Sprint Drops Clients Over Excessive Inquiries. *Wall Street Journal* (2007). at <http://online.wsj.com/article/SB118376389957059668.html>

83. Hatley, J. Creating and Implementing a Client Experience Blueprint. in *Customer Futures South Africa 2004* (2004).

84. Capon, N. & Mac Hulbert, J. *Managing Marketing in the 21ˢᵗ Century.* 29–30 (Wessex, Inc., 2007).

85. The Retail Bulletin. Tesco Homeplus expands trial of virtual stores in South Korea. *FastMoving* (2012). at <http://www.fastmoving.co.za/news/supplier-news-17/tesco-homeplus-expands-trial-of-virtual-stores-in-south-korea-1289>

86. Kumar, V., Venkatesan, R., Bohling, T. & Beckmann, D. The Power of CLV: Managing Customer Lifetime Value at IBM. *Marketing Science* **27**, 585–599 (2008).

87. Clifford, S. Shopper Alert: Price May Drop for You Alone. *The New York Times* (2012). at <http://www.nytimes.com/2012/08/10/business/supermarkets-try-customizing-prices-for-shoppers.html?_r=0>

88. McWilliams, G. *Analyzing Customers, Best Buy Decides Not All Are Welcome.* (2004).

89. Exostar. Microsoft Customer Case Study - Exostar. *Exostar* (2009). at <http://www.exostar.com/About_Exostar.aspx>

90. E2open. *Boeing 787: Global Supply Chain Management Takes Flight.* (2007). at <http://depart.zzti.edu.cn/foreign/Files/File/Boeing_case_study.pdf>

INDEX